BLACK SILENCE

Also by Paul Polansky

Biography (Editor)
ANTONÍN DVOŘÁK, MY FATHER by Otakar Dvořák
(Czech Historical Research Center, 1993)

Poetry
LIVING THROUGH IT TWICE
Poems of the Romany Holocaust (1940 – 1997)
(G plus G, 1998)

Novel
THE STORM
(G plus G, forthcoming)

black silence
The Lety Survivors Speak
PAUL POLANSKY

G plus G
Cross – Cultural Communications
Prague / New York • 1998

Copyright © Paul Polansky, 1998

G plus G
Čerchovská 4
120 00 Prague 2
Czech Republic
Tel: 00420 2 627 33 32
    00420 2 227 152 24
Fax: 00420 2 627 33 32
e-mail: gplusg@gplusg.cz
http://www.gplusg.cz

ISBN 80 – 86103 – 08 – 0

Co - Publisher
Cross - Cultural Communications
239 Wynsum Avenue Merrick,
NY 11566 – 4725 / USA
Tel: (516) 868 – 5635,
Fax: (516) 379 – 1901
e-mail: CCCMIA@JUNO. com

ISBN 0 – 89304 – 241 – 2

First edition 1998

Bound and printed in Czech Republic

Contents

The Lety Story 11

Lety Village Chronicle 23
J. Š. 27
Anna Růžičková 28
B. C. 32
Alžběta Růžičková 35
Marie Čandová 39
Barbara Richterová 43
E. C. 47
Anna Čermáková 50
Berta Berousková 52
A. Č. 57
Žofie Dolíhalová 62
E. S. 65
Alžběta Danielová 71
Z. F. 77
František Janošovský 81
A. F. 88
Beatrix Pflegerová 93
R. H. 95
Jana Marhoulová 99
Vratislav Chejlava 106
Bohuslava Klocová 107
V. J. 110
Vlasta Růžičková 117
Antonie Kroková 120
F. K. 125
R. K. 129
J. K. 130
Tony Lagryn 131
Božena Růžičková 133
A. Š. 139
Marie Petrskovská 144
František Kejval 150

Marie Serynková 152
Karel Kloc 155
Helena Růžičková 161
K. V. 163
Marie Šlehoferová 164
K. P. 168
Adéla Studená 173
Robert Růžička 180
R. B. 182
Ladislav Stokinger 185
Marie Vrbová 189
V. V. 194
Karel Vrba 198
Terezie Hubená 202
V. R. 204
Antonín Vintr 206
Alžběta Lagronová 212
Eduard Čermák 218
A. N. 225
Helena Richtrová 231
Emil Khiel 234
Josef Janovský 237
František Kánský 241
Václav Studený 244
František Kuchař 249
Josef Koudelka 251
Mr. Končický 252
Josef Matějka 253
Mrs. Luzumová 255
Václav Veselý 256
Václav Stuchlík 260
Adolf Vondrášek 263
Zdeněk Bárta 266
Růžena 267
Lety 1996 268

Epilog 270

Acknowledgments:

This book would not have been possible without the support of these people: Lubomír Zubák who helped me find the Lety survivors and convinced them to tell us their stories; and Fedor Gál who had the courage and conviction to publish their stories as brothers and sisters who suffered in the same Holocaust as his family.

I am also indebted to several other translators who did not wish to be named.

But above all, I wish to thank the Lety survivors who according to Romany law are not suppose to tell their stories to gadžos. By breaking that bond of silence, I hope the world will learn what happened then, and what is happening now, to them. Hate and prejudice will never be conquered by silence. Only by people brave enough to let us suffer their tragedies with them.

Paul Polansky
Prague 1998

*In memory of
my mother
and father*

*"They were supposed
to die and leave behind
only a black silence.
But the system passes away.
The truth stays.
The truth prevails."*

Lech Wałęsa

■ Wooden cross made by Jan and Martin Čermák, survivors of Lety. Without government approval these two brothers put this cross up in the woods at Lety in 1986 to mark one of the mass graves. This cross was found in 1995 collapsed on the ground in the Lety forest by Paul Polansky and Ľubo Zubák.

The Lety Story
By Paul Polansky

The village of Lety in south Bohemia sent the first Czech pioneer to Cleveland, Ohio, in 1848. Thousands of families followed. I discovered this information in the State Archive of Třeboň in 1992 while researching the 19th century exodus of Bohemian peasants. I saw Lety as the cradle of Czech emigration to the American Midwest. The reading-room director where I worked perceived Lety in a different light.

"There was a concentration camp there during the war," she told me. "It was a Gypsy camp. All the inmates died of typhus."

I had visited Lety often, interviewing the local historian, the mayor, several old-timers. No one had mentioned a World War II death camp.

"We have more than 40,000 documents," the reading room director told me. "But no one is allowed to study them for fifty years."

A Gypsy concentration camp? Everyone died of typhus? It didn't make sense. Typhus wasn't the bubonic plague. They could easily control it. My dream of asking the Czech government to put up a monument at Lety to honor the cradle of emigration to America suddenly waned.

That same day I re-interviewed the local historian, a retired school teacher who had published seventeen books on the Lety region, from medieval families to stone quarries. I asked him why he had never written about the Gypsy concentration camp.

"Gypsies aren't worth writing about," he said. "But if you want more information, ask Dr. Kalbáč down the road. He was a doctor at Lety."

Eighty-year-old Dr. Kalbáč told me his mind was as active as ever. He still remembered all his Greek and Latin from high school. But when I asked him about Lety he couldn't recall a thing. "That was a long time ago," he said. Finally he told me Lety had been a recreation camp for unemployed Gypsies. "Unfortunately, they were a dirty people and brought disease with them into the camp." Dr. Kalbáč declared that he had left long before the tragedy because the camp commander wouldn't pay his gas mileage from Mirovice to Lety, a distance of three kilometers.

I returned to see the mayor of Lety. He revealed that the camp was where the pig farm is today. The mayor had been born after the war so he knew nothing else. He advised me to speak with an older person who would have been alive during World War II.

I drove out to the pig farm, a few miles to the east. I stopped an old man on a bicycle, and asked if he knew anything about the Gypsy camp during the war.

"Everybody knows about it," he said. "In 1942/43 I rode by it every day on my way to work."

"Was it a German camp?" I asked.

"Of course not," he said. "No Germans were in this area during the war."

"Who were the guards?"

"Czech policemen."

"Did all the prisoners die?"

"Most of them."

"How did they die?" I asked.

"That's not for me to say," he said, and pedaled off.

Two years later in January 1994, the director of Třeboň archives granted me special permission to study the Lety records. He hadn't seen the records himself, but he didn't think I would find anything very interesting in the thirty-one boxes that covered twenty-five feet of shelf space. He appeared tired of me pestering him and his staff. He also allowed my Czech assistant to see the records with me.

The first day I discovered a cover-up. The official camp book listing all the prisoners didn't correspond with the arrival list. Czech police brought thousands of Gypsies to the Lety camp, but only six hundred were given a number and listed in the official camp book. Among the documents, I found a book on prisoners shot while trying to escape. I also discovered several files of death certificates, thousands of death certificates. It took me two days to read them. Only eight people died of typhus according to those records. Many comical reasons were given for some of the deaths: "He laughed himself to death"—- "He died because he couldn't read or write" – "He was too drunk to live."

I uncovered hundreds of mug shots. Women in nice dresses with gold earrings and new hairdos. Men wearing suits, white shirts and ties. Later I discovered the transportation lists to Auschwitz. But again, those numbers were only a small part of the total population of the camp. What happened to the rest? Then I found the records on the staff.

All were Czech. All were born in Bohemia. All had served as customs guards or policemen before being recruited to serve at Lety. My Czech researcher got scared.

"We shouldn't be seeing this stuff," he said. "Some of these guards might still be alive. If they hear what we're doing, they might come after us." That afternoon my assistant quit.

I requested photocopies of certain documents when the director of the archive was not there to say no. The staff let me copy more than a thousand documents. The reading room director then brought me a book that a Czech professor, Ctibor Nečas, had written about Lety in 1981. I skimmed through the book. Nečas called Lety a work camp and inferred that the Germans had run it. He stated that those inmates who had not died of typhus were sent to Auschwitz.

Four months later, May 15, 1994, a newspaper in Decorah, Iowa, published a front-page article on my research. The banner headline read:

> *Researcher claims thousands*
> *of Gypsies exterminated by Czechs*

The sub headline read:

> *Paul Polansky uncovers horrifying tale of death*

Newspapers in Iowa City and Des Moines also published front page articles.

I took my research to Washington, D.C. to the Commission on European Security and Cooperation. According to the Helsinki Agreements, all death camps at the end of World War II were to be preserved in their original state as national monuments. I felt they should remove the pig farm at the Lety camp and build a proper, dignified monument in memory of those who had died there. I didn't plan to write about Lety. I already had too many projects on my plate.

Two weeks later, back in Iowa, I got a call from Washington, D. C. The Czech Embassy wanted to see me about the Lety documents. They invited me to attend a meeting along with a member of the Commission on European Security and the archive director of the United States Memorial Holocaust Museum.

The Czech Embassy had a copy of the Decorah newspaper. They didn't want any more publicity on Lety. They offered to form a commission with me to study the records. They promised to remove the pig farm and build a dignified memorial. They asked the Holocaust Museum if they had architects who could undertake such a project.

I left elated, but suspicious. The embassy officials had congratulated me on my work but had made no definite arrangements with me. The Holocaust Museum wanted to microfilm the records for their archives; they had never heard of a Holocaust camp with 40,000 documents. According to my description of the records, Lety was the best documented camp in the history of the Holocaust.

Over the next few months, I called the Czech Embassy several times asking when I should go to Prague to start work with their commission. They never gave me a date. Finally I sent a fax suggesting we look for survivors first. The records could wait; old people had a bad habit of dying. I asked the embassy to contact Prague and have someone check out all the names I had found in the Lety records. I knew every citizen in Czechoslovakia was on the police computer. The Czech embassy never contacted me again.

That September I went back to Prague. The country had split in two. I was now dealing with the Czech Republic instead of Czechoslovakia. I returned to the archives in Třeboň. The staff wouldn't let me in. I was officially banned.

The reading room director tearfully told me how several agents from the Ministry of the Interior had interrogated everyone about my work, threatening to fire the archive staff. Everyone feared they would not only lose their jobs but their pensions. The reign of terror lasted several weeks. No one in the archive wanted to be seen in my presence ever again, not even after working hours.

Why? I suspected atrocities had been committed at the Lety camp. If any of the guards were still alive, they could be prosecuted for war crimes. I sent a fax to President Havel explaining the situation and asked for his help. His office answered saying the President was following my work closely but Lety and war crimes were not in his jurisdiction. His office made an appointment for me to see an official at the Foreign Ministry. Why the Foreign Ministry? I took a translator along, mainly as a witness.

Dr. Havlas at the Foreign Ministry assured me that he had spent the past few months studying the Lety records. He had concluded that the Germans had run the camp. There were no survivors, not even among the staff. The pig farm was too large to be moved. The government was planning a small memorial in a nearby field and had asked several Gypsy organizations for ideas on a design. But Gypsies were uneducated. They didn't care about their own past, so why should others? It was difficult dealing with Gypsies. Ninety-eight percent of them were unemployed; very few went to high school. None went to college. I should find a better project.

I said I was committed to getting the pig farm removed, and seeing a proper memorial put up for the victims. I asked Dr. Havlas whom in the country might help me. Without hesitation, he suggested Prince Karel Schwarzenberg, President Havel's ex-chief of staff. The President had appointed Schwarzenberg to investigate the Gypsy problem in their country. I was shocked. Many Gypsies considered Schwarzenberg a racist. So did several members of the United States Congress. I called Schwarzenberg's secretary but never received an appointment. A personal letter to him went unanswered.

After Prague, I attended a human rights conference in Warsaw sponsored by the European Union and the Commission on European Security about Gypsy problems. Gypsies were the largest minority in Europe. Official delegations from more than a hundred countries participated. A delegation from Helsinki Watch in Prague denounced the Czech government for passing a new citizenship law designed to disenfranchise more than 300,000 Gypsies from Czech citizenship. Helsinki Watch also complained about skinhead attacks against Czech Gypsies that seldom led to prosecutions, even when murder had been committed. I then spoke about the Czech government's cover-up of Lety.

I went back to Iowa and forgot about Lety until I received a fax a few months later from the editor of the only Gypsy newspaper in the Czech Republic. He had published my Warsaw speech. The Czech minister for Minorities then accused me of inflaming the Gypsy minority against the government. The editor asked me for a reply to those accusations. I faxed that I was not the author of the new citizenship law. A few weeks later the Office of the President of the Czech Republic complained about my speech in the Gypsy newspaper and the editor was fired.

In May 1995 I returned to the Czech Republic to find a Lety survivor. I still wasn't sure what had happened there. The evidence pointed to a Czech camp where thousands of Gypsies died. The Czech government had not allowed the Holocaust Museum in Washington, D.C. to microfilm their records. Holocaust historians from Auschwitz had visited the Czech government to see the documents I had found, only to be turned away. What was the government trying to cover up?

While in the Czech Republic I discovered the government had built a small monument near the Lety camp and was planning a ceremony to be attended by President Havel and several cabinet ministers. A Gypsy Holocaust seminar was planned after the ceremony. I was not invited. The chairperson of the Holocaust seminar was Dr. Nečas. I went to see him in Brno. He said many people were disturbed by my investigation, but I had served one purpose. In twenty years he had not been able to get the government to put up a plaque at Lety. Now I had forced them to build a monument. I asked Dr. Nečas if anyone had survived Lety. He said he knew of three survivors, but he didn't know how to find them. They were Gypsies. They never stayed in one place for very long. I asked if he had interviewed them. He said only about their stay in Auschwitz. Lety had not been an important camp for a Holocaust historian. His specialty was Auschwitz and what had happened to the Gypsies there.

Back in Prague, a member of Helsinki Watch, who knew President Havel personally, called his office and negotiated with the president's assistant to get me an invitation to the memorial service. After several calls the President's Office agreed to send me an invitation if I ceased attacking the President's image. They didn't mind me attacking other Czech politicians such as Minister Nemec but I was to refrain from making bad press comments about the President. I agreed on condition that President Havel in his speech acknowledged that Lety was a Czech concentration camp, not a German one.

At the memorial service they invited me to stand in line with several cabinet ministers to greet the President. The Minister of the Interior, Jan Ruml, told me he didn't like what I had said in the press about his President but he admitted this memorial service wouldn't be taking place unless I had made public my findings about Lety. When they introduced me to President Havel, he refused to shake my hand. He just nodded his head and walked on.

Five or six dignitaries spoke that morning in the rain about Lety. All called it a Nazi camp. Three hundred and sixty prisoners, all Gypsies, had died there from typhus. No one should forget what the Germans had done during the war. Although all the Gypsies who died at Lety had been Catholic, the organizers invited no priest to say a prayer.

When President Havel spoke, he acknowledged that Czech guards had run Lety. He said some of them had not acted properly; some had been cruel; so had some farmers living nearby who had used the prisoners as slave labor. But he attributed all the deaths to typhus.

At the Seminar they barred me from entering until a Gypsy activist, Ľubomír Zubák, demanded I be allowed in. Before the speeches, the Písek organizers held a press conference. I asked Minister Němec why there was no road or footpath to the new Gypsy memorial. It was stuck in a field by some woods unseen from the main highway. There were no signs to the monument either. Minister Němec answered that the government had paid enough money for the memorial; if the Gypsies wanted a road or signs to their memorial, they had to pay for it themselves.

The seminar lasted four hours. Several people in the audience petitioned the chairperson to let me speak. They wanted to hear my version of Lety. Their petition was denied. Only Dr. Nečas spoke about Lety. The other speeches were about Auschwitz. They produced one Lety survivor. She spoke only about her experiences at Auschwitz. Dr. Němec then announced that seven Lety survivors had attended the memorial service that morning but unfortunately they couldn't be introduced now because they had already left.

At that moment, my life changed. I vowed to find the Lety survivors.

It took me six months to organize my personal life before I could dedicate myself completely to searching for the Lety survivors. But by November 1995, I was back in the Czech Republic with a beat-up camper-caravan determined to travel anywhere to find Lety survivors. I hired Ľubomír Zubák, the Gypsy activist who had forced the organizers of the seminar to let me in. Ľubo spoke excellent English and had Gypsy contacts all over the country.

With some effort we tracked down the seven survivors who had attended the Lety memorial service. They had also attended the seminar but since they were not allowed to speak they had sat out in the hallway reminiscing. Those seven survivors called Lety worse than Auschwitz. The Czech guards were more cruel than the Germans.

For the next two months Ľubo and I traveled across the country seeking survivors. One old woman claimed there were as many as three hundred survivors, but she had no addresses. No one kept in contact. No one wanted to remember Lety.

Ľubo and I worked the Gypsy ghetto in Prague, asking old Gypsies if they knew anyone who had been in a concentration camp. We found survivors, but it took a long time. We averaged two survivors a week until several showed us letters they had received from the government. Suddenly I realized that the government had a file on all Lety survivors. The government was offering compensation if the survivors could prove they were in Lety. The money wasn't much, only a few hundred dollars, but the survivors had to prove they were there. The proof the government requested was a certificate from Třeboň archives.

I had worked in Třeboň archives for more than twenty years. I knew every employee. I knew every office. If someone at Třeboň archives was now corresponding with the survivors, I knew what to do. I hired a Prague researcher to find the file in Třeboň archives for me.

We drove to Třeboň. An employee who still believed in my work told us they had sent the file to the state archive in Prague.

My Prague researcher visited the state archive in Prague and told the director that he had heard about me, the American historian who was telling lies about Lety. The Holocaust was a serious thing which Americans didn't understand. My Prague researcher, a journalist, told the archive director that he wanted to write an article against my research. The archive director offered assistance.

Within minutes his staff produced two lengthy reports about me. Dr. Josef Havlas of the Foreign Ministry had written them. They were written in the old communist style, saying how I was an enemy of the state and why I should be banned from all archives and given no assistance by any state employee. The archive director allowed my Prague researcher to make photocopies.

It didn't take long to find out that the state archive in Prague held more documents on Lety than Třeboň. From the boxes of records they allowed my researcher to see, we estimated another 60,000 documents existed in Prague on Lety. To prove Lety was not an extermination camp, they allowed my researcher to see almost anything he wanted to look at, except a few "sensitive" files that were on a permanent loan to the Office of the President.

They also introduced my researcher to an archive assistant who had been working on the Lety case since my revelations. She had spent six months doing nothing else. She was supposed to refute any accusations, but had found more horror than I had.

To this day, I am not sure how my Prague researcher did it. He not only found the file on the survivors (correspondence from 1973 to 1996), but was allowed to make a complete photocopy. I now had the addresses of more than two hundred Lety survivors. Overnight we were interviewing two survivors a day instead of two a week.

Ten days later, my Gypsy translator, Ľubomír Zubák, quit. This is what he said:

"Look, I must tell you, I can't go on with this project. Nobody in my family understands what we are doing. They think it's a waste of time that I'm not working at a proper job. My wife wants me to go out and find a proper job. Every night when I come home she's yelling at me to do something worthwhile.

"I tell you, this work is not good for my health. I'm starting to dream, every night, about these stories. I can't forget what these people have told us. My life seems to be getting mixed up with theirs. I wake up in the middle of the night and I think I'm in Lety, I think I'm the one being beaten to death.

"I tell you, this work is getting too dangerous. We're getting things out of the archive we're not suppose to see. We're talking with people we're not suppose to talk to. You know, it's very easy for the government to stop us. When they find out what we're really doing, they will stop us.

"So I can't go on. I'm sorry. I really wanted to help you, but this country's not ready to hear these things."

I too was tired, emotionally and physically. It was May. We had been interviewing survivors for six months. Their stories had taken a toll. It was impossible not to cry with the survivors. Crying every day leaves you drained.

The government knew what we were doing. I had already heard remarks from government supporters: we really hadn't found any survivors; I was making up the stories; I had no proof; I hadn't recorded the Gypsies speaking; I had not videotaped their testimonies; and if I had found Gypsies, well everyone knew Gypsies lied; you could never believe a Gypsy. Even Dr. Nečas spoke out against my work, saying stories by survivors couldn't be trusted because survivors never remembered very well. Yet he had published a book of interviews with survivors about Auschwitz.

Did I believe the stories I was finding? There were too many details, too many tears, not to believe. After finding the government's correspondence with the survivors, we were discovering former Lety prisoners in every corner of the country. They were not in contact with each other. No one wanted their neighbors to know they were even Gypsy, let alone that they had been in a concentration camp. That was still a stigma in the Czech Republic. Most survivors had never even told their own children about Lety. They didn't want them to know the horror, to live with the stigma. Most of the survivors told the same story. I had no doubt that some of the survivors were mentally deranged, had been since Lety. I wondered what kind of story I would tell if I had been a prisoner in Lety.

Our critics were right about one thing. We were not recording the oral histories. The survivors refused to speak in front of a microphone or a camera. If the police detained me, the survivors could deny they told me about Lety. But if it were recorded or taped, they feared retribution. So while Lubo translated, I typed down their stories on my laptop computer. My reply to our critics was this: if the government thought I was making up the stories, why weren't they interviewing the survivors?

After Lubo quit, I used several different translators. The stories were too horrible, the tears too much for anyone to last very long.

I never made an appointment with a survivor. Whenever I called over the phone, they told me no. If I showed up, told them I was an American who wanted to help them get justice, I had a better chance of getting in the door.

Unfortunately, many survivors who had corresponded with the government were now dead. More than once I missed a survivor's death by only a few days. From the time I asked the Czech Embassy in Washington, D.C. to help me find survivors until I got the government's file on the survivors, more than half had died. Later I heard that several survivors died shortly after I visited them.

After hearing from the survivors the names of the most sadistic guards, guards who killed every day, I tracked down several, still alive, unrepentant. I also found the director of all the Czech camps during World War II still alive, living in Prague. Although he tried to fabricate a new story for himself, his information only collaborated what others were saying. I also found the widow of another camp director who confirmed the Germans had nothing to do with Lety. In her innocence, her story might be the most horrific of all.

My Prague friend made several hundred photocopies of the Lety documents in Prague. The SS report commissioned by the German high command in Prague after the typhus outbreak in Lety, confirmed that only thirteen prisoners and two guards had died at Lety from typhus. Also found were minutes of a meeting of camp commanders conducted by the Czech Minister of the Interior about how they should treat Gypsies in these camps. No Germans were present at the meeting. The Czech Minister insisted that the Gypsies be starved and beaten until they were almost dead.

The survivors' stories are the real stories of Lety. These people were there. They saw. They suffered. They may not get any compensation from the Czech government today for their suffering, or for the loss of family members, but they have a right to tell their stories. These are their words, not mine. These are their stories, not the government's. I believe them because I saw the horror in their eyes, heard the terror in their voices, while they told me their stories. Then we cried together.

Lety Village Chronicle[1]

Since 1 August 1942 the Gypsy camps have been in existence. The main purpose of these camps is to teach Gypsies and Gypsy half-breeds order, discipline and how to work. Therefore, all men, women and children without permanent work are suppose to be placed in these camps.

Gypsy camps came into being through a transformation of the already existing disciplinary working camps or so called "reception camps." Persons over the age of eighteen, hating work or without proof of a permanent job, are suppose to be placed in camps such as this.

According to the records, 1,852 healthy people and 383 other persons have been considered candidates for these camps in Bohemia. In Moravia, the numbers were 1,348 healthy people and 266 others.

For their education, the disciplinary work camp I (Lety) was opened in Bohemia, and the disciplinary work camp II in Moravia on 10 August 1940. The Czech work camp was placed not far from the village of Lety by Písek; the Moravian work camp was placed in the village of Hodonín by Kunstát.

The Lety working camp was built of 50 small wooden barracks suitable for summer accommodation, with one big barrack for winter. The camp capacity was for 80 people in winter and 240 people in summer. From the beginning there was great anxiety for the winter season because there wasn't enough clothing and there were no warm working shoes to replace the wooden shoes for summer.

In spite of these unfavorable circumstances, the disciplinary working camp in Lety was renamed the "reception camp" in March 1942. From this date, the number of people brought to the camp was much higher than the camp capacity, so a couple of new barracks were added. The director of the camp reported: According to present possibilities, it is possible to accommodate 300 adult people in this camp."

The construction of the camp was carried out by the inmates of the "reception camp." These people were released on 31 July 1942 (15 people). On 31 July 1942, at night, only 19 Gypsies remained in the camp at Lety.

Between 1 August and 3 August, a list was made of all Gypsies and Gypsy half-breeds in Bohemia. Families destined for the camp lost all of their property and assets. This property was given to the villages and towns where the Gypsies were living at the time of their order to report at the camp, or it was sold in public auction. Individuals were allowed to keep only their most important personal items, such as clothing, eiderdown, linen, blankets, dishes and the food necessary for transportation to the camp.

Coming from all over Bohemia, the first individuals began arriving on 2 August. Some of them arrived on foot, others in their nomadic wagons. Some were also transported by train or trucks, especially from the furthest places.

By the end of August 1942, the number of men, women and children in the camp was four times higher than the planned capacity. Therefore, it was necessary to extend the buildings.

Step by step, three wooden buildings were added. In this way, the capacity was doubled, so that it was possible to accommodate 600 people instead of 300 prisoners there.

But all of these adaptations were not good enough, and the superfluous prisoners had to live in unsuitable stopgaps until the end of January 1943.

After their arrival at the camp, all the prisoners had to go through a medical examination, and have their hair cut. Men, dirty women, and children were not allowed any hair. Clean women were allowed short hair. The men received second-hand prison clothes. The women and children were allowed to keep their civilian clothes.

The men's civilian clothes were put in storage where the personal effects of the prisoners were kept. The worthless things were immediately destroyed, while the valuable things were hidden. Later these valuable things and the money confiscated from the Gypsies were used to cover different camp expenses.

By the time the camp was liquidated, 8,367.45 crowns had been paid into the District Agricultural Savings Bank in Mirovice. Some personal property of the Gypsy prisoners (29 savings books, 3 sil-

ver pocket watches, 2 gold rings, 1 pair of gold earrings, and one watch) was taken by the District Office in Písek.

After their medical examination, and after receiving their clothes, the Gypsies were divided into three groups:

1) Men and boys older than 14 years of age.

2) Women and girls older than 12 years of age.

3) Children.

Each of these groups had their own separate accommodations.

The camp commander was a former police captain who had been the director of the Disciplinary Working Camp. He did not have a good reputation. Clerks and guards working at the camp didn't have a good reputation either. There were many frauds, and two were brought to court.

The camp leadership paid special attention to making strict camp rules. All games, especially cards or gambling games, were prohibited in the camp. It was also prohibited to make a campfire. Smoking was allowed only in an approved place.

According to the camp rules, all contact with the outside world was prohibited. Prisoners were not allowed to speak with other people coming from the outside. Prisoners were not allowed to receive any visits, correspondence, or packages.

The daily regime of the camp began at 5 a.m. with wake up time. After that, all prisoners (adults) had to get up, make their bed, wash themselves and clean their shoes. Children were allowed to sleep one hour more.

After a special signal, all prisoners had to stand at attention. Roll call was taken. After a health report had been taken, everyone had to report for work. Men and women worked separated. At work it was prohibited to eat, talk or smoke. Prisoners were required to work 10 hours daily. Work was interrupted only at noon for lunch, given at the work place.

The only place in the camp where the prisoners were allowed to congregate was next to the wash house. There prisoners could enjoy the fresh air. They were not allowed to congregate at any other place in the camp. They were not allowed to visit other barracks. Once in bed they were not allowed to talk or make any disturbance.

All prisoners had to be in bed with lights out at 8 p.m. After that time, absolute quiet was the order. Prisoners were not allowed to *leave the barracks after 8 p.m. Prisoners outside the barracks after 8 p.m. were warned by a shot. If they did not stop, they were killed. The same ruled applied in the case of escapes.*

Misdeeds in the camp were punished by the camp commander or any other superior person. The Gypsy language was prohibited in the camp. Gypsies were allowed to speak only German.

Criminal acts committed before coming to the camp were punished by the German Reich's courts. Criminal acts committed after coming to the camp were punished by the Criminal Center in Prague, with prisoners being sent to Auschwitz.

Copy of report supplied by Mr. Čanda, keeper of the Lety chronicle.

(1) By law every village in the Czech Republic must keep an up-to-date written history. Normally a local teacher is appointed to keep up this history which is filed in the town hall. During the main period of emigration to America (1850-1890), most Czechs sold their property to raise cash for their journey and start up in America. The village chronicles normally noted these sales and sometimes the reason the person was selling their ancestral cottage, "because they were emigrating to America." These chronicles are another source (besides the baptismal records) to document the exact date when families left for the United States. This is the official record about the Gypsy camp in the Lety village chronicle.

J. Š.

I don't want to talk to you about Lety. That was a long time ago, I don't want to remember those things that happened there. Those are bad memories. I was fourteen. What are you going to do with this? It's too late. Justice? There's no justice in this county. Compensation? It's too late. Havel gave us 23,000 crowns trying to show he's a humanist. What's 23,000 crowns today? It's like telling us to go buy a cup of coffee. In 1945 that was real money. Today it's nothing.

Many Romany died in Lety. Every day. Every day there were deaths. I was walking around the camp because I was working in the kitchen and in the laundry, so I saw many dead bodies. Every day dead bodies. They were all murdered. Murdered every day.

There were no Germans there. Just the Czech police. I think it's too late today to make some justice. You should have been here early in the 1950s to take care of what happened in Lety. When we moved to Prague after the war in 1948, I saw a Lety guard. He was a policeman. I told him I knew him. His name was Novák. He was in the police station, in the registration section. I recognized him. When he asked me my name, I told him Chadrabová. "You are a Chadrabová?" He knew my name was a Gypsy name. The next day he was gone.

I remember the guards Fejfar, Fejkl, Havelka, Černý. They were all bad. They beat and killed people, every day, every day there were dead bodies.

It was a hard time to be there. I don't want to talk about it. I don't want to remember those bad memories. I'm an old woman. I'm seventy now. The guards must be a hundred, at least eighty or ninety. What can you do to them today? If I was forty, that would be different. We could do something together. But nothing can happen now. What can happen? It's too late.

I don't want anything from anybody. No money, even if somebody wants to give me a million. I have good children. They help me. I don't need anything. They support me every month.

I want to live in peace. I'm sorry I don't help you, but I can't talk about this. I went there with my sister a few years ago. The government had built a pig farm where our people died, where they were murdered. Our relatives' bones were scattered in the field. The big pit was still there. Animals were shitting on the bones of our people. You talk about justice. There is no justice in this country.

The guards who were killing our people in that camp are already dead. So what kind of justice can you make?

You have found four guards still alive? What do you want to do with them? They're too old. They are like children today.

Photos? Can I recognize them? I don't want to see any photos. I don't want to see them again. I don't want to think about these things again. Please leave me alone. The people who can tell you these things are already dead. You're twenty years too late.

Anna Růžičková

I don't know why you've come to see me for information about Lety. This country is very well informed about Lety. There are lots of museums and archives that have information. Six months ago I took the bus to Třeboň and found my papers there. The archive staff was very helpful. They showed me all the papers about my stay in Lety. They gave me a certificate to prove that I was in Lety. Four months ago, I received 20,000 crowns compensation for being a prisoner in Lety.

My maternal grandmother Božena Růžičková was the first one in our family taken to Lety, but she was only there a few days before she was sent to Auschwitz. I don't know how she died. She wrote to us from Auschwitz asking for bread, garlic and onions. That's all she wanted. Of course we sent things to her until we never heard from her again.

I was born on the 28 December 1928 in Prague. My brother Jan was also born in Prague in July 1930. My sister Karolína was born in 1934, and Barbora in 1936. Josef was born in 1943 before we were sent to the concentration camp, and Jana in 1948. We all had the same parents. My father married my mother when he was 19 and my mother was 18. Our father took care of us very well. Our sister is a professor in Switzerland. She has her own ballet school in Geneva. Johanna Čermáková was my mother; my father was Robert Růžička.

We lived 30 years in Příbram. We had a big house there. My mother was half-Gypsy, my father one hundred percent Gypsy.

I was lying in bed one night when a Czech policeman visited them. He said that the police would pick us up the next morning. He also told us that the men of the Serynek family, our next door neighbors, had already escaped, that the police had only picked up the women and the children. The Czech policeman told us to pack a few things, that we were going to be picked up to go to a work camp. We thought it was strange because our father had a job. We knew people were being picked up, but only because they didn't have jobs. But three months before some Jewish friends had warned us that they were being taken away and that Gypsies would be the next to go. After the Czech policeman left, we went to a bread store and bought supplies.

It was 3:30 or 4:00 a.m. in the morning when the police came. We had to go by foot to the criminal police headquarters in Příbram. There we were fingerprinted, the whole family, our parents and all the kids. We were two or three days there at police headquarters, sleeping in the cells. After that we were taken to the train station and put in cattle cars. There was one Czech guard and one German guard in each wagon. I saw many other families, all Romany. The police weren't picking up anyone but Gypsies.

We were taken by train from Příbram to Prague with hundreds of other Gypsies. From the train station in Prague we were all taken by bus to a big wooden building. In this big hall there were hundreds of Gypsies from all over the Czech lands.

The wife of my uncle was living in Lysá nad Labem so my father wrote to tell them what had happened to us. He wanted someone to know.

While we were sitting in the corner of this big hall, I saw for the first time some SS men. They escorted all the families out of the hall. We were the last family left. All the other families were taken by bus to Lety. We wondered why we were the only family left there by ourselves. A few hours later we found our aunt from Lysá waiting outside for us. She had paid money for our release. We then went back home to Příbram.

A month later the Czech police came again and took the whole family except my mother who was pregnant. We were taken again to the train station near Příbram. When the train pulled out for Prague, I escaped and made my way back home. I asked a friend to send a telegram to my aunt in Lysá for me. I then stayed with my mother for three or four days. My aunt again went to Prague and again paid for my family's release.

After the family returned, we lived again our normal life in Příbram. I went back to school. My brother was born. We had no problems. Then in July when no one was in school my father took several of us children to his mother's place near Příbram to stay. While we were there, the Czech police arrived and arrested all of us in my grandmother's home on 7 August 1942. This time we were taken by train from Příbram direct to Lety. My mother and father with the rest of the children were not picked up. They were left alone for the whole war. I was with my aunts Josefa Vintrová and Antonie (Růžičková) Janošovská, my sisters Barbora and Marie Růžičková and my grandmother Filomena Růžičková.

When we arrived at Lety I was looking for my mother and father. I thought we were there to work. I was very naive. I found two of my uncles cooking in the kitchen. We did not have a good life in Lety but because of our relatives working in the kitchen we got extra food. After four days, some of our relatives disappeared. I never saw them again in my life.

When we entered the camp, the women had to have all their hair shaved off their bodies, everywhere. The guards watched this and then picked out the women they wanted. My two aunts were very beautiful, so they had to sleep with the guards.

I was thirteen years old and my job was to look after the small children, cleaning them, combing their hair. I was with my sisters. One was six-years-old, the other nine.

We seldom left our barracks. I never knew there was a small lake by the camp. I remember relatives coming to the camp and throwing food over the fence for their loved ones. I don't know if the guards arrested them or not, but I don't think so. My parents never came. My mother had a small baby and my father was working. Later I learned that my aunt in Lysá told my parents never to go near Lety. She told us that we were saved from going to Auschwitz by a lawyer in Prague 6, Dr. Benda. He was working with the authorities. She knew him and got him to save us.

In the morning we only had black coffee with bread. For lunch we had potatoes, sometimes watery soup. In the evening, soup or bread. There was hunger, but we had more food than the others because of our uncles in the kitchen.

I never saw anyone beaten at Lety. I never saw anyone hung up on a post. I know that there was a typhus epidemic in Lety but I never saw anyone die of typhus. None of the children died of typhus. I seldom left our building. I was really stuck in this barracks for nine months. Actually, my aunts always told me never to leave the barracks, never to go out. So I didn't. For nine months I never left that house. My aunts always told me to be happy that I was in the building, that I never had to see what was going on outside. They told me that my life would be much worse if I left the house. My aunts really looked after me at Lety but I never knew what happened to them. They never came back after the war. I don't know if they died in Lety or in another concentration camp.

There were many people in Lety who were not supposed to be there, many white people, many Czechs who were not Gypsies.

After nine months I left the house because my aunt from Lysá was outside the gate waiting for us. She had obtained the release for me and my two sisters. It was 4 May 1943. Later I learned that my grandmother had died in the camp.

My aunt had a car and drove us back to Příbram. In the car was my aunt, myself and my two sisters, Barbora and Filomena.

In 1944 a Czech policeman came again to our house in Příbram and warned my father to hide all the children because the police were coming in the morning to send us to Auschwitz. My cousin and my uncle were staying with us so they went into the woods to hide. I never saw them again. I think they were caught and taken directly to Auschwitz. Our parents took us to the attic to hide but the police never came.

My aunt really saved us from being sent to Auschwitz. Her

name was Františka Blumová. She had about five houses. She and her husband sold the best horses. They made their money with horses. They saved our whole family with their money. She died about fifteen years ago. Her husband was the brother of my mother.

I have a lot of Czech friends, but yesterday one of my relatives had to go to school because her beautiful child was being called a dirty Gypsy by the other children. There is a lot of racism in this country. Whenever I am in Switzerland visiting my sister, I never feel racism. But here I feel it all the time.

When we came back from Lety, there was no racism. We went back to school and all our friends and teachers were asking us about Lety. They were happy to see us. We didn't have any problems with discrimination and racism until after 1989. These problems didn't exist under communism, but today it's bad.

Some of my relatives are professors and they never had any problem finding work. But today they have problems.

I heard on TV that two Italian women were taken to a hospital after being attacked by skinheads. They thought these tourists were Gypsies. That's how bad it's getting in this country.

B. C.

My husband and I, along with our twelve children, were in Lety for only ten months, but it was long enough for six of my children to die.

I was born on 21 February 1904 in Zehun, in the county of Nymburk. My husband Antonín was born in 1901 in Černčice. Our oldest child Antonín was born in 1923. When we arrived in Lety our youngest child was only eight months old.

We were arrested in August of 1942, in Golčův Jeníkov, in the county of Čáslav. We had our own house but for his work my husband still maintained a wagon and horse. He worked the local area sharpening knives and scissors. I couldn't do anything except look after our 12 children. We didn't live like other Gypsy families. We didn't take things to markets to sell, we weren't nomads, we didn't steal. My husband sharpened knives for butchers and restaurants.

One day a policeman came to our home. We were worried by his visit because many Gypsies living in wagons had already been arrested. But he told us that we wouldn't be arrested because we had a home. We weren't vagabonds.

There were many Gypsies in our area, but we didn't consider ourselves Gypsies. Perhaps our ancestors were Gypsies, but we didn't live like Gypsies any more. We didn't steal, we didn't live in a wagon. We had our own home. Our skin was white. We didn't consider ourselves Romany. Maybe the police did, because of my husband's job. It was a job always associated with Gypsies.

In the town where we lived, where we were arrested, there was another Chadraba family that was not related to us. They were on the list to be arrested with the other Gypsies in town, but they were friendly with a policeman called Mák. He was a real Hebrew son-of-a-bitch. I think he was having an affair with this man's wife, so she got him to cross off the name of their family and put on our name. One day this policeman was telling us that we weren't going to be arrested, and the next day the Czech police came with a big truck and took us to Kutná Hora to the abattoir. We spent three days there until the police came with another truck to take us to Třeboň. We saw lots of lakes and fish at Třeboň, then they took us to Lety.

We did have a beautiful new wagon with a horse. The police killed our horse, but they liked our wagon so much that they sent it to Lety. In the camp I often admired our wagon until I saw the guards were using it to store dead bodies. Then one day they had to take the body of my eight month old son to our wagon. They just threw him in with all the others.

At Lety we got only a piece of bread for the whole day, nothing else. My seven year old son was working in the stone quarry with me. He kept asking for bread while he worked beside me. So I was always saving bread for him.

One day I came back from the woods where I had been working. My clothes were very dirty so I went to the laundry room where a good friend of mine was working. A policeman heard me say I wanted to wash my clothes so he beat me. I don't remember his name but he was very small. He beat me so badly that he broke my eardrum.

At the quarry, the beatings were bad for the men who had to push these four-wheel carts filled up with stones. Going up hill, the guards beat these men like horses, to make sure they didn't stop pushing. But some of those men weren't very strong. If they fell down and let the cart roll backwards they got beaten to death. Many men died from beatings at the stone quarry.

But one of the worst things I saw at Lety was when all the people were brought together to watch the guards beat my best friend, Marie Vrbová. She was from Prague. She was beaten in front of everyone by the guards because she had stolen a piece of bread. She was beaten so badly that she died in front of us. The guards brought water to get her up. Then they brought her a cup of tea, trying to revive her, but she was already dead. There were a lot of people who died like that, from beatings, but I don't remember all their names. There were so many people we couldn't know everybody's name.

One policeman by the name of Fiala was very nice to me. He told me his story once. He told me that he was in Lety because a high ranking policeman found out that he played cards for money during working hours. So he was punished for this by being sent to Lety. But he was a nice person and sometimes he brought me a piece of bread because I was working very hard. Sometimes he gave my husband cigarettes.

We didn't have any gold with us because we were afraid that the police would take it away from us. My husband had 60,000 crowns at that time. He hid this money in our scrub board. We took this scrub board with us along with our clothes. We thought we might use this money to bribe the guards and escape. But what happened was that somebody stole the scrub broad when we arrived the first day at the camp.

The beatings were very bad in the camp. The guards even beat the children. But I can not talk about this. I lost six of my children in Lety. I really don't want to talk about it.

My children got typhus in Lety. So did I. The older ones survived. It was the younger ones who didn't make it.

My husband and I had to work very hard in the camp. We were separated a lot from our children. I wish we could have looked after them more. But the guards wouldn't let us. They beat me once when I asked to see my children.

You shouldn't ask about Lety. We don't want to remember the past. We are afraid that if the Czechs know about Lety, they will make another concentration camp for us today.[1] I don't want to talk because I am afraid if I say something it can be used against us. The situation is not so rosy for us today.

After the war, the Czechs didn't receive people very well who had been in concentration camps. It got better under the communists, but now it's bad again.

Have I ever received compensation for being in Lety, for the death of my six children? Let me tell you. My daughter went to the government office to get an application for compensation when the newspaper articles appeared last year saying that parliament had made funds available after fifty years. But the bureaucrats in the office told my daughter that I had no right to compensation because I was not a political prisoner. I lost six children in Lety. My husband and I were beaten badly by the guards. We caught typhus in Lety. But we have no right to compensation.

(1) Ludvík Vaculík, a famous Czech dissident writer and journalist, wrote in 1994 that since the Gypsies have their own culture it might be better to find a place for them where they can realize their own life such as on a reservation. Karel Pecka, another dissident writer, suggested special laws in the Czech Republic for Gypsies.

Alžběta Růžičková

I was born 8 April 1924 in Dolní Slivno, county of Mladá Boleslav. My father Jan Růžička bought and sold horses. We lived in a wagon all year. We were Czech Romany and traveled all the time, mainly in northern Bohemia.

I was eighteen years old when I heard that my mother and father and my three brothers and two sisters had been arrested by the Czech police and taken to a concentration camp. I didn't really know where they were or what had happened to them, but from that moment on I tried to avoid the police. One day my husband had to go to Semily to the hospital for treatment for his back. We lived in Loukov. I stayed at home with our six-month-old daughter. That was the last time I ever saw him. After the war, I heard he died in Auschwitz.

A policeman came that day and told me I was under arrest. He put me on a train with my child, a train to Mirovice, with other Gypsies guarded by the police. From Mirovice we walked to a camp called Lety.

I entered the camp on 14 August 1942. Of course, the first thing they did was shave your head and change your clothes. Much to my surprise, I found my parents, my brothers and sisters and my grandfather there. They had arrived two months earlier.

My child was allowed to stay with me, but she died shortly after we arrived in the camp.[1]

Everybody in camp had a job. Some people worked in the stone quarry, others in the woods. I looked after the children, and cleaned the barracks. I was also allowed to look after my mother who was very sick in the camp. Ironically, she survived Lety only to die in Auschwitz.

We did not get much to eat in Lety. Potato soup and bread. The potatoes were never cleaned. We got as much dirt as potato. The water was always brown.

There was a lot of illness in the camp, some typhus. Many, many people died in the camp. I cannot tell you how many because there were so many people there. But they had a big pit behind the camp and bodies were taken there every day and covered with white coal.[2]

My father died in Lety, the guards said from bronchitis. I don't know. I seldom saw him. I didn't know he was sick. But I can tell you, we were badly treated in that camp. I won't say that Lety was worse than Auschwitz, but maybe it was. The Czech guards were certainly the worst of all the concentration camps I was in. If you were sweeping and didn't do it well, you got beaten. Jesus Maria, the number of times I got beaten, you have no idea. I'm black. You see my face. But at Lety I was even blacker from the beatings.

I can't remember any of the guards by name. Maybe I knew some names once, but those are names I don't want to remember. I heard about more beatings, more killings than I saw. You had to be careful at Lety. All day long you worried about your own life. You were afraid to see things, what was happening. You were afraid to see other people being beaten, because you could be beaten for watching. You tried to look away or close your eyes every time there was a beating, or a dead body was being carried away.

Some people escaped from the camp, but most were captured, then taken back to the camp and beaten to death. Many were shot trying to escape. My grandfather was once taken to a wagon where they chained prisoners together before they beat them. My grandfather died in Lety. I don't know what he died of. He just disappeared one day like a lot of people at Lety. I know he didn't escape.

I don't remember the name of the commander of the camp, but he was always telling us that there were only two roads in Lety: one to enter, and the other to heaven.

Many children died of starvation in Lety. They looked like those pictures you see of the starving children in Africa today. But so many horrible things happened in Lety every day that you would not believe it. If a guard didn't like a prisoner he would either beat him to death or send the dogs after him. Then there was the execution post. You seldom knew the reason why people were sent to the execution post. The reason was usually secret. You were afraid to look at the people hanging there. Most who were hung up died there. I only know of a few who survived the execution post.

There were only Romanies in Lety when I was there. I don't remember any other people. There weren't any Jews, or Czechs except the guards. There weren't any Germans there. All the guards were Czech.

In Lety we lost everything: our gold, our money, our wagons and horses, but especially our lives. You have no idea how many lives were lost at Lety. The Czechs at Lety were the real Hitlers.

Did the guards abuse the women at Lety? Daily. Every day. It was in their personal program. Not all of the guards, but most of them.

My worst experience in Lety? Starvation and the discipline of the guards. Being afraid all day long. You always feared a guard would beat you at any moment for no reason at all, just because of his mood that day. We were always victims of the guards' moods.

You say there's a pig farm on the camp site today? I don't believe you. I can't believe that. There were too m   people buried there. They couldn't have built a pig farm where so many people are buried.

After Lety, I was sent to Auschwitz. From there to Buchenwald, then Ravensbruck. I ended up in a camp where we made parts for airplanes, some place in Germany. I don't remember the name of that last camp.

Last year I got compensation from the Ministry of Defense: 100,000 crowns for my husband dying in Auschwitz and 80,000 crowns for my time in the German concentration camps. I never got anything for being in Lety where I lost my child, my father and my grandfather. Out of our family of seven, I was the only survivor of the concentration camps.

How do we live today? I still work. I go door to door selling pullovers. I used to make clothes to sell but I can't do that anymore. I'm seventy two years old this year (1996).

I have four children but none of them have a job except one son who buys and sell antiques. Look how black we are. We can't get a regular job in this country because of the color of our skin. My other son is a stone cutter. Under the communists he had a job. Later in Germany he made many fountains, cutting them out of stone. But here in the Czech Republic he can't get a job, not even as a garbage collector.

There's no discrimination in our town of Horice because the people here know us. My husband was born here. All my kids were born here. During the communist times we couldn't go to the Hotel Beránek, Gypsies weren't allowed in. But today we can go anywhere in Horice. There are no skinheads here to bother us. But the treatment elsewhere is bad in this country. Things are almost as bad as when I was arrested back in 1942. The Czechs have hated us for many centuries.

(1) Alžběta refused to say how her child died. Her eyes swelled up with tears and she refused to answer any more questions for several minutes.
(2) She probably means lime.

Marie Čandová

The conditions at Lety were very bad. People died there every day from hunger. Five of my brothers and sisters (Antonín, Stanislav, Anna, Františka, and Jana) died there.

I was born on 15 August 1925, in Hokava (Podbořany). My father's name was Josef Čanda, and my mother was Božena Hospodářská. When the police arrested us we were living in Hostovnice (Sedličany). My father was working in the mines in Krásná Hora. My mother was a housewife. She had eight children to take care of. I heard that my parents moved many times because we always had money problems. We were a lot of children and they had to move.

One afternoon the Czech police came and picked us up.[1] I can't tell you the date. To tell you the truth I can't read and I can only write a little bit. They told us that we were going to work on a farm. Each of us could only take 20 kilos of things. So they took us directly by truck to Lety. There was only one truck.

I heard that my father, before we went to Lety, hit a German man, or defended himself from a German who attacked him. I think that is why we were all taken to Lety. None of us were Gypsies. None of my ancestors were ever Gypsies. We had no relatives in Lety. Just my parents and eight of us children.

From the moment we arrived we were treated badly. They immediately shaved off our hair. They separated us and put women, children and men in different houses.

And then we saw the horrible situation in the camp, how people were falling down on the ground from hunger, and how people were dying every day. I was almost seventeen years old. I can't tell you how many people died in the time I was there, but there were many deaths every day. People were beaten all the time, and also they hung them up on the execution post and left them there for half a day.

We were tortured for every little thing we did wrong. When we were standing in line to receive our food and one of us didn't stand like the guards expected, the guards would beat us with a stick right away.

In the morning we received black coffee and a quarter piece of bread that had to last for the whole day. For lunch they gave us one potato in a small dish with a bit of sauce; in the evening sometime we got a bit of burnt potato with black coffee.

I was working on the road construction. The guards didn't care if our shoes were too big or too small for us. My shoes were too small so I told this to the guards because my feet were hurting. They sent me to the doctor who cut off a big part of two of my toes. I can't remember this doctor's name but he was a Jew. He was very nice. Later came another doctor who was not so nice to us. I was sent back to the hut. I didn't work for quite awhile.

My father worked in the office of the guards as a cleaner. My mother did everything, any kind of work they ordered her to do. She worked in the stone quarry and carried wood from the forest. My brothers and sisters also worked like my mother.

I remember working on a farm, in the fields. We got a room there and stayed for a couple of weeks. We received more and better food there and our life was much better than in the camp.

At the farm we also got a piece of bread every day that we could save to take back to the camp. We baked our own potatoes in the fields. We took our bread back to our mother who was waiting for us in the camp. The food we saved we were allowed to take back.

Visitors were not allowed to enter the camp.

Some of the guards spoke Czech, some German. I remember the guards Strnad and Maxa. Both were very mean men. When we wanted to drink a bit of water while we were working Maxa hit us right away. Once he slapped my face so hard, my earring felt out. At that time I was working in the stone quarry. I also remember Pešek. He was a good man. The first guards were worse, the ones who came later were better. Koudelka was one of the new ones who came to the camp. He was a nice man.

There was only one big latrine for all of us. It was always very dirty because there were so many people there. We all had to carry away the shit from the latrines in buckets. We stood in line and one gave the bucket to the other. The last one threw it on the garden. We were all dirty from that. When one of the guards saw we didn't do it fast enough he hit us. Afterwards we were allowed to wash our hands in cold water but without soap. Soap didn't exist in the camp.

I don't know what happened to the mothers who gave birth to babies in the camp. My mother's youngest child, Jana, was ten months old and my mother had to leave her in another house and go to work. We don't know if they fed the child or not; she died after two months. I am sure she died of hunger. She was always screaming and crying.

The guards used to take us on Saturdays and Sundays when the weather was nice to the pond so we could wash ourselves. During the winter there were a few showers in the camp we could use only a few times. It was very cold there in the winter. There was no heating inside the camp.

Everything was terrible there. During the time we were working and we asked a guard if we could go to the bathroom and came back a bit late they hit us. My mother once was with my little sister and a guard found her there and beat her until she bled. Her whole arm was covered with blue bruises.

We heard many times that some of the women were together with the guards. The women who worked as cleaning ladies for the guards and the ones who were cooking in the kitchen were treated nicely by the guards because they went with them.

Some of the prisoners had to take the dead bodies to the cemetery in Mirovice by horse and wagon. I heard that in Mirovice there wasn't enough space so after that they threw them somewhere in the forest.

They tortured us all the time. Only the women working in the kitchen received normal treatment. We had to work very hard all day long just for a quarter piece of bread.

I don't know what my brothers and sisters died of I think it was from hunger. People were very skinny there. I didn't have typhus in Lety, neither did my parents. We were very sick, me because of my feet. The overall health conditions were very bad.

When old people were afraid to go into the pond to wash, the guards threw them in. But I don't remember anyone being drowned there.

I don't have nightmares about Lety, but I think about Lety often, how we suffered there. My grandchildren want to have everything today; at that time in Lety the children didn't even have enough bread and were starving to death. I think about this all the time.

I remember the Gypsies beating each other in the camp, fighting over food. Everybody only looked after himself, no one stuck together, everyone went their own way trying to survive.

The women and the men wore prison clothes. I didn't see anyone in civilian clothes.

There are a lot of Gypsies living in Cheb today. But there are very few living here. I never see them. I can't tell you anything about racism. I don't know if there is a problem.

In the end they released those prisoners who had their own homes, especially the whites. The people were released by names also. The ones who didn't have homes or were black were sent to other concentration camps. A lot of people were released, especially whites and even some of the mixed people.

My parents and three of us children were released. My maternal grandmother died in Terezín. I don't know why she was sent there, but she died there while we were in Lety. My grandfather never told us why she was sent there. He just said that people were gassed there.

When we were released, we walked for about one hour to Mirovice and from there we took the bus to our home. All the things we took to the camp they took away from us so we left the camp without anything. Just the clothes we stood up in. We found our house the same way as we had left it. We all separated and went to different places looking for work. I worked as a servant in a farmhouse.

Two or three years ago I received 19,000 crowns for being in Lety. My two siblings that also were released with me had already died so they received nothing.

My worst experiences at Lety were the beatings. They happened all the time, every day.

I can't remember anymore, and I don't want to remember – all that suffering there. After the camp was closed, I never met any survivors from Lety. I only talked to my brother about it, but he died two years ago.

(1) Tenth of August 1942.

Barbara Richterová

I was born on 18 March 1926, in Prostějov near Olomouc. My father's name was Robert Richter. My mother's name was Anna Richterová.

My parents made their living by traveling around the country in a horse and wagon, selling clothes they made. There was never any time to go to school. We were always on the move. Although I grew up learning to speak German and other languages from my father, I've never learned to read or write. I've always been good at numbers, but never at words.

I was fifteen when we were arrested and made to drive our wagons to Lety. It took us three days. We couldn't stop even to rest the horses. In every village the local police followed us to the next village.

Our first introduction to Lety was a speech by the camp commander, Janovský. He always addressed the new prisoners from his balcony: "There are only two places for you Gypsies, here or in hell."

The first day at Lety they cut our hair. My hair was very long, down to my waist. My father begged them not to cut my hair. A guard by the name of Baloun took a small club out of his boot and hit my father across the face, opening a big wound, a big gash across his cheek and jaw right down to the bone. That was our second introduction to Lety.

I worked in the stone quarry, breaking up the stones, making them smaller, with a hammer. Older children carried the stones to the road the Gypsy men were building, Highway 19.

A German Gypsy worked next to me but she could only speak German. Her people had escaped from Hitler only to find the Czechs hated Gypsies more than the Germans. The guards at Lety didn't understand German so I had to translate for her. She was a Sinti and didn't understand Czech. The guards gave her a hard time because she couldn't speak Czech. They beat her because she couldn't learn Czech fast enough.

In the woods there was a big pit where they put dead bodies

■ Josef Hejduk, the most notorious killer at Lety, according to many survivors. Hejduk lives today in Kvilda, south Bohemia. To date the Czech government has refused to charge Hejduk with war crimes although many survivors are willing to testify against him. *Photo by Paul Polansky.*

every day. Today if you dig only a few feet down you will find thousands of bones. Hundreds of children were thrown in that pit. If you were a good mother, you threw yourself in with your child. Of course, many mothers didn't. They wanted to survive.

In the beginning there were cheap wooden coffins for the dead, but later the bodies were just thrown into the pit and covered over, layer after layer, with lime.

In the end everyone had to collect wood, all the men had to collect wood instead of working on the road. The wood was never brought to the camp. But at night we saw the fires. I heard those fires were to burn the bodies because there was no more room to bury them.

I remember the German Gypsies sent from Auschwitz to teach us order. They were Rupert and Vinily. They were happy to be out of Auschwitz, but they had to prove themselves so they wouldn't be sent back. For a time the Czech guards didn't have to beat us at all because they got these German Gypsies to do it while they laughed about Gypsies beating Gypsies to death. To amuse the guards, the German Gypsies called us Czech dogs.

I worked all day in the quarry or in the woods so I didn't see a lot of the horror in the camp. But when I returned at night, I heard about it, stories about Hejduk taking young girls to his office and making them take their clothes off and then beating them and abusing them. No one was ever seen again if they had to go to Hejduk's office. I remember him well. He was a tall, strong man with a big mole in the center of his forehead. My cousin worked in his office. She always had to mop up the blood from his beatings.

After five months I couldn't take it any longer. I knew my turn was coming. I heard talk that I was on Hejduk's list, that he was going to take me to his office and do things to me.

My aunt worked in the kitchen as a cook. She took me to the gate and told the guard the kitchen needed water. The guard let me go to the pond to fetch a bucket of water. When he wasn't looking, I dropped my bucket and ran into the woods. I slept that night in the woods. Although it was already May, it was cold at night. Early in the morning I walked to the Mirovice train station about 3 miles away. There were Czech soldiers there but they didn't bother me. With my blond hair and white skin they thought I was Czech. I didn't have any money for a ticket but I got on the train anyway and hid in the toilet. I rode the train to Benešov, then transferred to the Prague train. On the Prague train I sat across from a SS officer. I spoke German to him.

In Prague I went to stay with relatives. I went out every day and in a coffee shop I sat across from some more SS. They weren't looking for me or my people. That was our problem in our country during the war, the Germans didn't bother us, only the Czechs. That's how I got caught again. The Czech police paid a relative who informed on me.

I went through many concentration camps (Lety, Auschwitz, Ravensbruck, Belsen-Bergen, Buchenwald) but the Czech guards at Lety were the worst, much worse than the German guards in all the other camps.

Lety was worse than Auschwitz because you could be beaten to death at any moment, for any reason. In Auschwitz you only had one bad moment in the morning, to hear if your turn had come for the crematorium. The German guards weren't bad, they didn't push you, they didn't hit you. At Lety you had to be careful all day long looking out for a guard that could hit you at any moment, beat you to death for no reason at all. In Belsen-Bergen I was weak, sick, and my fellow prisoners held me up for roll call. The German guards said nothing. If that had happened in Lety I would have been beaten to death and so would the people holding me. I was in many death camps but Lety was the worst.

Half of my family, our clan, died in Lety. To this day we don't know what happened to them. At least two hundred couples died in Lety from our family, not counting the children. None of the children survived. There were five, six, seven children in each family.

Did I see the Czech guards drowned children in the pond? I can't tell you that because I didn't see that, I only heard it. Our Gypsy law doesn't allow me to lie.

I could tell you enough to fill several novels with stories about what happened but I am afraid to talk. I still fear the Czechs will come after me.

When they had the Lety memorial service two years ago (1995), Czech TV interviewed the Lety priest. He said, "Why are you reporters so interested in Lety? Only Gypsies were killed here, no one else."

The Czechs today keep talking about how bad the Germans were but in Lety there were no Germans; all the war crimes committed at Lety were done by the Czechs guards, the Czech police. But no one has been investigated, brought to trial. Some of the guards are still alive. Why isn't there any justice in this country? Gypsies who steal to eat are sent to Czech jails for years. But war criminals are still free in the Czech Republic.

And why hasn't the Czech government given us compensation for being in Lety? The Germans didn't take us there. The Czechs did. The Germans didn't beat us, kill us there, only the Czechs. What happened to our horses, our wagons, our clothes, our gold? All Gypsy families had gold in their wagons. Why doesn't the Czech government just pay us for that? Forget the work we did while we were at Lety, just pay us for what they took. Our dead ones, our loved ones, they can never pay enough compensation for those murders.

I will go to jail if I have to, fighting for our compensation.

A Czech jail is surely safer than the Czech streets.

In the Czech Republic today I'm scared. I'm not frightened in Austria or Italy or Germany, although there are skinheads there too, but in the Czech Republic I'm really afraid. A man called me the other day, speaking Czech. He frightened me. I hung up. I want to leave here. I never want to come back.

E. C.

(as told by his widow)

My husband was born 17 March 1930, in Staré Hradiště, Pardubice. He was my cousin but his family traveled a lot with their horses and wagon selling things in markets: clothes, pottery, cooking utensils.

All my husband's clan was sent to Lety, about 150 people, except for my family. My family was lucky. We weren't sent there because we had a small house. We weren't living in the wagons. We didn't have any horses.

Officials from the town hall came to my husband's people to tell them about Lety. It was a nice place to stay, warm homes, good salary, easy jobs, so our people said yes. The men went first by train, then later the police came and got the rest of them who were looking after the horses and the wagons.

The horses were left behind, but the wagons were taken on the train with the people. Later the wagons were used to haul dead bodies to the pit in the woods behind the camp.

On another visit to our village, a German came with the Czech police; if you had a small forehead you were arrested but those with a high forehead were considered of a different race. Since my family had big wide foreheads and we had our own home, they accepted us as different from our Romany cousins. Of course, we also had very white skin.

My brother was the only one in our family that they took because he didn't want to work for the Germans. He even cut his own legs so he wouldn't have to work for the Germans or go into the army. But the Czechs came and got him and we didn't see him for four years.

My husband told me that the first day at Lety they shaved their heads, took away their clothes and shoes for prison clothes and wooden sandals. The children had to break stones for the road the men were building. They also had to collect kindling from the forest.

According to my husband, the Czech guards drowned the children, and beat the adults. The guards beat you for no reason at all. If they didn't like your face, the way you looked, the way you acted, they beat you to death. My brother who was in many concentration camps (Terezín, Auschwitz, Ravensbruck) said the guards at Lety were the worst that he ever came across.

The brother of my father, my uncle, and his five children died in Lety. The guards said the children died of typhus, but my husband told me they died of starvation. Oranges were brought to the camp but only the guards got them. That was the way it was with all the food. The guards ate well, but many of the children starved to death.

The prisoners had to stand outside for hours whenever it rained. In winter on the coldest days the prisoners had to stand outside to attention while they got sprayed with water to make them sick so they would die faster. But the beatings were the worst. I don't want to lie, I don't want to say something that is not true, but my husband was there, my brother was there, they both told me these things. There were many sicknesses because the prisoners got nothing to eat.

I heard that everybody had to go to the pond to wash themselves, everyone together. They saw bodies in the pond. They had to wash among those bodies. They had to get their drinking water from that pond.

My husband told me about a big pit where many, many bodies were dumped, then covered with lime, layer after layer.

The sister-in-law of my mother, married to the brother of my father, she's about 98 years old. She was at Lety and lost five of her children there. She is alive today, but I don't know where she lives. Her daughter lives in Lysá nad Labem by Brandýs. The sister of this old woman is also alive; she was in Lety too. Františka and her sister were young children in Lety. You should talk to them. They were all there.

My husband never received any compensation for being in Lety. We had seven children. We could have used the money. He died in 1971.

We started living together in 1953. That's when I discovered my husband had nightmares every night because of Lety. Automatically, every night he had these bad dreams. He always woke up screaming. So did my brother. They thought they were still being beaten with truncheons at Lety.

My husband saw food delivered to the camp, coffee, lemons, apples, oranges, but the guards always got them. The prisoners never got anything.

My husband talked about one very bad police man, worse than all the rest. My husband had nightmares about him too. The policeman killed a lot of young people, but I'm afraid to tell you his name. When my husband's mother was dying, this policeman wouldn't let her have any water. There was also a very good police man who tried to help. But I can't remember his name.

My husband was twelve years old when he was at Lety. He was beaten many, many times for nothing. Just because he was a Gypsy. He wasn't a fascist or a communist or anything, just a Gypsy. This camp, Lety, was for the genocide of the Gypsies.

My husband told me that he and some other children once snuck out of the camp to get food in the village of Lety. When the villagers saw them, they gave them bread and jam sandwiches, but when the children returned to the camp they were beaten for taking this bread.

Things are no better for us here today. Skinheads break my windows every week. They toss bottles with gasoline at our home. The police laugh at us. They never catch the skinheads who break our windows every week. Today there is racial cleansing in our country just like in 1942.

Many Romany families have had to leave this city of Příbram because of the beatings. The skinheads have chains and metal pipes and they wait for us, to beat us. My husband had nightmares about what happened to him in Lety; now I have nightmares about what is happening to me today in Příbram.

You can see on TV how the Czech police defend these skinheads, escorting them to their meetings, never defending us against them. My son once caught a skinhead who threw a stone through our window. The young man apologized; he said he was ordered to throw stones through our window. His organization ordered him to do it.

We told the police but they never investigated. They told us to be quiet or we would have more problems.

Anna Čermáková

I am not a Lety survivor. My husband was in Lety and so were my parents and my three brothers. But I escaped Lety, thank God.

My father's name was Josef Winter. I don't remember when he was born or where. My mother's name was Josefa. Her maiden name was Růžička. My three brothers were František, Jan and Jaroslav.

My parents lived in the traditional way with horses and wagons. They traveled, visiting markets, selling things. When they were arrested I was in Lysá nad Labem visiting relatives who had given up the Gypsy way of life and were living in a house. They also had whiter skin than my parents and many people thought they were Czechs. They were never arrested during the war.

After my family was sent to Lety, I never received a letter from them, so I took the train to visit them. I had heard the prisoners at Lety were starving so I took them a basket of food, mainly bread with some salami. We didn't have much in those days either. Everything was rationed. I took what I could. I was sixteen years old at the time.

I was not allowed into the camp to visit them. I had to wait outside until they came out with a work gang to work in a quarry in the next village. Even then I was not allowed to approach them, to talk to them. I watched them from afar and then asked one of the guards to give them the food. I never saw them get it but I prayed they would.

Of course, I was very afraid that the guards would arrest me, that they would find out I was a Gypsy too. But I had to see my family, I had to take them food. I was afraid, very much afraid but I went. I was whiter than the rest of my family, I could pass for Czech.

I made three or four trips like this to Lety until one day the Czech police came to Lysa and arrested me for being a Gypsy. I was not sent to Lety. They took me to Kolín and put me on a transport straight to Auschwitz where I spent the next three years.

When I arrived at Auschwitz I learned from some other Gypsy prisoners that my entire family had arrived from Lety but had already been sent to the gas chambers.

After the war I met my husband. His name was Antonín Čermák. He was born on 20 December 1920 in Nové Strašecí (Rakovník). He was arrested in Lysá because his was there with his parents. He was the only one arrested because he didn't have a job. He was in Lety for only five months then he went to Kolín. He escaped the transport there to Auschwitz by hiding in Lysá. He was lucky. When they closed the camp at Lety he was one of the few to be let go.

He had a hard time at Lety. He didn't like to talk about it. He had some nightmares. He mentioned something about the beatings. He worked in the stone quarry.

He really arrived at the end. When he was there most of the children were already gone.

Behind the camp there was a forest where there were many bodies. Most had been beaten to death. There was a big pit where the guards dumped the bodies after they ran out of room to bury them in the forest. My husband told me most of the people died from the beatings, not from the typhus although there was some of that too.

Even if he told me stories of the horror there, I can't remember anymore. I don't want to remember because there is no justice in this country. The Czech government won't even accept my application for compensation for Auschwitz. I lost my whole family there and I was there for three years but the Czech government won't even accept my application.

Now you want me to talk about Lety, why should I? They would probably come and kill me. Look at my tatoo on my left forearm. Here. Z-2012. And the Czech government still won't accept my application for compensation.

I don't dare go outside after dark in Prague. I never go outside. I am afraid. The skinheads are outside yelling, "Kill the Gypsies, Gypsies to the gas chambers." Today in Prague is like the Hitler times all over again for us.

I would like to leave this country, but I have no place to go, no family to go to. I'm 73 years old. Haven't I suffered enough already?

Berta Berousková

I was born in a wagon by Prostějov (Olomouc) on 27 October 1928. My parents were Anna Richterová and Robert Richter. My only sibling was a sister, Barbara, two years older.

Before World War II all Gypsy people in Czechoslovakia had to have permission to be in the country so you had to go back to the village where you were born and solicit your permission from there. We were sent to Pacov to get our permission because our background was from there.

We moved to that area before the war about 1939 and in 1940 they started to pick us up. We had permanent papers to stay but still the Czech police picked us up. We were six families living together, all descended from my grandfather Robert Čermák and his sons. My father used the name of his mother, Richter, since in those days most Gypsies didn't marry, they just lived together. My grandfather was the first to be detained. He was already over there in that work camp in 1940 for playing cards instead of working.

The Czech police came one morning and told my father we had to leave everything, that they were taking us away for three months to work on a farm where we could make some money. "After three months you can come back," the Czech policeman said.

My father and his brothers took our horses and our wagons from Pacov to Pelhřimov. We traveled all the way in our wagons but we were always escorted by the police. At Pelhřimov we were turned over to the police there who followed us to the next town. At each town we were turned over to the local police who followed us to the next town. From Písek we went to Mirovice where the Czech police came from Lety by motorcycle. They escorted us, one motorcycle in front, one behind, until we arrived at Lety.

We had two wagons and four horses. The trip took us about three days. We were not allowed to stop, not even at night. The horses ended up crippled because they couldn't rest either. This upset us the most because our animals got nothing to eat or drink. But we couldn't stop because the police kept screaming at us. My father loved his coffee but they wouldn't even let us stop to brew up.

When we arrived at Lety our horses and wagons were taken from us by Romany prisoners who were already there before us. They were ordered to take our things by the Czech police. After these Romany cut all our hair cut off, we had to take off all our clothes and have them disinfected. When we were all nude we were sent to the lake to wash ourselves. After we washed they gave us clothes which were not ours. They were civilian clothes from some other people. The Czech police took all our gold, all our belongings.

The Czech policeman in charge of the new arrivals was a man called Hejduk. In his boot he carried a truncheon and he went up to the prisoners and said: "You must be good prisoners or there will be something bad for you. If you try to escape you will end up in hell." He enjoyed his speeches to us, he enjoyed terrorizing us.

We were all separated. The children in their barracks, the men in theirs, the woman in theirs. We were never allowed to get together again. The men went off to the stone quarry every day. I never saw my father again for six months. Even the children had to work there, pushing the carts filled with stones. The woman also worked there breaking the stone in small pieces with a big hammer.

We women also worked on the road going past the camp to Orlík, and for rich farmers in the area, bringing in their crops. The guards stood around us while we worked so we couldn't escape.

For breakfast we got black coffee and bread, but no butter. For lunch we got red cabbage with a small piece of potato that had not been cleaned. It was all boiled in water and tasted terrible. For supper we got nothing except what bread we had left over from breakfast.

One policeman didn't like this kind of treatment for us and he complained on our behalf. I don't remember his name but he had a mole in the center of his forehead and on his cheek. He warned the officials that we would get typhus from this bad treatment. He was a good man. He looked a bit like a Gypsy, a tall man with dark skin. He was the best policeman in the whole camp. He was about 30-35 around that time.

After we started to have problems with our stomachs, four doctors came. We were always leaking blood from our noses so they started giving us injections in our chest just above our heart. After the injections, many people died. The prisoners who lived had to make holes in the forest behind the camp for all the bodies. Behind the lake was the forest and many, many people were buried there.

The men covered the bodies with lime. For sure, 2,000 people or more were buried there after the injections.

Sometimes a prisoner was taken to hospital in Písek or Mirovice but they always died and their body was brought back to be buried in the woods.

After these injections, we had high fevers and again I have to say that that good policeman tried to help the old people. He was always sneaking garlic to them so they could rub it on themselves for protection.

I saw many people killed at Lety. The guards beat many people to death. They had a wheel to string people up. They hung there until they died. The guards called all of us together to watch those things.

If someone tried to escape and were caught, they were taken into the woods where some of our Gypsy wagons were still intact. There the guards nailed the escaped prisoner to a wagon like they were trying to crucify him. For three days the nailed-up prisoner wasn't given any food or water, so, of course, not many survived this ordeal. When my father was nailed up, they put nails in his ankles and... [1]

When my sister and my cousin escaped no one found them the first day. Then she made it to Prague but they found her there and sent her direct to Auschwitz.

Most of the Czech guards were bad. Pešek was a real son of a bitch. I don't want to tell you what he did. Cerny, don't ask me about him. Hejduk...[2]

There was one guard with a big nose, a man called Boda. He was a good policeman. He gave the old people cigarettes or bread, but he was always protecting himself. He never did anything if the other policemen were watching.

The first director of the camp, Janovský, told the baker in Lety to put poison in our bread. That policeman Boda told us not to eat the bread that day. There was a big scandal and in the morning the baker was shot by the Czech police in front of his house. The son of this baker is still alive and is living today in Orlík. The bad director Janovský was sent to Hodonín and the director of Hodonín was sent to Lety.

I was thirteen years old at that time. I had to carry the rocks for building the highway. After the new director came my grandmother was working sewing sacks with a machine that he brought. Times were better under the new director. There was some milk for the children, better bread. But it was too late. People still died.

After the new director was there, a German officer came to the camp for the first time. He was the only German I ever saw in the camp. We had to come out and line up. The German officer came and touched everyone's face. He pronounced us all Gypsies and then they started to send us away in trucks; every day people were sent to the train station at Písek or Mirovice to go some place. I didn't know where they were sending us. They had decided to destroy the camp because of disease so every time a barracks was destroyed they put the prisoners in trucks and took them to the train station. I wasn't sure where we were going. I actually thought it was the end, and everybody was going home.

Since my family always stayed away from most of the prisoners, we were among the last in camp to leave. When our turn came, they took us to the trucks. But the trucks were full. There were about 80 of us that wouldn't fit in the trucks and since they had already burned the barracks they told us to go home. We walked from the camp to the train station in Písek. As we walked through the village of Lety people came out of their homes to give us food, milk, clothes. We refused to take anything from them. We started to run because we were afraid the police were still behind us. I don't know where my father got the money but he had some. We went from Písek to Pelhřimov and from there to Lukavec, our home northwest of Pacov.

My father went to the police station in Pacov to get his papers. We got jobs in the fields. In the woods we found that two of my grandmother's wagons were still there. After the war we were able to buy horses again.

I've been back to Lety many times to visit the graves in the woods. There are no markers but I know where all the graves are. Two years ago I met the son of the baker in front of the pig farm. I talked to him. "What have the people done here building a pig farm where so many people died? This is terrible."

During the communist time I was there also. Oh my God what have they done here? I asked everyone. Why did they make a pig farm where so many people were killed? I asked the people in the office of the pig farm. When I told them what had happened about four of them started to cry. They apologized but they had their jobs. They felt sorry for me but they could do nothing about it. This was about 1980.

When I was there in the woods behind the pig farm I was also looking to see if I could find something from our wagons, but

I couldn't find anything. I just saw a piece of brick, some bones. I was there all day. I left many candles burning around the lake and in the forest. I spent all day lighting candles.

Where the pig farm is today was exactly where the labor camp was. The entrance is still the same but the big gate is missing.

I never received anything, any compensation, for being in Lety.

I tried to escape once when we were working on the road. A Czech policeman shot me in the back. An older Gypsy woman put some grass of some kind on the wound and stopped the bleeding. When I got back to the camp, I was afraid to go to the doctor. The guard didn't report the shooting.

In 1946 I had a big pain in my leg so I went to the hospital and there the doctor told me that the bones in my leg were crumbling because the bullet was still in me. So I got an operation to replace part of the bone. I have the bullet they found in me.

(1) At this point, Berta cried and said she didn't want to talk about these things anymore. It took several minutes before we could continue.
(2) Berta cried, and again we had to wait several minutes for her to dry her eyes.

A. Č.

No, I don't want to talk to you about Lety. I would have to cry. These are not stories you can tell just like that. It was horrible. I'm not exaggerating. Okay, come in, come in. I will tell you something, only what I want.

I was born 30 June 1914 in Milevsko, county of Tábor. My parents were Jan Kloc and Marie Růžičková. My father worked on a farm. He was a day laborer. I never asked if I was born in a house or in a wagon, but I suppose it was in a house. My father never traveled like other Gypsies. If we didn't like our work or our house we moved on, but we always worked. My husband never traveled either.

The night before I was arrested, I traveled to Jicin with my six-year-old daughter Růžena to stay with relatives. It was the beginning of August 1942. The next morning the Czech police came while we were still sleeping. They woke us up, made us put on our clothes and told us to come with them. My relative Josefa Černá was arrested with us. The Czech police took us by car to Jičín. We were kept for two days in the court hall. There were lots of Gypsies there that had been rounded up. From Jičín all of us were taken by train to Lety.

During the train trip one of the Czech guards told me that he would take my daughter as his own right away if I would give her to him. When I refused, this guard said: "You don't know what will happen to your daughter, you have no idea what is going to happen to you."

I remember a small road that went around the whole camp. It was covered in small stones. We had to sleep on that road, on those stones, the first night until they could prepare a barracks for us. A lot of Gypsies from Jicin were with us. All their children were crying. Then my daughter started. I remember one of the guards told my daughter, "if you don't stop crying I will lock you up and you'll never see your mother again."

The next morning I was combing my daughter's beautiful long hair when a guard started screaming at me that I was wasting my time because they were going to cut it off. I told him he couldn't cut it off unless he found lice, which I knew she didn't have. But in the end they cut the hair off both of us.

When we entered the camp, they took our gold from us, but I was allowed to keep a few small coins. I used these to buy tobacco. You could always buy tobacco from one of the guards.

The camp was divided up, with all the prisoners separated by sex. The worst moment I had in Lety was when they took my daughter away from me. My daughter was so nervous that day that she chewed the tops of her fingers until they bled. See. I still cry when I think about it.

All the guards were Czech. Most of them were really bad, terrible. But Maxa and Janda were good men. I was working in Maxa's labor gang. He was a wonderful guard who took care of us while we worked in the fields or in the stone quarry.

When I came back with the work gang in the evening, my daughter was always waiting for me by the gate. We could only meet at the gate. If the guards had seen me near my daughter's barracks, they would have shot or beaten me to death right away.

I always had some bread for her that I saved from my own breakfast. I was suffering a lot of hunger but I couldn't eat the bread, I had to save it for my child.

I always feared for my daughter's safety. The children had to go to the lake. Even if they couldn't swim, they had to take off all their clothes and go into the lake to wash. I don't think any of them were killed or beaten by the lake. But in other places there were lots of deaths.

Whenever you went to the toilet, you saw dead bodies lying on the floor, so many people were dying you wouldn't believe it.

Either the guards beat people to death, or they died of starvation or other illnesses.

Prisoners who claimed they were sick were thrown out of bed in the morning and beaten to death. If a prisoner couldn't walk or talk, they were beaten to death.

I was never beaten, but I remember one woman who got a terrible beating. Two German Sintis came to the camp and they were beating many Gypsies. One woman by the name of Vrbová was in charge of the children's barracks. She received the food for the children but she didn't give it all to them. She kept a lot for herself and her friends. When the Sinti found out, they took her to the center of the camp. While one held her, the other beat her with a stick in front of everyone.

Prisoners died every day in Lety. Every morning when I got up I saw dead bodies in our barracks. You couldn't go from one barrack to another so I don't know how many died in the other places, but in our barracks there was always at least one dead person every morning.

In the camp there were two Gypsy caravans where dead prisoners were put in storage until they could be buried in the forest. Many prisoners were always digging big holes in the forest for these bodies.

I once spoke to the prisoner in charge of burying the dead prisoners in the forest. It was about four months after I arrived, before the typhus epidemic started, and he told me that he had already buried about 680 people in the forest. I know for a fact that many hundreds were buried after that. I saw lots of people die. Small children, old people.

One day it was snowing and there were drifts where the snow had been shoveled off the road. A short Czech guard, about 40 years old, caught a young boy who was always trying to find his parents. This Czech guard took this boy and put his head into one of the drifts, then kicked him with his boots. I couldn't stand to watch this guard almost kill this young boy. That night I told all my friends that I was going to pray to God to kill this guard. The next morning the guard was dead. He wasn't taller than one meter fifty.

The director of the camp, I don't remember his name, was a bad man. I think he was a German.[1] The man who came after him was better. When new prisoners arrived in the camp, this bad director would have the guards bring them to his house which was just outside the camp, and there he would stand on his balcony and make a speech. He said: "Don't think you were brought here for only one or two months. Your way doesn't take you home. It takes you only to heaven or hell."

I remember once the cooks were giving a piece of butter to some kids and Janovský caught them. He took all the butter away from the kitchen and put it in his private basement. A lot of food was found in his basement when he was transferred to another camp. That was the reason the Gestapo took him away, because he was hiding all our food.

My daughter and I received no injections against typhus. We both caught it. I had a high fever and couldn't hear anything for a long time. I couldn't walk. I had to crawl on the floor like a small child. In the end I was lying in my bed for three weeks. I never saw a doctor. I never heard of a doctor in Lety. After the typhus disappeared, I was weak for many months.

When the epidemic was over, we had to take showers in a new hut and then have our clothes disinfected. Then we lived for three months in new barracks.

Near the end, I missed my daughter so much that sometimes I snuck over to see her. I no longer cared if they shot me.

After ten months we were released on 4 May 1943. I don't know why they released us. We walked by foot to Mirovice then took the train home.

Two of my brothers were in Lety, František and Václav Růžička. They arrived after us. František was sent to Auschwitz, but survived and came back home after the war. Václav was released with us and went to live in Prague with his wife. But one day he said something in a restaurant and two men there denounced him. Václav and his wife were arrested, taken to jail in Prague and later both were guillotined.

The rest of my relatives all died in either Lety or Auschwitz except my husband Antonín. He spent the war in six different concentration camps, but he survived and came back home. My cousin Františka died in Lety from typhus, my mother died in Auschwitz.

Some people talk about their experiences, but when I got out of the camp I refused to talk about it. I wanted to forget Lety. I've never looked back. I've never remembered Lety until now.

We have lived in this village since 1964. We have Czech friends, they do not look at us like Gypsies, they are friendly to us, we have no problems.

We have never had any skinhead problems here. Even in the nearby towns we have no problems. We just hope there is enough work and medical assistance, that's all we want.

My children and my grandchildren don't have any problems once they get a job and the people see that they are good workers. Sometimes they tell me that people look at them in a strange way until they see that they are good workers, then they are accepted.

In January 1995, I applied for compensation for being in Lety. It took a long time, almost a year to get the certificate back that we were in Lety. Later my daughter received 20,300 crowns as compensation, but I was told that I would have to wait, that the youngest must receive their compensation first, that the older people have to wait. I will be eighty-two next month.

(1) The director of the camp was Josef Janovský, a Czech police captain. He spoke German, dressed in a black uniform like a German and insisted that his guards salute him in the German manner.

Žofie Dolíhalová
(as told by her husband)

Žofie was born 24 April 1928, in Hranice na Moravě, on the Czech-Moravian border. Her parents were František Chadraba and Anežka born Richterová. The family went from city to city, market to market, in their horse and wagon, selling whatever was possible to sell in a market: clothes, cooking pots, whatever.

On 9 August 1942, in Klasder (Choděboř), the Czech police arrested Žofie along with her family, her whole clan, and held them in Lety until 27 May 1943. She was in Lety with her parents and three brothers and two sisters.

From Lety came back only Bohumil, Emanuel, Františka and Žofie. All the rest died in Lety, about 150 members of her clan.

They all died of beatings. The Czech government today says the prisoners died of typhus but this is not true. All the members of my wife's family and most of the prisoners in Lety died of bad beatings

Žofie had shoes with buttons and from time to time the guards would count the buttons on her shoes. If one was missing, she got a bad beating. Her head was broken on many occasions and both her legs got broken from beatings with a garden hoe.

Žofie was in Lety for a year. I was in Lety for only one month. Then I got transferred to another Gypsy camp, at Hodonín.

In Lety the guards sent the prisoners to the lake to wash themselves. In the lake were many snakes swimming around the dead bodies. Many people were afraid of these snakes. Today you can still find thousands of human bones in the lake. The farm tractors are always plowing up bones in the fields.

I was told there was compensation for survivors of Lety. Prague told me to apply in Písek and Písek told me to apply in Prague. I was sent back and forth so many times I gave up.

My cousin Antonín was transferred from Lety to Terezín when I was transferred to Hodonín. I don't know why they transferred us. The rest stayed in Lety where most of them died.

All of my uncles and aunts and cousins, all my relatives, about

150 people from our clan, died in Lety. Only my cousin Eduard Chadraba survived Lety. He died about ten or fifteen years ago in Kolín. He never married.

We were all arrested in the same place at the same time as my wife who was my cousin. We lived together after her first husband died.

I heard from my cousin Eduard and from my wife that most of our relatives died of beatings. Typhus was only the third or fourth cause of death at Lety.

Our people were arrested because in 1939 came the new law about the permanent residency. Every Gypsy had to return to the place where he was born to get a traveling permit. Our original home was in Klasder so when we all arrived there to register, the police arrested us. The law was made to round us up.

In Klasder, some of us lived in metal shacks, most of us lived in wagons. The Czech police came with trucks and drove us to Jeníkov (Čáslav) to the train station. We were put in wagons, cattle cars, no one told us where we were going. From Jeníkov they sent us to Kolín. In Kolín we saw our first Germans. There were four wagons and the Germans separated us, sending some directly to Germany; others joined our group of about 350 people for Lety. We then were put on another train for Mirovice. From Mirovice we walked the last five kilometers to Lety, guarded by Czech police.

Recently, I went to Třeboň archives to find papers about my arrest. All my brothers and sister are in the records, but I am not. So they say I can't get any compensation.

When we arrived at Lety they shaved everyone's head first. You had to give them all your clothes and shoes, watches and gold, whatever you had on you. We got striped prison clothes and wooden sandals. Some of the children were able to keep their own clothes and shoes.

I had to break rocks with a sledge hammer. The children had smaller hammers for the smaller stones. Others carried what we made to the prisoners making the road, highway 19. We also had to collect wood, cut wood, split wood.

Although I was only in Lety for one month, I saw the beatings. Every ten or fifteen minutes there was someone being beaten, usually to death, for no reason at all. There was never a moment when someone was not being beaten. If you stepped out of line it was one type of beating, if you did something bad, like stealing potato peelings, you had your hands locked behind you and you were hung up, then beaten until you died.

Hodonín was much better. We had to work hard in Hodonín but there were no beatings, certainly not bad beatings. We got more food in Hodonín. It was more of a labor camp. You had to work hard, but survival was possible. Survival was not possible in Lety for most prisoners because of the beatings.

On 19 December 1995, there came to the post office in Příbram 100,000 crowns compensation for my wife whose parents died in Lety in 1943. But since my wife had died on 17 December 1995 she could not sign for the money, so it was sent back to Prague. I swear the government was waiting for her to die before they sent the money. She had been fighting for more than twenty years for this compensation. I've heard from other Romany that the government has sent compensation only when they know someone has died and then the check has to be returned.

I remember the guards Soukup, Malina, and Hejduk who was a son-of-a-bitch. He was the worst of all. From block C, it was possible to see prisoners being beaten, killed. Hejduk was always there.

I saw beatings in the quarry, in the fields, on the roads.

My wife knew all of the guards. She told terrible stories about the guards. You could not find one place on my wife's head that had not been broken. She lived her whole live with bumps on her head from those beatings at Lety.

For example, if people were standing in line to be counted and my grandmother was missing a button on her dress, my mother would take off her sweater to cover up the missing button, and when the guards saw this, they beat her. Her arms were broken. Her legs were broken. She had bumps all over her body for the rest of her life from these beatings.

When the latrine was full of waste, small children were drowned in there. The guards took great delight in drowning Gypsy children in shit. Then we had to haul the bodies to a big pit where lime was thrown over them, lime, bodies, more lime, more bodies.

President Havel put up three stones at Lety as a memorial to close people's mouths. No one knows what happened at Lety. Our government doesn't want anyone to know.

My wife and I never heard about the memorial service at Lety. The government knows about us, they mail us letters saying we have the right to compensation, but we never get it. Why didn't they send us a letter about the memorial service at Lety?

We have written many letters to the President's office but nothing happens. If we go in person, the people joke about us, they laugh in our face. They say we have to wait. We can't have things so fast. We have to be patient. It's fifty-three years since Lety, how long do we have to wait? Until we are dead like my wife?

I was released from Hodonín in the summer of 1943. My wife was released from Lety in May 1943; neither of us was sent to another camp.

Who told you there were only seven survivors living today from Lety? There are still many, many survivors. They are dying faster these days, but you can still find them. I know a woman, Anna Čermáková. She lives in Prague. She's 73 years old and knows everything that happened at Lety. She remembers the names of all the guards.

She hasn't received any compensation either. The government told her she can't ask for compensation because she was 18 and one month old when she left Lety; compensation is only paid if your parents died in Lety while you were a minor; all her family died in Lety, she was the only survivor. She was a minor when her parents died in Lety, but she was one month too old when they released her from Lety to receive compensation.

The government is always looking for tricks to play on us. We suffered at Lety and now they want us to suffer some more. That's the kind of government we have, that's the kind of President we have.

E. S.

I was born on 20 April 1925 in Plavsko. My father was Václav S., my mother Anna N. He was in World War I for four years fighting at the front. When he came home, he had something wrong with his arm, he had been shot or something. He walked a bit strange the rest of his life.

We were all born in Plavsko. My father bought and sold horses, cows and all kinds of farm animals. I heard that my paternal grandfather was a director in a school. I went nine years to school. I had eight brothers and sisters and they all went to school like me. After that I went for two years to a school for economics. At that time there didn't exist any discrimination or racism in our village. We had a good life.

On 3 September 1942 the Czech police rang our door bell and arrested us. We were only able to take some bed linen with us before they put us in trucks and drove us away. They took us direct to České Budějovice, to the train station where many Gypsies families were already waiting. I also saw some German Gypsies there that had been picked up. We were told we were going to a work camp.

From České Budějovice we were taken by train to Mirovice. From there we had to walk five kilometers to the camp on the other side of Lety village.

First they told us we were going to work there, that they had jobs for us. But when we arrived we knew where we were. The first days were very strange for us. There were little wooden houses for ten people and in front of these buildings was the building for the guards. In the middle of the camp were two storage houses. The second day they gave us old army clothes that had been died black. We were separated from our parents: the women on their own, the men on their own, the children on their own.

My parents were very old at that time, about sixty. So my father had to carry wood to the kitchen to make the fire for the cooks, that was his job. My mother worked as a cleaning woman in the guards' house. Some of my brothers and sisters and I worked on the road, highway 19, that went from Lety to Staré Sedlo.

For breakfast we received brown water, colored by a bit of coffee and a small slice of bread. For lunch, hot water with a little bit of cabbage swimming in it. For supper we got what we called Hitler's goulash: a bit of potato mixed with cabbage. Many times there were worms in this mixture. I laugh now because that was the only meat we got.

The guards I remember very well. Most of them were very bad. I remember especially Hejduk and Maxa. Janovský was the director of the camp. He was a pig, a mad man, an asshole, an animal. Two or three times German SS men came to make a control and I saw Janovský was a very good friend of theirs. Most of the guards were Czech. But I remember when three Germans came to the camp; they came in a SS car. They wore German uniforms. They spoke German. I saw them only once or twice and they only stayed for a few hours. But in that time they hit my sister. I will never forgive them. My brothers and I wanted to strangle them but our father wouldn't let us.

In my first days I heard about a Romany man who saw a dead carp in the lake. He was so hungry he ate it. Right after that he died. Everybody knew him. He was the first man to die in Lety. He also ate mice. Whatever people found, they ate. The first week we were starving to death.

I can remember that they took me and another 25 kids to Nevezece to a bar and from there to the forest to work, cutting wood. The guard Bláha was with us. He was a good person, a real Czech. But he got sent away because one of the prisoners in our work gang escaped.

Josef Serynek was sleeping with me on the hay in the barn and he wanted to escape. He ran away but I didn't follow him. He went directly to the front and joined the Russian partisans. He saved a lot of people and later built bunkers in Moravia. Serynek personally killed twelve German soldiers and was decorated. He opened a restaurant in Brno after the war.

Because Serynek escaped from the work gang, Bláha was replaced by Kurka who beat the hell out of us all the time, for no reason at all. From time to time Kurka put a rope around our necks, made us sit on the ground, then tied us up and kicked us.

In January 1943 we were taken back to Lety just after the typhus epidemic broke out. I cannot remember that people were hit or beaten in the camp because we went out early in the morning and returned late at night. One time when I was 17 years old I saw a guard wearing three coats. I called him a Frenchman and he ran after me and beat me.

Later a friend and I were in charge of making the coffins, simple wooden boxes. We couldn't make these coffins fast enough.

People were dying at the rate of 25 people a day, so behind the kitchen they piled up the bodies and later took them to mass graves in the forest. I think six or seven hundred were buried at that time in the forest, maybe a lot more.

Everyone in my family had typhus. Vojtech Vrba, the father of my sister's husband, died of typhus. The guard Havrda put my brother and me into snow banks when we had a temperature of 42 degrees. He saved us. He was an excellent man.

Dr. Bohin was also an excellent person. He gave some kind of an injection to Karel Vrba which saved him. Luckily no one in our family died of typhus.

Hejduk was in charge of the trucks that brought the prisoners to Lety. He was a tall man. But I was never in the camp to see what really went on. I tried to stay out of the camp as much as possible.

I heard in the camp that the Germans were building a crematorium near Smetanova Lhota but when the war ended the Americans and the Russians blew it up; it was never used. They were just finishing it. I also heard that women from France were in a concentration camp near Lužnice, not far from us.

I saw a wall, part of a building or something near the forest in Lety. But I don't know what it was, I don't know if it was a bunker or what.

There was a big warehouse with food. Kouželka was in charge of all the storage in Lety. He was a good person and he asked me to help him work there. After Kouželka was in charge of the food and Janovský had been taken away, we got better food. In fact one time I remember getting some oranges. Kouželka told me to take a little wagon with oranges and to take them to the children. Blahynka was a good man, a Moravian, worth a million dollars.[1] He saved whom he could from the Auschwitz transports.

There were four or five Czech prisoners from Prague. I don't know why they brought them into the camp, with them was Věra, Anežka and Marta and another older woman. Kuželka got married to Věra after the war. I also remember that Walter, a German guy was with us. He was taken to Auschwitz. He wasn't a Gypsy, but a normal German. I don't know why he was in the camp.

The guards always found a woman to sleep with. They made controls during the night. They walked in and got whomever they wanted. The women in the kitchens and the women cleaning the barracks had to sleep with the guards to save their families.

When prisoners were sent to Auschwitz they had to stand in line while a man from Prague looked at them and selected them for the transport. He was a Czech. I can't remember his name. Maybe it was Stuchlik. I know he was a Czech. A man by the name of Beran was with him. They selected the typical Romanies because of their dark skin. The Svetskys, those with whiter skin, were normally not selected. Blahynka was a good friend of my parents. He did whatever he could for the Gypsies. He even falsified the lists to save people; he even took some of them away in a truck to save them.

Only fifteen or twenty people were kept behind when the camp was closed. Most were released in May. I stayed for another three months. I came home on the 30th of August but then was taken straight to the hospital in Písek. I was there for two weeks until I got stronger.

My parents with my brothers and sisters left in May. They didn't return to Plavsko. My eldest brother Jan was never in Lety. He worked in a factory in Prague making airplanes. Then the Germans took him to Germany but he returned after the war.

Jaroslav was taken in 1940 straight to Mauthausen; he was speaking out against the politics in the Protectorate; he came home as a political prisoner rescued by the American army.

We were working in Zbonín by Varvažov working in the forest. I went to see them in 1943. That was the time the Gestapo came and took my brother and me to Čížová, then to Klatovy, then to Plzeň. They put us in jail in Plzeň. We stayed there until the 30th of March 1945, when the Americans bombed the beer factory which was the Gestapo headquarters and the Germans came and opened the doors and told us to leave. They knew it was finally the end of the war.

Antonín went to Prague to see a girl he met on a work gang in Lety while I returned to Varvazov. A few months later I went to Prague to visit them.

In Varvazov my father received a note saying that someone had tracked Janovský down in Prague. He was working in a bread factory. I was eighteen years old, and we went looking for him. My father wanted to go by himself but I insisted on going with him. My father went to kill him. He had his knife with him. He told me the minute he saw Janovský, he would kill him. But the men at the factory wouldn't let us see him. They made us leave the factory. We came back home. Later we heard that Janovský was taken to court. Sometime in 1945 or 1946 my father was called to court in Beroun to give a statement against Janovský. They finally had Janovský in jail there. I went with him to Beroun to the court to make that statement. My father said that Janovský beat everyone he saw. He was always ordering people to be hung up on the execution post. Karel Vrba was hung up but survived. Children died because they didn't have enough food. But that was the last we ever heard of Janovský. My father never retracted what he said about Janovský. Father never forgave Janovský for his sins. My father never would have retracted his statement against Janovský. We never heard any more about Janovský after our visit to Beroun.

We had a forty-year school reunion two years ago in Plavsko. Everyone was hugging, kissing each other. Whites, Gypsies.

I applied for compensation in the beginning of 1995. A month later, I received 29,900 crowns for being in Lety. But my friend Stokinger who escaped from Lety and whose mother died there has received nothing. I know of many people who have received nothing.

I can't understand why the Czech newspapers are publishing Sládek's articles.[2] He's a real racist. Why do they publish this kind of article?

The Gypsies who live in Tábor are very good workers. They have worked there in the factories for 25 years and are very much respected. One of them has a big agricultural company there.

We are Svetskys. Because we are white, the Czech people don't look at us like Gypsies. I have lived 40 years here. I have no problems. I have sung in a restaurant here. There is no racism or discrimination around here.

But in the rest of the country the situation is very bad at the moment. The Republican party and their leader Mr. Sládek is leading the young people toward violence. They are supporting the skinheads. Violence against the Romany. Sládek said that when he gets to the castle he will throw out all the politicians there including Havel. Sládek says when he gets power he will take all the Gypsies in the Czech Republic and send them to Spain.

In the program of the Republican party published in a full page ad in our newspaper today (17 May 1996), I saw this. Listen to what the ad says: "We will make a law that no one in our Czech State has the right to be a parasite. We consider the Gypsies to be parasites and that the Gypsies have the highest percentage of criminality in the Czech Republic. The Gypsy clans kill, rape, and steal. We consider the black racists are parasites on our whole society. It is our aim to stop this."

Hitler had the same plan in 1932 to liquidate all the minorities like Gypsies and Jews. I believe that this can easily happen now in our country.

I really can't talk about Lety any more because I see the piles of dead children in front of me and I get depressed. We must stop talking about this. Now I'm living alone with my wife. We have only a short road left until our death.

(1) He replaced Janovský as the camp director in the spring of 1943.
(2) Head of the Republican Party in the Czech Republic. His party published full page ads in the most important Czech newspapers during the 1996 election promising to provide the "final solution" against parasites (Gypsies) if elected.

Alžběta Danielová

I was born 21 July 1924 in Nová Hospoda (Plzeň). My mother was Marianna Serynková. She was born 20 February 1898 in Jindřichův Hradec.

I was in Lety with my mother and my little sister, Antonie. We were taken by train from Plzeň to Lety on 2 August 1942. I was sent to Auschwitz in September or the beginning of October after the potato harvest. I was seventeen years old. My mother was forty-two.

We were a large family. The police came unexpectedly. We lived on Jateční Street, number 45, and had a 3-room apartment. They came in the morning, the Gestapo with the Czech police with dogs. They told us to open the door. So we did and they told us to take as much as we could carry. It was terrible to tell you the truth.

Sometimes the Czechs were more cruel than the Germans, showing off among themselves.

They didn't tell us where we were going or anything else. They took us to a school over the train station on Jiráskova Street. There we had to wait for three days until the railroad wagons came. Then they made us get into these wagons and we started on our way to Lety by Písek, though they sometimes called it Mirovice.[1]

At Lety we had to work. There were all kinds of jobs. They forced 50 children into one building and someone had to keep an eye on them. We also had to tidy up inside. Later on they loaded us into trucks and took us to a farm where we worked during the potato harvest. Stones had to be picked up from the roads. That was the main road from Lety to Písek. With all these jobs, there was no time to rest.

We had one meal a day. In the morning they gave us a kind of black coffee and a piece of bread. At noon they gave us beetroot with potatoes. That was at two or half past two. That is why there were those illnesses. We didn't have enough to eat. In the evening we got nothing.

We lived in wooden barracks with three beds stacked over one another. There were three beds on the right, and three on the left. We slept two in each bed with some people sleeping on the floor. There were 24 people in each barracks. I slept in one bed with my mother.

When you entered the camp on the left-hand side there were eight barracks, and on the right-hand side there were six. Also, on the right-hand side there was a very large two-story building. The men were there. My brother was there.

Actually this high building was arranged into a circle. So when you viewed the camp from the gate, the kitchen was on the left and on both sides the barracks, rather small ones. They put 20 to 25 kids into a barracks and in the morning you would find five to ten dead, suffocated, or beaten to death, because their parents weren't allowed to take care of them. The kids were always taken away from their parents.

At six or half past seven p.m. they closed the barracks and let the dogs loose so that nobody could escape. It was truly terrible.

Prisoners were brought to the camp all the time. A transport came, then left again. Old people who were incapable of working were transported to Auschwitz. The young ones were kept at Lety to work. This is why they took my mother away. I never saw her again. Later I was in Auschwitz for a year and a half. My mother had already gone to the gas chamber. Then I was sent to Ravensbruck but only for a week before being sent to Wittenberg. I was there when the Red army liberated us in May 1945.

How often did transports leave from Lety? About twice a month. I do not know how many people were in those transports. You weren't allowed to peer out. I just heard the cries, and people saying goodbye.

Transports bringing prisoners to Lety arrived all the time. One transport arrived and another left. All the time. At night, in the morning. I do not want to speak about it any more because it was so terrible. It happened fifty years ago but nobody has been interested in it during all this time.

At Lety there was an execution post and when someone did something the guards would let him hang there like they did to my brother.[2] My brother tried to escape. He was in the forest, digging something, and he tried to escape. So they caught him and hanged him on the post. He had been hanging there for half a day when my mother came to tell me this. She was crying, then we were both wailing for him but we could not go see him.

He survived and in the evening they let him down and locked him in a bunker. That was horrible, you know. We could not help him. They gave him a choice. To survive the post hanging or not.

The Czech guards were cruel. I was going to get some food and a guard did not like something about my cup so when I was just about to get some soup, he took my cup and threw it in my face and told me to go back and wash the cup once again. Things like this, or we would have to stand outside whether it rained or not. They didn't care. If they told us to stand, we had to stand. They didn't care when someone fell down.

I never heard of Janovský because they never told us their names.

I was seventeen at that time and the young people had to spend most of the day working on farms. Where we worked, we got water and potatoes. We worked only on German farms. The Czechs took us there and on the farms we were guarded by Germans and Czechs together. The Czech guards interpreted. We were in the fields so I don't know what was happening in the camp during the day. Sometimes my mother would tell me: "Listen, another transport left Lety."

Were people dying in Lety? Of course. Many people were dying there. And do you know what they did with the dead bodies? There was a huge pit behind the camp near the forest. The dead bodies were thrown into it and lime poured over them. They loaded dead people into a cart, six to ten bodies, and then threw them into this pit and poured some kind of lime over them. People were not buried in a cemetery, nothing like that. Every day there were many adults and children who died.

Where was this pit? It was when you went out of the camp behind the camp in the forest. I heard that they have destroyed it by now, that the barracks are gone, everything destroyed by the Communists. They should have left it as a memorial like Terezín. But they didn't. I think there is only a little monument in the middle. I heard from somebody that there is a pig farm there. That shouldn't have happened. There should have been a memorial place as it is in Terezín and Lidice.

How did people die? They got beaten up and there were illnesses. People were shot. I never saw anyone shot, but I could hear shots, at night. I also heard cries at night. Those who stayed in the camp were killed the most. We, the young ones, worked on the farms. It wasn't so bad there. We got enough to eat and drink, that's why we could survive.

Did people die of typhus? Oh yes, many people were dying and for different reasons. Diarrhea, typhus. There were all kinds of illnesses there.

We had Gypsy wagons in the camp. They were used to store the dead bodies until they could be taken to the pit. But I didn't see everything that went on in the camp. As I told you, we were working in the fields during the day.

Some people were released from Lety, those who were white and had blue eyes. Once a Czech said to me: "You don't belong here. You are a young Czech girl. Your father is Czech." But I said I was staying with my mother. My hair was blond. I was an illegitimate child. My mother had been living with my father. They were going to get married. My father was from Plzeň, a white Czech, not a Gypsy. My mother's family was comedians mostly. We were not like the Czech Gypsies. We were more like the Slovakian Gypsies. I was silly to have refused to go back home. But I said to myself: "What would I do at home as an orphan? I have nobody." My father hung himself when he heard that they took us away and not him.

There were many Romanies in Lety. Most of the people were Romanies. There are various sorts of Romanies but they did not care. A Gypsy was just a Gypsy for them. Nobody had any privileges. Once a person entered Lety and the gate was closed behind him, that was the end. My family died there. No one returned except me. Lety was terrible. Out of ten people one survived. We were a large family and only I have returned. My mother had four sisters and two brothers; all of them had three or four children of their own. They all died in Lety. I would like to have some compensation for my mother's death at Lety. But nothing is happening. Today I have no relatives, just my own family, four children and eight grandchildren. But I fear the way this country is going, they are going to have to live through exactly what we experienced. My husband is already dead. He was from Poland.

A short time ago Czech TV was here to film some skinheads. Fascism continues to exist. There are again people who beat each other. When I hear something like this, I don't know what to think about it. They murder one another, you know. It should not be like this. I am against it. You know, I was traveling and there was this young boy, they call them skinheads, and he was teasing this girl because she was black. But it's not her fault. Her blood is red like anybody else's. And he started to beat her on the tram. So I stood up and said to him: "You are only sixteen, you did not even know Hitler. What are you doing?"

Would you believe, he wanted to hit me on the head with his chain. People saw this but they didn't care. It really should not be like this. One should not have to be afraid to go on the tram or into the city center.

If they only knew what it was like, when we got up in the morning and the police came and said: "Come with us."

It was terrible, it is still terrible. We have democracy today and we enjoyed it at first but I have grandchildren and I don't want them to experience what I had to go through. People beat each other up. Czech, Slovak, Pole, we are all the same. Even if someone is dark-skinned, the blood and the heart are the same. But people don't see it this way. That's bad. Even Gypsies have something to say, but we don't make it known anywhere.

Sometimes I regret that I've lived through all this when someone says a Gypsy is not allowed to enter a pub. Why? The Gypsy is not doing anything bad. People are afraid to take their father to the tram station. When three skinheads attack one person, that's not just. Somebody should do something about it. It is not like this in Germany or America. I have a son who lives in Germany. He has never experienced anything like this. They don't have discrimination there. There is no difference between us and white people there. But in our country it isn't like this. One is afraid to open a window in the evening because somebody could throw something in. We live with fear. Sometimes I have this feeling that I am living in another concentration camp, and there isn't any help coming from anywhere. It's terrible. The laws should be stricter.

I am afraid of the skinheads. The government doesn't want to do anything against them. I have a granddaughter who has dark black hair. What if they don't like black hair and they think she is a Gypsy? One is afraid. Only the skinheads attack. So I would like to ask Mr. President to make them illegal. This should not be happening. It's like Hitler's time all over again. Look, I'm now 71. I was born in 1924, on 27 August. Soon I will be 71. Do you know what it would be like for me if my granddaughter was hit and killed? I still want to live for sometime. I want to enjoy my grandchildren.

So much suffering and fear. I lost my sight from crying. I have been in therapy with my eyes since 1945. I have a white stick, but nobody pays any attention to it.

---

(1) Mirovice was the nearest train station to Lety. All transports to Auschwitz left from here.

(2) A prisoner's hands were tied behind him with a rope and then with a pulley and a wheel he was hauled up on the post and left hanging, usually for 24 hours. Most prisoners did not survive this torture.

Z. F.

I have hated Germans all my life because I thought the guards in Lety were Germans. You have left me speechless by telling me that all the guards in Lety were Czech. Do you know how bad they were? My mother went to Lety with all her daughters healthy and I was the only one who came back alive with her.

I was born on 11 August 1936 in Touškov, county of Plzeň. My parents were V. F. and M. L. My father sold textiles in the markets in different villages and my mother helped him. We were three girls so they had a lot of work with us. We used to live in Osvračín near Domažlice. We had a house there but most of the time we were traveling in an old car we had.

The end of July 1942, we received a letter saying that we should come to Klatovy a week later, that the authorities were sending us some place to work. We traveled by car there and were put in a large patio with several other families. The director of the police station was a man by the name of Kotek. He had a daughter and a son. He was a very bad man. He was Czech but he had a German wife. He lived in Osvračín and was responsible for sending us to Lety. I don't know why we were taken to Lety. My father was never a communist. I suppose because he traveled and sold his things in the markets. My father had ten siblings but none of them were taken to Lety. We are not Gypsies. We are Czech. We never found out why they sent us to Lety.

We stayed one day in that big patio until they took us by trucks directly to Lety. The guard who brought us to the camp was a short man and he always told us that the way out of Lety led through hell. The first thing I saw was a big wire fence around the camp. Then the director of the camp told us, "the only way out of here leads directly to hell."

They separated us from our parents, I didn't want to stay with the children so I snuck in and stayed with my father. I didn't want to stay with the children because they all had fleas. There was a lot of dirt in the camp.

There were dogs in the camp, mainly German shepherds, which

were used to capture the escaped prisoners. I saw a woman who tried to escape because she wouldn't do what the guards wanted. They shot her. They shot everyone they wanted. It was normal that prisoners got shot in Lety. I saw many people shot there.

My father worked in the stone quarry, then on the road. Later he had the job to bring the bread to the camp every day. My mother worked in the forest collecting wood. At Lety we all had to wear prison clothes and the same work shoes.

My sister Marie died in Lety from a lung infection two months after we arrived and my other sister, Jaroslava died a month later when she was just six months old. My mother told me that the woman in charge of her just dropped her on the floor and let her die. But my mother never saw the dead body of her baby. She had blue eyes. Maybe the Germans took her away. Maybe my sister is still alive somewhere in Germany. No one in our family ever saw the body of my sister Jaroslava.

Both of my parents got typhus in Lety. We stayed in the camp for about six months before we were released. My grandmother paid a large sum of money for us to be released. That was the only way you could get out of Lety.

The guards took us to the pond to wash. I do remember that my father had to make the coffin for my dead sister Marie and later he was slapped in the face by one of the guards because he was late to pick up his food because he had been making this coffin.

Most of the time I was hiding under the covers in one of the barracks. On Christmas day I went to join the other children to get some Christmas cake. I don't remember any woman taking care of us children, but really I was always hiding. I was old enough to take care of myself.

I remember the transports. We all had to line up. Luckily we weren't chosen. My maternal grandmother came from Vranov to see us. I think she paid some money to save us from the transports.

They were torturing and beating people a lot in Lety. Whenever anyone tried to escape and was caught he was put in chains.

There was a lot of hunger in Lety and the little food we got was terrible. Mostly we received cabbage soup and some bread. We suffered cold there. Relatives used to visit us, sometimes they brought us food. Once when we went to the pond, we begged a farmer to give us some potatoes. He got into trouble because he gave us some.

Before my father brought bread to Lety he worked on the road going around the camp. My father also worked in the stone quarry where they took the stones to build the road. He had sore bleeding fingers all the time from this work. He suffered in Lety very much.

I remember that people were hung up on the execution post. One woman after she was tortured by a guard swallowed a spoon to kill herself. I never saw her again.

They used to take the dead bodies to the cemetery in Mirovice. My sister Marie Flachsová is buried there. My sister Marie died in my mother's arms when she was three years old. Later everyone was buried in the forest behind the camp in mass graves. Before the bodies were taken away, they were put in wooden coffins. My sister Marie was also laid in one of the wooden coffins.

There was no heating in the winter. We used to sleep on wood just covered by a few blankets. We suffered terribly from the cold. That is how my sister got her lung infection.

My father was lying in bed with one of his friends who froze to death over night.

People died of several sicknesses, hunger, the cold. I don't know how many people died every day, but people were dying every day while we were there. I was told most of the people died of typhus.

The people in the camp, Gypsies and whites, used to stick together. They were very much afraid of the guards. Each guard had a truncheon. I don't know what happened to my sister Jaroslava. I don't know where she is buried.

The guards took my gold earrings and also the gold from my parents but we got it back when we were released. All the girls had earrings and rings.

My father left all his money at home when we went to Klatovy. I don't remember what happened to our car. We took it to Klatovy. When we were released, we took the train home.

My grandmother paid a big sum of money for us to be released from Lety. She was a powerful, short woman. She used to come into the camp and walk right through the guards, bringing us food.

We were supposed to be sent to another concentration camp if my grandmother had not saved us. I heard we were going to Terezín. Later a lot of people were released from Lety. Mainly white people.

There were rain barrels in Lety and from them I think we got the typhus. When the typhus epidemic broke out, they shaved off our hair. My father and I were taken away to the hospital in Písek, but when my mother got typhus they didn't even want to examine her in the camp, or take her to the hospital. After we were released, we went to see my grandparents in Vranov.[1] From there I was sent to another hospital to give me a complete cure. When we finally went home, we found our home in the same condition as we had left it.

My mother was so weak after she came back from Lety, she couldn't have a baby for five years.

Only one distant relative went to Lety, Antonín S. He must be about seventy years old today. He was there about two months. He was white like us. One of his relatives also paid to get him out. Money was the only way out.

Last year I received about 13,000 or 14,000 crowns for being in Lety. My mother received the same amount just before she died. It was enough to pay the funeral, that was all. All her life she suffered from her time in Lety. My father had liver cancer after he was released. We think he got it from the typhus in Lety. He died about ten years ago. He was seventy-four years old. My mother died last year.

Our family came from Kajovice, county Plzeň. They have always come from there. I don't know why we were sent to Lety.

My mother used to go to Mirovice to visit the grave of my sister Maria. My mother never spoke about our time in Lety. She always started to cry when Lety was mentioned. My father hardly ever talked about those times either.

I still have dreams about Lety. I was afraid of all the guards in the camp. If you could see these tall men with their sticks, they gave me nightmares for the rest of my life. Even today I cannot see any movies about the war.

My worst experience was when I could not recognize my own father in the hospital. I had a very high temperature. My father wanted to kill me before he would let them send me to another concentration camp. He was crazy with his nerves in Lety.

I cannot imagine that all the guards in Lety were Czech. You have told me something new. It must have been horrible for my father to put his dead child into a wooden coffin. My father didn't do anything bad. The only thing he ever did was play cards in pubs. Maybe that's why they sent us to Lety. He didn't work a lot.

I can't tell you anything about racism in these days. I don't want to hurt anyone. But not all of them are the same. We have darker skin so maybe that is why they took us to Lety. But we never heard that we had Gypsy ancestors. Our relatives the Lagrons were Svetskys, I guess we knew that, that we also were Svetskys. I don't want to lead you astray. We were Svetskys. My grandparents on the side of the Lagrons also had a circus. I remember now that the Flachs used to work with the circus Bonello.

Once in Lety I was sent to the garden to fetch a red cabbage. I was supposed to wash the worms off the cabbage but I didn't know how to do it because I was only six years old. So a guard beat me with a truncheon. If my father was still alive, he could tell you much more.

I heard that they built a pig farm where the camp used to be. Is that true? Do you know how many people are buried there?

(1) On 18 January 1943.

František Janošovský

I'm not so sure I want to talk to you. The last time I gave a statement about Lety I was arrested. A few years after the war, two men came to our apartment to investigate what happened in Lety. My mother was afraid to talk, but I told these detectives the truth. A year later some policemen came to arrest me because they said I had told lies about Lety.[1] They took me to police headquarters in Prague 1. From there they took me into police custody in Prague 6. They kept me there for ten months trying to get me to change my statement. They wanted me to say that Lety was run by the Germans, not by the Czechs.

There was no trial. They just detained me. When they took me back to the police station in Prague 1 for questioning, I escaped. The policeman went to find someone and left me alone for a few minutes so I just walked out. I took the train to Asch trying to escape to Germany. But a few hundred yards from the border the soldiers caught me. I was taken back to Prague where they convicted me for trying to leave the country. The judge sent me to prison for five years.

But you're here with a Romany so I guess I can trust you. I want people to know the truth about Lety. I think it is terrible that people don't know about Lety, what happened there, what the Czechs did to us.

My mother was Antonie Janošovská, born in 1906 in Benešov. Her maiden name was Čermáková. My father was Karel Janošovský. He was born in Brožánky by Prague also in 1906. He was a horse dealer and also sold textiles in the markets. We traveled a lot with our wagons. We had two wagons: one to live in, the other was like a shop; you opened it up and you had a shop.

I had two brothers and two sisters. We also had a house in Brožánky where we were all born. I was born there in 1933. We traveled only in the warm months.

My father was arrested in 1939 when the Germans came to our country because he was in a group of partisans. They had weapons and were determined to chase the Germans out of our country. For the next six years my father was in five concentration camps, but I can only remember four: Mauthausen, Auschwitz, Birkenau and Buchenwald. Luckily, he survived and came back to us after the war.

In 1942 the rest of the family was in Popovice with our horses and wagons. The Czech police arrested us there and escorted us to Hostěradice by Jílové. We were kept there in a house owned by the town hall for two weeks. We weren't allowed to go home, but for two weeks we had our horses and wagons. Then we were escorted with our horses and wagons by Czech police from county to county until we arrived at the camp in Lety. This trip took us about four days. We were allowed to stop at night and cook our supper and sleep.

The Czech police always told us they were taking us to a nice place where we could work and earn some money. They told us we

■ Jan Šmíd with his accordion in happier days, after Lety.
His brother on far right bought the entire Šmíd clan out of Lety.
Photo circa 1955, from family archive.

wouldn't be there very long. It was just a place where they needed some workers for a short time. We children were very happy, we wanted to travel and see a new place. We thought we were going on holiday.

But when we got to Lety and the gate was closed behind us we saw everything. There were Czech farmers waiting for us with the police.

The first thing that happened was the guards told us to unhitch our horses and give them to these farmers. I didn't want to because they were our horses, but a guard came and beat me and my brother with a wooden club until we unhitched the horses and gave the reins to these farmers. They didn't want our wagons. I don't know what happened to our wagons. They were very nice inside. Later I saw that some wagons were kept to store dead bodies in until they could be buried or burned but they didn't use our wagons for that. Our wagons just disappeared.

After that we were sent to some barracks. We had to take off our clothes until we were nude. There was one man, a prisoner, who had to shave all the women, all their hair, even between their legs. His name was Šmíd. He hated to do these things but the Czech guards made him. After they cut everyone's hair, all our clothes were taken to a warehouse. Then they gave us some dark clothes. Then we were all separated, the men to one block, the children to another and the women to another.

The men were sent to work in a stone quarry. I didn't have a job. I was about ten years old but I remember Lety very well because it was my first concentration camp.

Once a week the guards took us to the lake so we could wash ourselves. We children were afraid of this lake because there were eels in it. We all had to wash together, all nude, men, women and children.

The food was terrible. Potatoes in dirty water. Some cabbage. A little bread. Some people got enough to eat because they had relatives working in the kitchen. But most people had to steal something to survive.

In the middle of this camp there was a small vegetable garden. Sometimes we were so hungry that we children used to raid this garden to get some cabbage leaves to eat. But if the guards caught you they beat you so badly that many children died of these beatings.

My grandmother once went to steal a cabbage for us and the guards beat her to death. I had to help carry her body to the wagon.

The guards were terrible but some of our own people were almost as bad. At the kitchen there was a long line where you waited to pick up your food at a small hatch. I had an uncle working in the kitchen so when I got to the hatch I called out to him. But when my uncle heard me, he hit me over the head with a ladle. He hit me so hard I fell down. Then the guards made me go to the back of the line. By the time I got to the hatch again there was no more food. So what I am telling you is that there were good and bad prisoners too.

In all the barracks there were capos. These capos didn't have to beat us, but they did. They wanted to show the guards how good they were so our own people were beating us too. But they didn't beat us to death like the guards. When a guard beat you, he tried to kill you.

Later there were these Sinti capos from Auschwitz. These capos were already trained like guards. They were really bad, worse than the Czech capos. One of these Sintis escaped from Lety with a Czech family he was related to. After about a week the guards called us all out and showed us a picture of this Sinti. He had been caught and shot in the head. We saw the hole and the blood and we were told this is what would happen to us if we ever tried to escape.

I never saw the guards drown a child in the lake, but after the war I heard from some Lety survivors that newborn babies were thrown in the lake. I never saw this but I know the people who told me this. They were my relatives. They would never lie about such a thing.

I can tell you that I saw many old people beaten to death. The guards really wanted to get rid of them. There were so many dead bodies you can't imagine. These wagons were always full, every day, of these dead bodies. There were also dead bodies on the ground around these wagons. In the beginning these dead bodies were taken by truck to the Mirovice cemetery and buried next to the wall. But later they said there was no more room so they made big holes in the woods and buried the bodies there.

There was a special wagon for prisoners who did bad things like stealing food. My brother once stole some food and was taken to this wagon where his legs were put in iron clamps. Then he was beaten until he passed out. But he was lucky because the director of the camp was from Jílové. When he heard we were from Jílové, he ordered my brother released from this wagon.

There was a metal chamber in the camp where they disinfected clothes to get rid of the lice. I know they used chemicals in this chamber but I don't think this chamber was used to kill people. I never heard about a gas chamber in Lety.

In Lety the guards were always sexually abusing the most attractive women prisoners. These women got special privileges. Good food, no hard jobs. We all knew about this. I could tell you names, the names of many of these women, but it wouldn't be right. If the woman was married, her husband also got special privileges, a good job in the kitchen.

There was a post where people were hung up and beaten. I remember this well. They tied your hands behind your back and hauled you up. Some people hung there overnight even when it was raining or snowing.

I had typhus in Lety. There were two doctors in the camp during the epidemic. One was Czech. The other was a foreigner. They were good doctors. They saved a lot of people. I don't think very many people died in Lety from typhus. There was an epidemic but the doctors saved us.

One day my mother was taken to work on a farm to pick up potatoes but that night she never returned. Later I heard she had been put on a transport to another concentration camp. Only after the war did I hear she had been taken to Mirovice and put on a train to Auschwitz with hundreds of other prisoners from Lety.

A month later I was sent with my brothers and sisters on a train to another camp where they spoke only German. I don't know where they sent us but they tried to teach us German. I think this was a camp where they prepared children to be given to German families. We were all white so I think they wanted to educate us and make us German. That's how I learned German.

I hate Germans. I would like to blame them for Lety, but there were no Germans in Lety. Everybody who died in Lety, the old people, the children, was killed by Czechs. The Czechs did these terrible things to us, not the Germans. Most prisoners who were in Lety could have survived if they had better treatment. There didn't have to be so many deaths. But the Czech guards were so bad that most inmates found it hard to survive.

If you just looked in the wrong direction, the guards might beat you to death.

You know that things were so bad in Lety that until now, even today, I still have nightmares. It's like a movie in my brain. Every night I see the same film. I can't forget those bad things that happened at Lety.

In the 1960s we went looking for some of the guards. We wanted to kill them. I heard about a guard living in Mirovice so we went there. We heard that one of the worst, Pešek, was living there. We never found him but we broke his windows and his front door. The house was empty. A neighbor told us he had moved away, because he already knew people were looking for him. We weren't the first ones.

Two months after they built the pig farm over the camp site I heard about it and I went there with ten members of my family to protest. I went to see the mayor of Lety to complain. I asked him if he knew how many Gypsies had died there, suffered there. He told us that they never should have closed the camp, that we should still be there. That we were parasites. I got so upset, I beat him up. My family had to pull me off him.

The worst thing for me at Lety and I think for most of the prisoners was the hunger. Many children and old people died because there was not enough food. The guards were stealing this food from the warehouse and selling it. Of course some of the prisoners got enough to eat because of special privileges, because some wives or mothers were sleeping with the guards. But most of us starved. Sure, the beatings were bad, very bad. And many people died of these beatings. But for me it was the hunger that was the worst.

There should be special compensation from the Czech government for Lety survivors because only the Czechs killed us at Lety. It was a Czech camp. But I got only 18,000 crowns for being at Lety. They paid me 18,000 crowns last year (1995). Our horses and wagons were worth more than that, so where is the justice?

Sure, I think the Czech government is still covering up what happened at Lety. Why didn't they invite us survivors to the memorial service last year? Why weren't some of us asked to tell the audience what really happened at Lety?

Today people are saying we have democracy in this country, but for the Romany there is no democracy. Look what the skinheads are doing, attacking us. The police do nothing. The politicians don't say anything. This can't be democracy. I keep telling our people we must fight back. If someone hits us, we must hit them back. It's going to come to that. I don't care who is in Prague Castle, saying nice things. If the skinheads keep attacking us we must fight back. My father found weapons to fight against the Germans. We must now find weapons to fight against the Czechs. If we don't, there's going to be a new Lety. If the Republican party wins power in this country, they'll be chopping off our heads.

(1) The communist government stopped an investigation into Lety in 1948.

A. F.

My daughter and I were in Lety for eleven months. It was the only camp we were ever in. What can I tell you? Not too much.

I was born on 20 November 1917 in Eger, Hungary. My father a Czech soldier in the Austrian army in Hungary. He met my mother there. Before being a soldier, he was a marionette player. He didn't make his own marionettes but his profession was to work with them, traveling with a little marionette theater and playing for the children in schools.

I was the only child. My mother died when I was three years old, in Církvice near Kolín. I had two sons and my daughter who is sitting here beside me. My two sons died when they were very little. Later I married my husband present husband with whom I didn't have any children.

My husband was working in a factory in Líšné making linoleum and carpets when three Czech policemen arrived at our door one afternoon in August 1942. They told us we had to go to a work camp. They let us pack only a few things. My sister from my father's second marriage was with us. Later in Lety we found my husband's sister and her husband.

The Czech police took us to Jicin by car where they put us in the town jail for one week until we left by train for Mirovice. Many other families were with us in prison in Jicin. I don't remember any families from there, none of our relatives and none of our friends. Most of the families were Gypsies and Svetskys but there were also lots of white people.

There were different guards on the train than in the prison. The train was full of people. Now I remember we were taken to Písek, not Mirovice. I can't remember how we got to Lety. I don't think we walked all that way. We probably went by truck. There were many of us.

The first thing I saw at Lety was a big gate. Wooden houses. A high fence. They immediately separated the families. The children refused to go away without their mothers so they were beaten by the guards with truncheons. The guards had dogs that they used to take out of the camp once in a while.

They shaved all our heads. At first we could keep our own clothes but later in the winter we received black army clothes and shoes. The shoes hurt me so much that I couldn't even walk in them.

In the morning we received a black coffee and one-sixth piece of a small round bread that had to last the whole day; at midday we got hot water with a few cabbage leaves swimming inside; when the potatoes were big we got one, when they were small we got two, without salt or butter; in the evening, I don't think we received anything. I cannot remember. There was very little to eat there.

No one could escape. Some of the guards were outside of the camp walking around the fence in a circle with their dogs to watch us.

The guards inside of the camp used to beat us very often. They beat us without a reason. Maybe they were also afraid that they were in the camp. I think they were also prisoners. About five or six times during the time I was there, German guards came to control the situation in the camp. They wore German uniforms and spoke German. They never spoke to us. They only went through the barracks to see if everyone was there.

Later four capos came from another concentration camp, two men and two women. They were all German Gypsies, Sinti. They were very, very mean. They used to beat people all the time. The two women were even worse than the two men. The two men escaped with one of the women; they never came back. The one who was left turned crazy after a while. I don't know what happened to her.

They also brought six or seven women prisoners from Prague who were sewing for the camp. I heard that five of them died of typhus. The other two stayed there.

The guards hung up people on the execution post, tying their hands behind them. They left them there for a couple of hours. I remember one woman who was hung up, but I don't know why.

Everyone had to save his own life. We didn't want to see what was happening to the others. We were happy when we weren't beaten.

There was a long wooden latrine with six holes on each side. There were people who died while they were going to the bathroom. That's the only thing I remember happening at the latrines except that we had to clean it out. The children had to stand in line passing the buckets of shit down the line; the last one had to throw it on the fields.

I worked in the stone quarry. My husband was there just a short time, until he was taken to work in the forest; I don't remember where he was taken but he stayed there during the whole time we were there. He returned to the camp two weeks before we were released.

The children were taken to the pond to wash themselves; I remember watching down from where I was working in the stone quarry and saw how the little children were freezing. They were also taken there in the winter time. There were a lot of blind snakes in the pond.

We carried the stones in wheel barrows to the road that was being built at that time. Women were in charge of the children at the lake; they didn't beat the children, but the children received less food than the adults. In the morning they got black coffee, but without bread. I don't know what they got for lunch, but later most of them got diarrhea and then got nothing. I always gave my bread to my daughter. I think some of these women stole the children's food for their own families. Some of the children were so skinny that they couldn't even move their hands to put food in their mouths.

A lot of people died in the camp. I can't tell you the number. They died of hunger. Later a lot of them died of typhus that they got from the dirty conditions of the camp. The bodies were taken to the forest where they were thrown into some kind of mass graves. People died every day in the camp. The conditions there were not to live, but also not to die. We were told that about 1,100 people were in the camp when we arrived, but I believe we were many more. I am positive that about three-fourths of the people in Lety died. Later when they were suffering the typhus epidemic they fell on the ground like dead flies.

A few people were taken to a hospital, but only very few. The camp had its own doctor who was half-Jewish. He went to see the people a lot but he really couldn't help them because he didn't have the necessary facilities and no medicine. He lived in a small house near the guard's house, in front of the gate. He was a good person, also a prisoner, but he couldn't do a lot for us. He just didn't have the possibilities. I don't remember any other doctor.

Whenever a prisoner went to see the doctor, this prisoner was beaten by the guards with truncheons. I don't think they wanted the prisoners to see the doctor very often.

There were three Gypsy men cooking in the kitchen but actually there was nothing to cook. Some of the Gypsy women were helping in the kitchen. Later we found out that the warehouse was full of food that we never received. I heard from one man who broke into the storage house and stole some butter. He told us that there was lots of food, not only butter but smoked meat, and other things all meant to be for us.

The prisoners working in the kitchen all died. One of the Gypsies who was cooking went to the doctor to get himself an overdose of something to kill himself. He died later. If they didn't die in the kitchen, they were sent to Auschwitz.

A lot of Růžičkas were in the camp. The family Richter also. The four capos were also named Richter but most of them were sent away to Auschwitz.

There must have also been kitchen for the guards outside of the camp, but I never saw it. I believe that the guards got better food than we did; who would eat our food which was worse than the pigs received?

Sometimes a guard came and took a young beautiful girl away with him. He gave her a piece of bread. Some of the women had to clean for the guards, and I suppose sleep with them.

We suffered very much from the cold in the winter. Each barracks had a small coal stove; there was a small bag of coal but it was more like dust. It was so dusty that when we wanted to burn a fire the cold dust put it out. People died of the cold also, but our organisms were so weak, we were so skinny, that we really weren't people, just skeletons. So anything could kill us: hunger, cold, all kinds of sicknesses.

I don't know if the people who were badly beaten ever breathed again. They were taken away and we never saw them again.

Most of the pregnant women died. I don't know why. When a woman did give birth to a baby, it died right away. From hunger I suppose.

Everything was bad in Lety. My whole stay there was bad. The work in the stone quarry maybe was the worst. We had to break rocks and then carry them.

My husband's sister and daughter died in Lety, supposedly from typhus. Her husband and her other child were sent to Auschwitz where they died. We have never heard how they died.

In the end, most of the people in the camp were sent right away to Auschwitz. We were also selected for Auschwitz, but I told one of the guards we weren't Gypsy and that we hadn't done anything wrong. Finally we were separated from the transport and later released with four other families.

We were never told why we were sent to Lety. No one in my family was ever a Gypsy or a Svetsky.

After the war, in about 1947, my husband denounced one of the guards in Prague. He was not the director. The police told my husband that he would need a lot of witnesses to prove the accusations and that nothing that he had written was true. I don't remember the name of the guard. It's too long ago. Later my husband received a letter from the police saying that the guard had a good record and that his file contained no bad reports.

After the war, I refused to see any movies about the war. I could never see a German movie about concentration camps. My daughter tells me she sometimes still sees Lety, a picture of the camp in front of her.

We don't have any contacts with Gypsy people, but here in Turnov we don't hear anything bad about them. It's quiet here. The Gypsies are already at home here.

I applied for compensation last December (1995); I got a letter saying we were going to receive something but until now (June 1996) we have received nothing.

I saw on TV that they constructed a pig farm on the camp site. They complained on TV about the pig farm on such an important historical place. We also think that it wasn't right to put a pig farm there. They should have made a decent memorial there or at least a cross.

I think I have told you enough. I don't like talking about Lety. It brings back too many bad memories.

Beatrix Pflegerová
(as told by her son)

My mother was a prisoner in Lety. Her name was Beatrix Pflegerová. We called her Bozena. She was born 23 February 1921 in Boskovice (Blansko), a village in Moravia near Olomouc. Her father was Josef Sigmund who was from Benesov. Her mother was Emilie Pflegerová. She was born somewhere in Moravia.

My mother's family had horses and wagons and made their living by traveling, selling different things and sharpening knives and scissors. Neither her parents nor her four siblings were sent to a concentration camp because by that time they were living in a house. The Moravians in their village protected them, saying they were good people.

Only my mother was unlucky because she was in Prague living with a man. When they rounded up Gypsies in Prague, they got her, but her man, Jan Čermák, escaped. Later he was caught and sent to Terezín. He survived and died about ten years ago in Prague.

My mother was arrested in 1941. She was pregnant and had her son Vlastimil in Pankrác prison in Prague. After she gave birth, both she and her infant son were sent to Lety.

She told me that in Lety there were no Germans, only Czech police. From time to time the Germans came to visit, to check on the camp but the whole staff at Lety was Czech. The Czech police abused the women all the time, especially if they were nice looking.

Beatings were normal. Most of the people who died at Lety died of these beatings. The Czechs tried to get the Gypsies to kill their own people. For example, some of the Gypsies were capos. There was one Romany man who was a capo in both Lety and Hodonin. He was a Czech Gypsy. After the war, he escaped to Germany and died there. Šafránek was his name, from Moravia. He beat his own people, the Czech Romanies, so badly that after the war many Romanies tried to find him, to kill him, but he escaped to Germany.

My mother found it very hard to talk about her experiences in

Lety. We had the tradition in our family that the old people never talked about those things in front of the children, so we never heard all the horror stories. I was only told they were treated like animals, worse than animals.

My mother was only in Lety for three or four months, then she was transferred to Hodonín. After that she was sent to Terezín where they subjected her to experiments and measurements to confirm that she was a Gypsy. She was in Terezín for two and a half years, then sent to Auschwitz.

My mother always said it was a miracle my brother survived Lety. Most of the children there starved to death or were killed.

My father's first wife was also sent to Lety with her four children. Later they all died in Auschwitz.

How did my mother feed her baby in Lety? I don't know. She just didn't talk about those things, but he is still alive. He lives today in Cologne, Germany. Many Lety survivors are there today. They never wanted to remain in Czechoslovakia after Lety, after what the Czechs did to them. They prefer to live in Germany.

There is also an old man about 78 years old called Ruvrli. That's his nickname. He lives about 100 kilometers from Cologne. He was in Lety and Hodonin and then in a concentration camp in Germany. After the war he said he'd rather take his chances with the Germans rather than the Czechs.

Alois Hauer has a son (Václav) in Germany who was with him in Dachau. Alois was in Lety. Václav lives today in Munich. His nickname is Tiknu Venu. You can find him in the Gypsy market. There are several descendants of Lety survivors also in Munich.

Anna Růžičková lives in Brandýs. She's about 70. Her husband Gustav was in Lety for sure. She might have been.

I have some photos of the relatives of mine who were killed in concentration camps.

I would like to tell you more but the old people just never discussed these things in front of us.

My sister might know more because she and my mother talked more. She lives in Toronto. She is 51 years old. The last ten years of her life, my mother lived with her in Toronto. My mother went to Canada in 1979; she died there in 1995.

For many years my mother tried to get some compensation for

her time in the concentration camps, but she never got a penny. I have a cousin whose mother lost all her family at Lety but she got nothing either, even for her time at Auschwitz. My cousin is still fighting to get something because he wants the money to make her a better grave. It is against Gypsy law, tradition, to take money for the dead, but he would like to make her a better grave for all the suffering she went through. He would like to put up a small family memorial for those who died at Lety. But the Czechs are against a real memorial at Lety. They built a big pig farm there. They want that to be our memorial.

What is happening today in the Czech Republic? The situation today for the Romany is very bad. If you go out and the skinheads find you they try to kill you immediately, in front of all the people in the street. My cousin's son was beaten very badly in Prague about three weeks ago.

The Czech Republic today reeks of racism. We are in the same position as we were during the Nazi times. The Czechs hate us, they treat us like they treated the Jews during the war.

Thirteen years ago I went to Canada with my son. In the airport in Montreal the emigration officials asked us if we wanted to stay in Canada. They warned us then that things would get bad for the Romany in Czechoslovakia. They said we would have problems in the future because we were Gypsy. They told me we could stay if we wanted. After five weeks I returned to Czechoslovakia and have regretted it since 1989. I feel today I made a big mistake. My family is now suffering because I believed in the Czech nation. I believed in the Velvet revolution but it was not a revolution for us, only for the whites. Now I am tired of people calling me a "black face."

R. H.

I have written to the Ministry of Defense many, many times asking for compensation for being in Lety. I heard on TV and read in the newspaper that this was now possible. I earn only 3,000 crowns a month; my rent is 1,700 crowns, and all I get are postcards from the Ministry of Defense saying I have to wait because there are so many people applying.

I was born 30 December 1930 in Dvůr Kralové nad Labem. My father was a knife sharpener. My mother had a little store with textiles in Klášter.[1] I had twelve brothers and sisters. We always lived in a house. We never had a wagon. I don't know why we were taken to Lety. We weren't Gypsies.

A Czech policeman by the name of Mák came in the afternoon on 8 August 1942 to our home. We children were playing outside and our mother called us in. We were told that we were being taken to a camp. We had a lot of possessions at that time, so they allowed us to take money, jewelry, clothes. We took a lot of things with us. We gave our animals to our neighbors: chickens, dogs. The police put us in a truck. My father used to have a lot of horses, he used to be in the horse business but when we were arrested we were out of that trade.

The Czech police took us to Golcov Jenikov where we slept in the market square until the morning. There were many other families there: Gypsies, Svetskys, Czechs. I remember a Lety guard by the name of Maxa was there. He was a good man. Many times in my life I wanted to find him. I heard he was taken to Lety as a guard because he was caught playing cards at his police station. Also in the market was the Lety guard Havrda.

When we got to the market there were many people who had been there for several weeks. Many children came up to us to ask for food. They told us how long they had been there.

The next morning trucks took us to Lety. The first thing I saw at Lety was skinny, starving children. Lots of dirt. A very poor atmosphere. The minute we walked through the gate we had to stand in line and strip naked. All of us. I can remember that Mr. Havrda took our clothes away, all our possessions. We never saw them again. They cut off all our hair. The family was separated. The little children were together, the older children some place else, and the adults separated.

My mother worked with us children in the stone quarry. My father was working with some farmers in a field with my eldest brother. My youngest brother who was only a few months old was taken from us. We were carrying lots of stones every day. It was very hard work for all of us. A German was in charge of our work. I believe he was mentally sick.[2]

In the camp we had a small pot for our food. When another family stole our pot, we had to go back to this German for another pot. Instead of giving us another pot, he started beating us. He wore a German uniform. He was the only one. The other guards wore black uniforms. I can remember that one of the guards in a black uniform liked us children very much. But when one of the guards, I think it was Hejduk, saw that this guard was very friendly to us, he told him he was digging his own grave. We never saw this guard again. I don't know if they shot him or not.

In the mornings we got black coffee and a quarter of a loaf of bread which we had to share with five people. For lunch we had soup that was made out of water that had been boiled with red cabbage. Sometimes we also got two small potatoes. I don't remember if we got anything at night. They counted the food for each of us very precisely. But for lunch I remember we mainly got red water.

Whenever we got coffee, the kitchen staff threw away the grounds in the garbage. So we children used to go and find these coffee grounds and eat them. When we got caught eating these grounds, the guards beat us. They wanted us to die of starvation. I also heard that they put something in the milk for the babies so they would die.

My baby brother died shortly after we arrived in the camp. I remember my sister Josefa carrying his dead body to the pile while we all followed her, crying. When we arrived at the pile where all the dead bodies were, she said: "I will put him on top so he doesn't get squeezed by the other bodies."

I remember that two young boys by the name of Vrba ran away. They were hungry and went looking for food. After the guards caught them in the forest, they put chains on their legs and locked them up in a hut for two days. After that the boys were hung up on the execution post for another two days. After the guards let them down, they beat them. I never saw those boys again.

I never heard anything about a lake outside of the camp. There was a house with showers. About a hundred prisoners were brought there at a time. They shaved all the hair off our bodies, then we took a bath and came back where other people were standing in line for the showers.

I remember Mrs. Vrbová giving birth to a child. She herself threw this child into the toilets. I think Mrs. Vrbová was sleeping with the guards because she got pregnant after being in the camp for more than nine months. I think that was why she threw her baby away. She was a beautiful woman. She died in the camp but I don't know how. I am sure there were many women who had to sleep with the guards but this is the only case I know about.

When the small children went to the bathroom without using the toilets, the guards took them and dunked them in the rain water barrels. My four-year-old sister Božena was dunked several times and later died of lung problems.

All of us were beaten every day. I saw several prisoners beaten to death every day. I saw many new dead bodies every day, mainly children and old people. Every day at Lety was bad. Beatings, hunger. There were huge mass graves in the forest for all these bodies. I never saw these graves because we were not allowed to go into the woods, but I heard about them. Everybody was talking about them.

Near the end, typhus broke out. I got it. Two of my sisters Marie and Anežka died of typhus. That was the time when another director came to take over the camp. If Janovský had stayed, we would have all died. This new director gave the order to take all of us away to the hospital in Písek. This is how I survived Lety. I was about one month in the hospital.

I came back with my mother from the hospital. While we were gone, my brother Josef died in the camp but I don't know from what. My sister Antonie also died, I think from typhus. Altogether five of my brothers and sisters died, two in the hospital, three in the camp.

We were released at the end of May 1943. From Lety we walked without shoes to Prague where we caught the train home, back to Klášter. My father couldn't come with us. He had to stay in the camp. He had a better life than us because he was working on the nearby farms. But he joined us a few days later.

When we arrived back in our village, we no longer had our home. It was in ruins. We had to move into a little house that was in the yard of a friend who owned a shop in town.

When my mother returned to the village she found the policeman Mák and tried to denounce him for sending us to Lety. He denied it, then ran away and we never saw him again.

Many times since Lety I have had bad nightmares that someone is lying on top of me. Someone is lying on my feet and I am trying to escape but I can't manage it. I've talked to my friends and they told me to take a knife or a comb into bed with me and since then I haven't had a nightmare again.

I don't think we have a very good government today. I am still afraid to say what I think. I am afraid they would put me in jail. I am also afraid to tell you too much for the same reason. When I see our youth today, I don't believe in them, and I don't believe that they will have a very nice future.

No, you can't take my photo.

(1) County Čáslav, today Kolín.
(2) Josef Janovský, a Czech, was the camp commander. He spoke German.

Jana Marhoulová

Don't worry about my dogs, if they bite you they will only bite your foot. Lety? I am 64 years old, there is so much that has already fallen out of my brain. I can't remember a lot anymore. Lety was a camp for only real Gypsies. Since we weren't pure blooded Gypsies, they released us after a year.

I was born 29 April 1932. I had two sisters. We were all born in Prague. We were all in Lety except my father who was sent directly to Ravensbruck. The German Red Cross informed us after the war that he was also in Buchenwald and some other camps but they could not find a death record for him. He never returned after the war.

My father was a musician, working in Liberec when he was arrested. After he was taken, we were invited to the criminal office in Prague where they took our fingerprints. From there they took us away in green military trucks. We children were taken away to a monastery in Prague where we stayed for three days with the nuns.

We were all taken because of our father, this is the only explanation I can find. I don't know where my mother was while we were in the monastery. I think she was locked up somewhere with some other women. We were again taken away in green military trucks to the train station in Prague where we were sent straight to the concentration camp in Lety.

The train was full of people. Gestapo men and our Czech guards were standing near the windows and the doors so no one could escape. I was a small child then so I don't remember that much, but all the mothers were crying. Finally we found our mother on the same train.

In the train there were white and black people all together, only later when we were released did they make a difference between whites and blacks. The transport was coming from all over the Czech Republic with people that had been collected.

When we arrived at the camp, the first thing they did was shave our hair, wash us and look to see if we had fleas, which we didn't. Then they separated the parents from the children.

The babies were also separated from the little boys and girls. Most of the babies died. They were there under the worst conditions. The people in charge of the little children stole the food from them and gave it to their own children. At first they took the dead bodies to somewhere near Písek and later they buried them in mass graves made around the camp.[1]

My grandfather, the father of my mother, was also there. They asked him to bring water from the well. He had a pole across his shoulders to carry two buckets at a time. When he had the buckets full, they beat him. Then they kicked him into the well. After he climbed out, they made him turn the wheel and bring up water again. Then they kicked him in again. They kept doing this until he drowned. I saw this with my own eyes. I was screaming. The guards had a lot of fun doing this.

All the guards were Czech but a lot of them spoke German. The leader of the camp was German.[2] I can only remember one guard, Maxa from Prague. He was terrible. All the guards wore guns.

In every house there was one capo. A.I. was in charge of the women in the camp and Martin Richter, A.I.'s cousin, was in charge of the men. I am related to the whole family. We were a big clan. A.I. worked in the kitchen for a while but then she got into trouble over stealing food. Later she was in charge of the children. She was no sweetheart. But you had to look after yourself and your family, you had to see that they survived first. A lot of women were with the guards in Lety.

I was a small child then with my mother. She worked as a cleaning lady for the guards, so we were living with my mother outside of the camp. We were taken away to the guards houses to stay there when the typhus broke out. It was a big house built outside the camp. We women had our own home.

All the Istvans are from Germany, from the Sudetenland, from Liberec. That's why my father was a musician there. My mother saved the lives of a lot of women there because she spoke fluent German.

In the morning we received black coffee and a quarter of a loaf of bread for the whole day; during the day we got three little potatoes with a bit of grease. In the evening we got a little bit of sauce. Usually potatoes. We never saw dumplings.[3]

In the summer time the guards took us to a pond to wash ourselves. There were a lot of guards watching us with their dogs, standing around the pond, watching all the naked women.

We also had to go into the forest and cut wood. I can only tell you how I felt as a child there. Our mothers knew what was really happening, but for us everything was new.

We children were sent to the garden to pick the worms off the cabbage; we were very happy to do this; also to clean the tomatoes; we stole some cabbage leaves and ate them there. These vegetables were meant for the guard's kitchen. There was a lot of hunger and a lot of dirt there. A lot of people died of hunger.

My grandmother came from Prague to bring us some food. She was caught in the forest by the guards and beaten. She had bloody stripes on her back and on one arm. Two guards beat her in a very cruel way. My two aunts were also with her. When I saw how my grandmother was beaten, I ran away. The guards caught me and beat me for that. My aunts were able to run away, but my grandmother was more than seventy years old and couldn't keep up with them. My grandmother was not detained in Lety because the camp was already too full. I was in the pond bathing when I saw this. I saw my aunts and grandmother coming through the forest. The guards went after them with dogs.

I also remember the guard Baloun. I used to hear his name all the time. I think he was the one who beat me at the pond and Maxa was the one watching this. Maxa was the leader of the camp guards. I don't think all of them were the same. Some were good, some bad. It's difficult to talk about this. Later our own people were even worse than the guards. Everyone was out to save his own life. My uncle told me when he came from Auschwitz that there was a woman who sold her own husband to save herself and her children. It is difficult to say who was good or bad. They made animals out of people in Lety. But I don't want to judge anyone because you had to save your own life.

Many Czech Gypsies went to Germany in 1945 to live because they had been capos in Lety. They feared our people would find them after the war. Later my mother told me that people who really loved their children or their spouse seldom survived. Everybody, or most of the people, were only saving themselves.

I heard from the adults of our family that my father's uncle denounced us, that's why we were sent to Lety. He also denounced a lot of other families in Prague. He denounced them so he could save his own neck. When there was no one left to denounce, they took him. This is how the police did it. My mother said one would denounce the other just to save himself.

A woman named Bluma ran away from the camp. Robert, Frida and Ferstu were three capos who came to the camp. They were German Sinti. Ferstu was in charge of the children and Robert was in charge of the men; the other one, Frida, was in charge of the women. He was the one who ran away with Bluma. They ran away with her children. Later they were caught but I don't know where they ended up.

Two brothers of the Richter family escaped and were also caught. I took them food which I slipped through the bars. Each one of them was in a little wooden hut which looked toward the camp. I don't know what happened to them in the end. I think they were taken to Auschwitz. Later they ended up in Germany.

There was a latrine in the camp; there were five circular holes on each side. When people went to the toilet, they were sitting in front of each other.

Behind the camp were three Gypsy caravans. These caravans were used to store the dead bodies. There were loads of bodies, a lot of flies, dead meat and flies. The smell was terrible. Later they took the bodies away somewhere else.

When I was in the forest, Josef Vrba whom I knew from Prague and a friend of his ran away. I was in charge of looking after them but they ran away. In the evening we had to stand in line and I had to count the people. That's when I noticed that the two boys were missing. The guards beat me and locked me up for three days in a hut near the three Gypsy caravans. This is how I knew where the dead bodies were kept. My mother used to come and see me and bring me food. She also came at night because I was crying. I was afraid of the dead bodies. If I hadn't been locked up, I would never have known where they kept the dead bodies.

All of the children of my uncle Čermák died in the camp from hunger. They looked like skeletons. Two girls and one boy, Karlíček, Gizelka and Janička. They were beautiful children. Within six months of arriving in Lety they were dead. A lot of people died there. In the morning we had to get out of our house and stand in line. The dead bodies of the children who had died during the night were then taken away somewhere.

The cold in the winter was terrible. There was a lot of snow. We had a very thin blanket so all of us squeezed together to keep warm. There were little stoves that they heated once, and that was it.

My mother also worked in the stone quarry in the beginning with other women. Then she worked behind the camp as a cleaning lady for the guards.

I saw how people were beaten when they left their barracks before going on a transport. The guards were there with their dogs to make sure no one escaped. They called the prisoners' names from a list to come out of the barracks. When the prisoners came out they were all crying and didn't want to go, so the guards beat them badly with truncheons.

My paternal grandparents died of typhus in Lety. People first got diarrhea, then they had white gums and tongues. We were not allowed to go where all the sick people were. My grandparents were also taken to the camp because of my father. My grandmother was visiting us when they took her to Lety with us. I forgot she came to Lety with us. Later all the sick people were isolated. A lot of them had typhus. We all got typhus. When we were released, we went to the Bulovka hospital in Prague where we were cured. My mother and my sister Marie had it very bad. Many, many people died of typhus in the camp. Later they didn't know where to put the dead bodies, so they made mass graves. I would say that most of the children died of hunger, but later everyone just died, old people and children, from typhus, whether they were sick before or not. The water was dirty, that's where we got typhus from. I think 25 to 30 people died every day during the epidemic. They died like wax drops coming down from a candle.

I didn't ever see any doctors in Lety. Later some of the guards also died of typhus. There was no doctor in Lety. The prisoners washed the sick and helped each other.

They released us because we were not pure Gypsies. My grandfather was a Czech. We were sent there because of my father. My mother said that my father helped some people to escape to Germany. Istvan only knew this about my father so this must have been the reason why he denounced us. They took only pure Gypsies to Auschwitz.

We went by train back to Prague. We lived with our aunt until we got an apartment. The family helped us, only the family. The Czech police took everything away from us. But the family helped us start up again.

When I came back from the camp, I had a feeling that I had been sent away from life. People told me I had changed a lot. Instead of taking the tram, I just sat there at the tram stop, I just sat there on the ground.

My mother was in the hospital three months after she was released from Lety. It was a very hard time for her.

After the war my mother went to the main archive in Prague to find information on my father; my mother needed a certificate that she was a widow so she could get some compensation. In the archive my mother saw that Maxa was working there. My mother screamed, "Maxa is here!" I was fourteen years old. The archive was in the basement. We both ran up the stairs; we were still afraid of him. We thought he could still do something to us.

After the 1989 revolution, we applied for compensation. We received no money because they wrote from the German Red Cross that my father's death was not registered and that we could only receive money for a ten-year period after the war.

Last year in December 1995 I applied for compensation for being in Lety but I have never received an answer. Our family has never had any compensation. I also wrote a letter to the Ministry of Defense but never received a reply either.

I know of no racism in our community. We are not like the Slovak Gypsies. We have never had any contacts with people who wandered around. We are intelligent, civilized people since the time we were born. My grandmother always told us we were born with intelligence. There are some racial problems in Brno with the Gypsies who moved there. I never had problems in Prague. My whole family lives there. If the situation would come back like it was before the war it would be terrible. I can't imagine it.

Sometimes I listen to Sládek who studied under the communists, but he hasn't a clue about what happened during the war. He is a stupid man. How can he say something like, "Gypsies to the gas chambers?"

There is no one in our family who was ever in a fight with a skinhead. We have been here from our childhood. The Gypsies from Slovakia do have problems with the skinheads. Now the borders are open. Anyone can come in the country.

I think President Havel is a good man, but a bit naive to be a politician. If I tell you the truth all politicians are only interested in their own welfare.

I have never been back to Lety. I never heard about a memorial there, a service. No one invited me. It is terrible to think that they put a pig farm on the camp site. So many people died there. And so many were killed there. And they didn't even put a cross on the place where it happened.

Please, I don't want to remember Lety any more. I've had two heart attacks already. I am happy that I was a child there. The older children and parents lived, felt, this time in a different way.

If you take a photo of me, the lens will explode. I look like an old Gypsy now.

(1) Mirovice.
(2) Josef Janovský. Many prisoners thought he was German.
(3) The cleaning ladies ate in the guards' kitchen and received much better food than the other prisoners.

Vratislav Chejlava
(letter found in Třeboň State Archives)

Please, I want to appeal to the state archive in Třeboň to send me a certificate of my detention in the concentration camp of Lety by Písek where I was sent on 10 July 1940. I was released on 18 October 1940 from this concentration camp because of my sickness. I was born on the 19th of January 1908 in Plzeň.

From Lety I was released to the labor office in Plzeň where I received medical treatment by Dr. Chudáček and in November 1940 he sent me to the German clinic of Prof. Schlofer to diagnose my illness. He sent this information about my medical condition to the labor office in Plzeň. After this I was sent to the Czech clinic of Prof. Jirásek and from Prof. Jirásek I was sent to the Prague clinic of Prof. Henner for neurological treatment. I was in that clinic from 1941 until 1948 receiving psychiatric treatment.

After this Prof. Henner sent me back to Plzeň to the clinic of Prof. Hrbek where I remained until 1953. From Prof. Hrbek's clinic I was sent to Prof. Vencovský's psychiatric clinic. From there I was sent to the hospital to Dr. Jindřich Dvořák, head of the psychiatric department, where I have treated up until now.

During all this time I have been treated for what happened to me at the concentration camp in Lety by Písek where I was detained although I was guilty of no crime. I kindly ask you for some confirmation from the state archive that I was released as an ill person and that my bad health comes from my detention in Lety. Please send me this document as soon as possible because I have to present it before the 10th of April 1975 to the Ministry of National Defense in Prague.

Bohuslava Klocová

I was born on 4 January 1922 in Trhové Sviny in the county of České Budějovice. My parents had two wagons. We lived in one. The other was my father's work wagon. He was a grinder. We traveled around the country with our horses while my father earned his living by sharpening scissors, knives, and axes and making special knives for butchers. My mother and we children sold clay cooking pots.

My father's name was Ota Daniel. He was born in Salzburg, about 1900. My mother was Marie Klocová. She was born in Bohemia, but I don't remember the name of the village. She was three or four years older than my father. We were always traveling; there was never any time to go to school.

I was the oldest child. Next was my sister Blažena. Her married name was Kadalovská. After the war started she was sent to the Gypsy camp at Hodonín in Moravia. The next time I saw her, she was at Auschwitz. We promised each other that if we survived we would never again live apart. After the war we shared an apartment with our families in Prague 3 where she died in 1985. I still live with her son in this same apartment.

The next oldest was my sister Josefa Klocová. She was sent to the Gypsy camp at Lety with me. Later we met up in Auschwitz. I saw her for about three months there then one day I never saw her again in my life.

My sister Marie Klocová was also in Lety and in Auschwitz. She disappeared in Auschwitz too. My stepbrother František Růžička was also in Lety and died in Auschwitz. Adolf Kloc, my real brother, was in Lety, and died in Auschwitz. My youngest sister was Antonie Růžičková. She wasn't in Lety but in Hodonín and in Auschwitz. She lives today in Brno.[1]

My father was working in Písek in 1942, making butcher knives, when he was arrested by the Czech police and taken to Lety. We never saw him again or his horses or work wagon.

A month later we were with my mother in Třebeň by Tišnov

when the Czech police came to pick up the rest of us. We were picked up by truck and taken to Lety. I don't know what they did with the horses and wagon and all our possession we left behind.

When we arrived at Lety, they shaved our heads like the palms of our hands. They took our clothes and gave us some dark gray colored clothes with black stripes. We girls had a long sack dress; I don't know what happened to our nice clothes. We had such nice clothes; we weren't poor Gypsies.

The first day everyone was together, then the next day they separated us, men to one barracks, the women to another; the children were allowed to stay with their mothers.

There were seven or eight very long barracks in the camp, with 300 or more people in each one. There were double or triple levels of beds, overflowing.

Everyone had to work at Lety. I had to carry rocks in a basket to make a bigger pile. I didn't know why we had to carry rocks. It didn't make sense. I guess they wanted us to do something instead of wasting time.

Later I had to collect wood in the forest, kindling, but I wasn't sure what it was used for. Perhaps for burning bodies; I saw many bodies that weren't buried. Not too far from the camp there were many fires but you couldn't go there; the fires were always made when new transports came bringing people to the camp.

There were so many cases of beatings and killings that I could not count them. Nobody could count that many. But I don't want to remember them, I don't want to talk about it.

They gave me a tattoo at Auschwitz, Z-2320, on the left side of my left forearm. But look what they gave me at Lety for stealing potatoes. The Czech guards burned a swastika on my right thigh with a Bunsen burner. They also burned my left palm, under the little finger, here, this scar. I was starving in Lety and I stole four or five little potatoes and this was my punishment.

From Auschwitz they brought German Gypsies to look after us, three women and four men; Fasi and Nablo were two of the names I remember. They were forced to beat us, but they didn't hit us as hard as the Czech guards.

All the guards at Lety were Czech. The worst one was Josef Hejduk. He was a tall man with broad shoulders, a very strong man, clean shaven. I couldn't believe he was Czech because he was beating and killing his own citizens. He sexually abused the young Gypsy girls, but only those who were nice looking. This Hejduk took these young girls to his office where he made them take off their clothes. Then he beat them and abused them. He also did the same thing to young boys. Everyone who got in his way he just took them away and they were never seen again. If he came out of his office and anyone walked in front of him, that person disappeared forever.

In the camp there were six or seven wooden rain barrels. When a pregnant woman gave birth, the baby was immediately drowned in one of those rain barrels. No children were allowed to be born in the camp.

I never saw my father at Lety. When we arrived, we looked all over for him. We asked the guards about him. One guard said he had died of typhus, another said he had escaped. But the prisoners told my mother that the guards had beaten him to death.

After the war, I heard some prisoners say that Lety was worse than Auschwitz. I can't say that. I lost almost all my family at Auschwitz so for me Auschwitz was worse. But the Czech guards at Lety were worse than the German guards at Auschwitz. The beatings were worse at Lety, that's all I can say, except that many Romanies got better food in Auschwitz than at Lety.

When I was in Lety there were about 20 or 30 deaths a day; some died of typhus, some from starvation, but most died of beatings. New prisoners arrived every day, about the same number that were killed every day.

I don't remember when they sent me to Auschwitz; it wasn't cold, it was warm, maybe in the spring; I was only in Lety about three or four months.

I've never received any compensation for being in Lety. It wasn't a German camp so the Germans won't pay any compensation for being in Lety. I was also in Auschwitz, Ravensbruck, Wittenberg, Dachau, Mauthausen. All were bad, but the guards at Lety were the worst.

I ended up in a small concentration camp making parts for German airplanes. I don't remember the name of that place but we got a whole loaf of bread there. I remember that.

The worst thing at Lety was the beatings, the beatings, the beatings with the truncheons, and old gun barrels filled with sand; in no German concentration camp were we beaten like we were at Lety.

You got beaten at Lety for the smallest thing; men were tied on tables and beaten in front of all the people. Most of the men died of those beatings.

Young girls, eighteen and nineteen-years-old, were given injections at Lety so they wouldn't have any more children. I didn't get any injection but I knew many who did.

All these things that are happening today in the Czech Republic (the skinhead attacks, the hatred against us, the government's non-reaction) remind me of what happened at the beginning of World War II in our country.

You can't get a job today if you are a Romany. If you don't have money to pay your rent, they kick you out. If this government was a good government, it would not let these things happen today.

This government is always talking badly about the communists, but this government today is worse than the communists ever were. During the communist era no one ever kicked us out of our apartments; everyone had a job. Even if you can get a job today, they steal from you; they don't pay you what they promised.

(1) No member of this family was ever mentioned in the records of Lety, although the Auschwitz records list them as coming from the camp at Lety. How many Romany passed through Lety, or were killed at Lety, with no record ever having been kept about them?

V. J.

I was born on 28 January 1930 in Pavlíkov (Rakovník). My father worked in the forest; he traveled a lot. My mother was a housewife.

My mother worked as a cook in Rokycany in a German military base. My sister was Maria; my brother's name was Josef. We were all taken away to Lety excluding my father who was sent directly to Auschwitz, but including my grandmother whose name was Jana Krylová. At that time we were living in Strašice, county Rokycany. The Czech police came to our door, told us to take with us the most important things, then we were taken by truck to Rokycany. They told us we were going to Lety because we were Gypsies. They told us we were going to work.

In Rokycany there were already a lot of families waiting: some of them were Růžička and Serynek. There we stayed all of us together in a cinema. We slept for two days there, then we walked to the train station. From there we took the train directly to Mirovice. At Mirovice the guards told us that those of us who had money could take a bus to Lety, the rest of us had to walk.

I was 12 years old when I arrived in Lety. When we entered the gate they took all of our things away from us. They shaved our heads immediately. They separated the small children from the older children and from their mothers. All of the men they took straight away to farms where they had to work. Only the older men stayed in the camp.

When we entered the camp we had to stand in line. The director of the camp was standing there with all the other guards who had truncheons and dogs. The camp director greeted us and said that one way leads to the camp and the other way to heaven. A lot of women cried because they guessed what could happen to them. We all thought we were going to die in Lety, that's how we understood his message. This man is not alive today; he was an old man even then.

There was one guard who was a very good man. His family had a restaurant in a small village near Lety. We used to call him "brown eyes" because he had beautiful brown eyes. He came to the camp early in the morning and left in the evening.

Later in Auschwitz people who were together with me in Lety told me that our grandmother was not buried in the cemetery in Mirovice but was thrown into the mass grave in the forest behind the camp.

There were wooden houses in the camp. There were about 28 maybe more people in each house. About six children and sometimes even more slept in one bed together. My sister was three years younger than me. My brother was only two years old. There were women who were there to take care of us. We received one small loaf of bread that we had to share with five other children. The smaller children sometimes didn't receive anything because the women stole their bread from them.

My mother worked on the farms, leaving early in the morning and coming back in the evening. My mother never worked in the kitchen but almost the whole family Dubský worked there. They got better and more food than we did. They weren't related to us, but we knew several Plzeň families in the camp: Draský, Dubský, and Kocek.

In the morning when a guard rang the bell, people had to run out of their barracks. From each side a guard ran after the people, beating them to run faster. Then we had to stand in line for roll call. Later the prisoners went to work.

Prisoners were beaten there every day. When one of the prisoners made a mistake he was locked up in a small wooden hut that they called "the bunker." There the prisoner had to stay for two or three days and only received water in the morning.

On Saturdays the guards used to take us to the ponds. One day a woman, I think it was Zdeňka Serynková, went from the pond to the forest to go to the bathroom. She had asked one of the guards for permission to go. He nodded. We were all wondering why he was following her. After a while we heard her scream. The guard had beaten her to death with his gun. He came back and said, "Quiet, quiet."

At that time my mother was working in the stone quarry; she told us that she and several other people had seen the blood from that incident on the place where the woman was killed, but they never saw the body.

In the stone quarry the prisoners were forced to take the stones by wheel barrows two kilometers away, then they had to carry the stones back the same way. It made no sense. They just wanted the people to work.

There was a vegetable garden between the barracks; I saw a child running from this garden with a carrot. A guard caught him and beat him to death.

They hung people up on the execution post. The guards left them there for a long time. The little children were sent away but the older children had to watch what would also happen to them if they did something wrong. Many people died from these hangings. There were many deaths at Lety from things like this.

There was a man called Studený who was in charge of taking the dead bodies away to the cemetery in Mirovice. Some of the prisoners were in charge of making the wooden coffins. There was a small boy, eleven years old, who they took to bury in Mirovice; when Studený was about to put the coffin in the ground, he heard some sounds. He opened up the coffin and found the boy still alive. The boy asked Mr. Studený for a piece of bread.

I remember that once the two children of Tonka escaped from the camp to beg for bread in the village of Lety. When they came back to the main gate they were singing. The guards were so surprised hearing these happy songs, they didn't beat them. Of course A.I. had good relationships with the guards because she was sleeping with them. She had a beautiful body. She didn't mind who she slept with.

There was a Gypsy there, Eduard Serynek, who grew up in a children's home. He worked in the camp before the Gypsies came. He stayed because he heard Gypsies were coming and he wanted to get their gold. A.I. had a relationship with him also.

When there was a sick person whom they couldn't help anymore, the guards drowned him in the latrine. There were also a lot of babies drowned in the latrines. The child Maria Flachsová died there.

My mother was in charge of taking care of the sick people when my grandmother and I got typhus. She could write and read very well so she wrote down temperatures. I remember one night there was a nine-year-old girl dying; my mother told me to please take her out; I was a bit afraid but I carried her out and put her in one of the Gypsy caravans the guards used to store dead bodies. She died there.

A lot of people died of typhus. My grandmother died when typhus broke out around Christmas time. She was taken to Písek Hospital where she died. I was also in Strakonice for two months where they cured my typhus. My uncle Bohumil also died of typhus in Lety.

People who came from Lety to Auschwitz told me later that there had not been enough room in Mirovice and that the bodies were thrown in mass graves in the forest behind the camp.

All of the guards at Lety were very bad. They were already contaminated by the Germans. Their only aim was to beat people; they beat them without any reason. When they called us to stand in line, the people couldn't get up fast enough; the people were too weak to walk because they were hungry; this was also a reason for the guards to beat them.

I remember Dr. Kopecký, and one woman whose name was Vanda Studená who was assisting the doctor. I was never examined by the doctor but I knew he was there. They had too much work so they had to take a lot of the people to hospitals. If the doctors had been good, the guards would have been bad to them.

All the cleaning women and all the women cooking in the kitchen had to sleep with the guards. I was only a child then but I saw the curtains put up on the windows. I heard the women laughing, having fun. Today I wonder how those women could laugh knowing how many children were dying outside.

The children received a spoon full of potato goulash for lunch. Later outside when they were going to the bathroom many ate their own shit they were so hungry. In the morning we had white coffee and a piece of bread; in the evening sometimes some water with noodles or potatoes.

Alois Růžička had to feed the rabbits of the camp director. When one of the rabbits had babies, he ate them alive.

I was in Lety many times after the war, sitting in the woods, crying for my people. There was nothing left. Later they built a pig farm on the camp site. I can't believe that the government put a pig farm there. It is such disrespect for the people buried there. There are a lot of good people, Czechs and Gypsies but I still can't understand the reason not to respect the dead at Lety.

I talked to Mrs. Vrbková who is living on a farm near Lety; she said that a lot of inhabitants of the village felt the pig farm was a terrible thing, with no respect for the dead.

Some prisoners escaped and lived with their relatives. When they were found, they were brought back to the camp with their relatives. A woman called Chadrabová was caught in Prague and brought back to Lety. She came back with a small child who was killed in the camp. Later she was released.

During the winter we suffered very much from the cold in Lety.

A lot of children froze to death. Prisoners always had frozen extremities, especially their feet. Four of my toes got frozen at Lety until pieces of flesh fell off.

Every day there were dead bodies in Lety. Five or six people, I am sure, died every day while I was there.

The director gave the orders to the guards to kill people; he never wanted to get his hands dirty.

There were rain barrels filled with old, dirty water. That's why we got typhus.

All the guards were Czech. Before the winter time three Germans came to the camp, SS men. They were sent there to organize who would be sent to Auschwitz.

There were two or three German Gypsies in the camp as capos; they were very brutal; one woman I know was beaten to death by them on her way to work.

People died of typhus, starvation, cold, beatings.

Today I don't have any more nightmares about Lety, but I used to, very, very often. Whenever I remember Lety I start to cry.

In January last year (1995) I received some compensation, I got 75,000 crowns for being in Lety. They told me I would receive 100,000 for my father and mother, and 50,000 for each brother and sister. But I never got it. I was supposed to get 300 DM per month for being in Auschwitz from the German government. I believe that the Germans pay this to the Czech government but the Czechs only give me 300 crowns a month. I don't want to ask for compensation for my parents. I want to give the money to my three grandchildren.

It was so terrible, my mother was only 43 years old, she was such a young woman then. She died of typhus in Lety. My two brothers died in Auschwitz. My grandmother also died in Auschwitz. But for me, Lety was much worse than Auschwitz.[1]

My worst experience was when one of the cleaning women told me that my mother had died. At that time I had a very high temperature, and I didn't even realize what had happened. I was still asking for my mother long after she had died. My grandmother also died in the hospital in Písek.

We live in Stankov in our own house but nobody in town pays any attention to us. I can't understand it. I worked very hard for 30 years as did my husband who was a white man. Today we are

Czechs, why don't the Czechs mind the Vietnamese who are here? The Czechs only hate us Gypsies. I have given up speaking to them. They tell us that we are different. I answer that I feel that I am a much better person than they are.

The government should do something about the skinheads. They kill Gypsies, we can't do anything about this problem, only the government can change this but they are doing nothing.

My children were raised to stay at home; we are a close family; we don't go out very often. I have six sons; they all work; we have our house in Stankov, but I travel with one of my sons, he is working in the forest.

My eldest brother went to a bar here in town to get some cigarettes. He doesn't drink at all. There were some skinheads in front of the pub and they ran after him; my brother was very lucky that he could escape; he called the police, but the police told him not to exaggerate, who would run after you?

There is enough work these days but the sad thing is that we have to move a lot. Two of my sons work in the forest; when I hear that the skinheads want to send Gypsies today to the gas chambers, I think they don't know what they are talking about. They are uneducated children. A tree in a forest knows how to behave better than they do; they are like trees that the parents just let grow without educating them.

My sons are employees of the state; they work in the woods with their own horses and wagons. The government makes contracts with them; when they like the contract, they work, when the government doesn't pay enough, they don't work.

They cut the trees down, take them on their wagons to the main roads, where trucks take the wood away. We have two horses. Sometimes we travel with our horses and wagons, and sometimes the employers pick us up with trucks and take us to our new place of work.

This is the same profession our family has worked in for many generations.

---

(1) Mrs. Procházková broke down and cried for several minutes at this point. Her mother died in Lety on 27 December 1942.

Vlasta Růžičková
(as told by her son)

According to the certificate I have here from the International Red Cross, my mother was in Auschwitz, Ravensbruck, Buchenwald and Bergen-Belsen. Her Auschwitz number tattooed on her left arm was Z-7960. The Red Cross certificate doesn't mention that my mother was in Lety, but that was her first concentration camp. She always said that the Czech guards were worse animals than the Germans. Lety was the worst place she was ever in.

My mother, Vlasta Ludmila Růžičková, was born 2 May 1919 in Třemy by Mělník. Her parents were Josef Růžička and Maria Hauerová. She had three brothers and four sisters. Her father bought and sold horses. They had a wagon and traveled all year long throughout the country. My mother was born in their wagon.

She was living in Staré Jesenčany by Pardubice when she was arrested and sent to Lety. The police arrived one day with trucks and took them to the train station in Pardubice. She went with her husband and three children. She was the only one who survived Lety.

The police told them they were taking them to a place where they would have good work and a nice place to stay, a place where they could make lots of money. My mother had no idea where they were taking them.

She told me that after her husband and her three children had died in Lety, she was beaten almost every day with a wooden club. She said the food was horrible; they had soup with red beets made with dirty water. Normally it would be impossible to eat this food but they had nothing else. She was sick in Lety. She had bronchitis. Her parents were arrested with her in Třemy but after arriving in Lety, she never saw them again. She wouldn't tell me how her children died. She would never talk about it.

She saw many people murdered at Lety. They were mainly beaten to death for no reason at all. People also died of starvation. She told me about all the dead bodies, she couldn't believe there were so many dead bodies stacked up.

I remember my mother having nightmares every night. When I was growing up, she had to have treatment for her nerves for more than seven years. She was marked for life by her experiences. But Lety was the camp that woke her up every night. She could never forget Lety. She lost her husband, her parents and her children in Lety. She always spoke about the Czech guards who were responsible for taking her loved ones.

My mother remarried in 1946. From her second marriage she had six children. I have two brothers and three sisters. We have always lived in Liberec. Life wasn't very nice under communism here. There was discrimination, racism. We were second class citizens under the communists but the fascists were under control. We were protected by the Russians; the Czechs couldn't harm us then. But today reminds me of all the terrible stories my mother told me about the Czechs during the World War II. My mother never expected the Czechs would take her to Lety, so I can't say what they are going to do to me. I fear the same thing may happen. She died in 1991. The last two years of her life she feared because of the Velvet Revolution that she would be taken to another Lety before she died.

I live next door to a restaurant where skinheads have a club. Three years ago in 1993, on a Sunday afternoon, there was a soccer match with Ostrava. About fifty skinheads came on a bus for the match. I was repairing my car with two of my sons. We didn't see the skinheads because they approached us from behind. Suddenly I was hit by a big stone on my back as I was leaning over looking at the engine. I didn't hear the skinheads because the engine was running. When I turned around there were fifty skinheads. I didn't know the exact number at that time. I just saw a big crowd. My two sons ran away. I tried to follow them but one of the skinheads hit me over the head with a metal pipe. He never stopped beating me. I had my face broken from my forehead to my jaw. My nose was broken, two ribs. My kidneys were damaged and I lost all my front teeth. According to the doctors, I also had brain damage. When the ambulance arrived to take me to the hospital the doctor refused to treat me because he said I was a Gypsy. After he walked away, another doctor who I knew helped me.

When the ambulance arrived the police also came. They arrested two skinheads. The next day in the hospital the police asked me questions. I couldn't talk to them because of my condition. The doctor also told the police I was not in any condition to answer questions. The policemen told me after I left the hospital they would visit me again.

I spent two months in the hospital but the police wouldn't let anyone interview me; no newspapers, no TV, nothing. A television crew with a camera arrived the second day I was there but the police didn't want any pictures of me.

Two months later the police came to visit me at home. I told them what had happened. They said my version was different from when they interviewed me in the hospital. I asked if the skinheads were in police custody, they said no. They said there was not enough evidence to prosecute. I insisted on a case. Half a year later there was a court case. Three skinheads were charged. There were fifty skinheads in the courtroom. The three skinheads who were charged now had long hair. The judge asked me if I could recognize them. I said yes. Despite their long hair, I could still recognize them. The skinheads said that they were not in that attack, probably somebody else. It was not a serious trial. The judge said the skinheads could only be charged for creating a public disturbance, not for assault. It was such a farce I told the judge it was nothing more than a theater play. The judge ordered two guards to throw me out. The fifty skinheads in the courtroom started laughing. Until now I am still waiting for my appeal to a higher court.

My mother was beaten in Lety in 1942 and I was beaten even worse in Liberec in 1993. The Czechs are out to kill us and I believe they will. We Romany are not united. When I was beaten, I lived in an apartment building full of Romanies, but no one would help. The Czechs are picking us off one by one. We have no hope.

I would like to emigrate to a country where there is real democracy, where there is no racism. I know that in the United States the blacks have problems but it can't be as bad as it is here. I see they make sport together. They are living together. But here it's not that way. I have no hope for us in this country.

Antonie Kroková

I am 70 years old. I was born in Doupov (Duppau), region Karlovy Vary on 29 September 1925. Because my parents weren't married, as was the Gypsy custom in those days, we children all used the surname of my mother. I was in Lety with my brother Antonín Serynek, my sisters Jana, Josefa, Marie, my father, Jan Vrba, my mother Anna Terezie Serynková and her parents who were Františka Růžičková and Eduard Serynek.

In August 1942 we were all at my mother's home in Beroun. The Czech police arrived with a German officer who wanted to take photos of all of us, head shots, mug shots. My father had a fight with this German officer. When all the men in the house saw this, they joined in. The Czech police then beat all the men and women in the house. When the Czech police started to put our men into a truck, my mother protested that if they were going to take our men they might as well take all of us, and they did. That was on 4 August 1942. There were three big trucks that arrived in front of our house, one already full of people. When we arrived at Lety these trucks were completely full. We weren't allowed to take anything with us.

The first thing that happened at Lety was that they cut our hair. They didn't shave people's heads unless they had lice. Since we didn't have lice they only cut our hair short.

After that we had to wash. They took us to a large wooden shed that had a log water trough as if they wanted to water lots of animals at the same time. They took our clothes and burned them. The men got pants and a work shirt with blue strips; we women got a gray striped sack dress with no buttons. Both men and women got wooden clogs for shoes.

In our barracks there were three levels of beds. We were eight or ten children to each bed. For a few days my mother was allowed to stay with us children; then she had to go to the women's barracks.

Everyone had to work at Lety. Every morning we children were taken outside to the forest where we had to pick up all the wood that could be used for a fire. We had to bring this wood and stack it up next to the dead bodies in another place in the forest so they could be burned.

Behind the camp the prisoners had to make a trench four or five meters deep so when people escaped from the camp they would fall into this trench. The trench was checked every morning and if a prisoner was found in the trench he was shot. We had to bring wood to burn his body too. We also had to bring wood to burn the bodies of the people who died from typhus.

I also saw every day the guards killing people by drowning them in the lake and in the rain barrels. The men (old and young) had to work very hard with the pick and the guards were always standing around them yelling, "Work faster, work faster, you dirty Gypsies." If somebody worked slowly the guards beat him with their truncheons especially around the head. If the man fell down the guards would yell, "Get up! Get up!" If the man did not get up after three calls to do so, the guards shot him. I saw this with my own eyes on too many occasions.

The only guard I remember by name was Hejduk because he was the worst. I know I could recognize him today but I don't want to talk about the things he did. I've tried to forget them.[1]

My father spent only ten days in Lety. He was among the first prisoners sent to Auschwitz. My mother also left on one of the early transports, so we children were alone in Lety almost from the beginning of our stay there.

Because we were without our parents, I remember one of the guards tried to use my sister Josefa. When she screamed he took out his pistol and said he would shoot her if she didn't do what he wanted. We were crying, she was crying. Then we started to run, screaming that this guard wanted to kill our sister. Another guard came and talked the bad guard out of abusing my sister. But I'm sure he went and found someone else. That was what happened in the camp every day.

Women in the camp who refused to have sex with the guards were either beaten, usually to death, or shot. I remember that shortly after the war, around 1946, I met with some other survivors of Lety in Plzeň and in Beroun. We traded stories, we talked about Lety. It was then I learned how often women were abused at Lety. Hearing it from the older women, I now know how bad it was.

■ Antonie Kroková, Lety survivor who believes Czech President Václav Havel is not speaking out against the skinheads who are attacking her people today.

My two cousins died at Lety from typhus. I also got typhus there. But none of my immediate family died at Lety. My parents and all my brothers and sisters died in Auschwitz.

When people got sick at Lety it was normal to give them an injection just above the heart. Most people died from this injection so we didn't like to tell the doctors when we were sick.

But everybody got sick because we didn't have enough to eat. For breakfast we got only a small piece of black bread and some black coffee without sugar. We got nothing else. For lunch we got rabbit food (some boiled oats), nothing else. We got supper only once and a while, hot water with some finely shredded sugar beets. Sometimes they put rock salt in the soup.

I remember the Romany capos at Lety. They were very bad to us. They came from Auschwitz and treated us worse than the Germans did in Auschwitz. I never talked to these capos, but our old people, the men, told the Romany capos that we would one day find them when all this was over.

The worst thing for me at Lety, was what happened to the children. Children who were sick received injections to kill them. And the small children, only two years old, had to drink sour milk that was poisoned. I personally drank this poisoned milk, but immediately threw it up. The children who didn't throw up this milk all died. Every day these things happened to the children in Lety. There were too many children in Lety for them to handle so one of the priorities was to get rid of the children. When the population of the children had fallen drastically then we were better looked after.

In the middle of the camp there was a small garden with overgrown, old cabbage heads. Sometimes we stole some cabbage leaves, but once I got caught and shot in the left leg. There was no hospital in the camp so I had to recover in my room. The guard who shot me called an old Romany woman prisoner to take care of me. I was happy I wasn't beaten because the guards always beat you around the head. Very few people survived a beating. I was glad they shot me instead of beating me. If they had beaten me I wouldn't be here today.

I remember a man who tried to escape and the guards sent the dogs after him. When the dogs caught the man, he cried out to surrender. The guards called the dogs off, then shot the man in every part of his body: arms, legs, head, chest, stomach. Two prisoners had to bring a wheel barrow to carry the pieces away. These two prisoners had to push this wheel barrow around the whole camp so all the prisoners could see what had happened while the guards yelled at us, "Everyone who tries to escape from this place will end up like this." Many prisoners were crying and we children were crazy with grief and fear. When they took his shirt off there was no body, just strips of flesh like spaghetti.

I was sent to Auschwitz after only five months at Lety. I was sent there because my parents were already there.

After the war, I never went back to Lety. I didn't even go for the memorial service this May (1995). That's a part of my life I want to forget. I have eight children, I must look after them.

I used to know many people who were at Lety, but all of them are dead. I belonged to an organization that kept records on survivors from concentration camps, and I think there were about 360 survivors from Lety. Perhaps the Red Cross in Prague still has a list. The International Red Cross in Geneva sent me a document showing that I was in Birkenau.

Last year I went to the funeral of Mr. Robert Ševčík. He was in Lety with me. He died very near here, in Kryry. I never kept in contact with anyone else. I can't read or write. But I know what's going on. None of us ever received any compensation from the Czech government or anyone else for being prisoners in Lety.

You know, my children are suppose to be living in a better world today. But what is happening with the Romany in the Czech Republic sounds like these skinheads don't have a heart or a soul. I see on TV how they are beating and killing people. It reminds me of the start of Hitler all over again.

My children are half Romany. I only have one son who looks dark and he has been attacked by skinheads in Podbořany. He is the only one with dark skin and he is the only one who has been attacked, thank God. But he was so badly injured that he had to spend two months in the hospital. He had to have surgery to his stomach and his chest because the skinheads drove a metal pole into him. On that day in Podbořany there were two busloads of skinheads. They drove into town and started attacking Romany wherever they found them on the street. Somebody must have invited them. There is a large Romany community in Podbořany. The police arrested somebody for the attack on my son but it never went to court. We were told there wasn't enough proof.

The police just laugh about it now. We heard a restaurant owner in Podbořany called friends in the city of Most and two buses loads of skinheads came from there. Why can't the government do something about this today?

I would like to personally tell President Havel that he is only for the whites. He is cooperating with too many people who are against us. I think he's a bad person because it's not right what is going on and he is not speaking out against the skinheads.

(1) In 1998 Antonie told CBS News researchers: "My father and my fourteen-year-old brother were shot in Lety trying to save my sister from being raped by Hejduk. My sister was trying to resist Hejduk. He was lying on top of her, slapping her. I was there screaming when my father and brother ran over. Hejduk shot my father, another guard shot my brother. Their bodies were buried in the forest." This statement was translated by PhDr. Vladimíra Žáková as Antonie spoke to the American television researchers.

F. K.
(as told by a younger brother)

My older brothers Josef and Ferdinand were in Lety. My brothers were detained by the police in Plzeň then sent to Lety. Josef came back from Terezín. Ferdinand never got back home again. After Lety he was in Mauthausen, Terezín and Auschwitz. The family got only his shirt and trousers back and they were both full of blood. The clothes from my brother Ferdinand were sent from Auschwitz with just a note saying he was dead.

Our parents weren't detained, although my mother was arrested for beating up some Germans. But they never sent her to a concentration camp. We were lucky during the war.

There was a bombardment of Plzeň. We were at the slaughter house. My mother was beating up the Czech and German policemen. She was detained for a long time. We all tried to get her out.

Our father had died before when we were very young. My father was a soldier and in the first war he was in the Dragoons. He died 59 years ago. After he got back from the war, he was ill and he died shortly thereafter. I was three years old so I can't remember exactly what happened.

My brother-in-law František Flachs went to Lety to rescue my brothers. He couldn't get them out but he got them some food. Without that food they never would have survived. There was great hunger there, they had to work hard, and Josef told me they were beaten very often. Josef didn't want to talk about his experiences at Lety because he said no one would believe him.

My mother never knew during the whole war where they were. She never knew how they had to suffer at Lety. The hunger they went through, eating only potato peelings. They talked about starvation, typhus, stacking the dead bodies under Gypsy wagons until they could be buried. The Czech guards also killed many people, beating them to death when they didn't work.

Josef was born in 1923; Ferdinand would be 75 years old today; Hynek was also in Lety. He escaped shortly after they arrived, he died not long ago. Jaroslav never went anywhere because he was too young; he is 61 years old today.

Hynek said they had to work even when they were ill; they had to work all the time. He had to escape because they wanted to kill him. Antonín Chadraba came back like a skeleton.

They remembered a lot about Lety but they never had any nightmares. They worked in the forest or in the stone quarry.

I was in jail during the communist times and had to work for nothing too.

I remember several families from here who were in Lety: Janeček, Bluml, Šlehofer, Draský, Dubský. Matěj Dubský is alive but has cancer and is dying. Šmíd was there also, and Josef Čanda. His kids are living near Slaný. Josef Čanda was kicked so badly in Lety that after the war they had to operate on his ribs and shoulder. He was never the same again.

My brothers had a lot of illnesses after the war because of Lety; liver, stomach, lots of things, which they always said were a result of their beatings at Lety.

Josef always told me that he never wanted to go through another Lety in his life. It was the worst thing that ever happened to him.

My father was in prison for 14 years after the First World War. He was in many countries as a prisoner of war but mainly was in prison in Russia.

My brothers were sent to Lety because they were always going to parties, raising hell. Ferdinand went to a party once in clothes that someone claimed were his; Ferdinand slashed the man who falsely accused him; the police were called and he slashed the police. After the Gestapo detained him, he was sent to Lety.

Antonín Bluml, he was in Lety. He came back but had big problems with his health and died on us. Karel Ulm was also in Lety, but he survived.

We were all fairground workers, not Gypsies. My father had a puppet theater and they traveled with the fair. They also worked in the circus. The Kludskýs were their relatives; they were on a ship to America that went down; everything was lost at sea, the animals, the people. That was the end of their circus, before the Second World War.

My people never associated with Gypsies; we were sent to Lety because of our own problems. We are very different from the Romany. We have our own special language, Hantýrka. We can communicate all over the world with our clan, our people.

This government is made up of burglars; the communists were gold compared to these criminals. Before 1989 we could buy much more with our money; today we get nothing for our money.

My mother's second husband rescued the younger kids so they didn't have to go to Lety. He rescued them by giving them his surname. The police wanted to send everybody to Lety with our surname. He gave the family a new name so they didn't have to go.

I was very little when the family stopped working in the fairgrounds. After the war, Josef was working in the brewery. Before that he had been in the uranium mines in Příbram. The communists sent him there after Lety.

No one in my family got compensation for being in Lety; they never asked for it either.

I was in a labor camp during the communist times (1955) but never got any compensation for that either. We built houses and an airport in Košice but never got a crown for our work; we were sent there because we weren't communists; there were many prisoners there: Germans, political prisoners. They called them PTP camps. I was there for 26 months, my brother Josef for three years. The first three months were like military service, doing the worst things in mud with full gear; once when we returned to the barracks full of mud they told us we had to be clean in five minutes; another time the guards threw all our clothes out of the windows, trying to make us angry so we would fight back so they could punish us even more.

My brother Josef said these communist labor camps were the same as Lety; the prisoners had to work all day, sometimes all night. Some of the young guys were not experienced. They didn't know how to work so there were some horrible labor accidents. Others killed themselves by hanging because it was too much for them. Whoever didn't toe the communist line was sent to these labor camps, handicraft men, private businessmen. We worked in the mines with bakers, men who were totally out of their depth; totally in shock the first time they went into the mines because they had never done these things before.

These camps were also our military service. You never knew where you were being sent to. We ended up in Bohumín (Ostrava). After they shaved us, we had to shower and then we went to work. Three months basic exercises, very bad, daytime and nighttime, then to Ostrava to build houses, make construction work, then to Bohumin again, then to Poprad in Slovakia. There we were split into groups and I was sent to Košice. My comrades were good guys, even the Germans among us. But some of the sergeants were very bad. One was so bad that if I saw him on the street today I would kill him.

After Košice I was sent to Mošnov, then again to Slovakia, to Horemlos where there were bears in the woods. But now we work for ourselves. My wife repairs knives and umbrellas; I have horses. It's my hobby. I have little ponies for the grandchildren. Five years ago I had five or six big horses. I bought and sold horses, now my son runs this business for us. I would like to buy more horses but I don't have a big yard. I like very much to ride. Horses are my real love in life. Bohumil Serynek was in the uranium mines for 14 years after Lety. His sons also work with horses.

R. K.

The German Gestapo arrested us. My mother, father, and two brothers (Hynek and Jan) were all taken to a prison in Prague, Pankrác, and hung to death there. I don't know why. The rest of us (me and my sisters Lída, Božena and Zdena) were taken to Lety.

We arrived in Lety in April 1942 and spent ten months there. I believe my ancestors were Romany but I'm not sure. Perhaps because my mother was living with a man by the name of Růžička, which is a Gypsy name, perhaps that's why they took us away.

What happened at Lety has now been covered up by a pig farm. Do you know that? I never went there to look, but I heard about it. All that suffering and now some inhuman beings put a pig farm there. Terezín is not like that. The prisoners there were human beings, victims of World War II. Why can't the victims at Lety be remembered that way?

Our first day in Lety our hair was cut off. We were in a special block only for children. A woman prisoner there took care of us. She looked after us well. She was a prisoner too.

I can't say how many children were there, but there were many. The older children had to work. They worked on the farms, picking potatoes and cabbage.

As you can see, I can't say anything about Lety without crying.

We were released from the camp in May 1943. Somehow we were released to the Czech Red Cross and they sent us to different orphanages. All of us spent more than fifteen years in orphanages. I went to Klánovice by Prague. My sisters went to a different place.

There were more children in that camp than old people. You know what they did with the children ... ?[1]

---

(1) At this point her husband came home and found us at the kitchen table interviewing his wife. Her face was wet with tears. She had again burst into tears over the last statement. Ľubo and I both jumped up to shake his hand and explain what we were doing. He sternly asked us how we got their name and addresses. We fumbled for an answer about getting a list of Lety survivors from Třeboň archive. He had

heard of me. He was happy someone was trying to bring out the truth about Lety. He then went to get his briefcase full of papers that he had been collecting for a year and a half, fighting to get his wife some compensation.

J. K.
(husband of Lety survivor)

Lety must have been horrible. Look at my wife's state of mind. She has never recovered from her experiences at Lety. Her sisters are even worse. One is in a mental home, the other is constantly in a hospital. Lety marked them for life.

I found the papers on her mother and why they were hanged. They were accused of listening to foreign radio programs. Someone must have informed on them. They were arrested in August of 1942 and hanged on the 23 January 1943 at 9:15 in the morning. The only thing they were ever accused of was listening to a foreign radio program.

It has taken me a year and a half to get my wife 23,000 crowns from this government. They tried to send me in so many wrong directions, hoping I would give up. But I didn't. I filled out the five pages of information they wanted, then I found all the documents they wanted. They sent me to archives that had nothing, they tried to send me on many unnecessary trips, but I got everything. Now I want to do the same thing for my wife's sisters and you know what the bureaucrats tell me? I have to start all over from scratch. None of the documents I have for my wife are valid for her sisters. None of the certificates which mention all their names are valid. This government I am sure hopes that all the survivors will die before they have to pay out. No one who works in those offices was ever in a concentration camp.

The Lety issue is really a national disgrace for our country. I am sure they have burned all the important papers. They don't want to pay compensation for Lety. They burned the most important papers and covered over the graves with a pig farm. They have no respect for the dead because most of the victims were Gypsies. This new government is just as bad as the old one when it comes to Lety.

The camp at Lety was built only to get rid of unwanted people. It was a racial matter, that is why it is still covered up today.

I went to the Antifascist League for help about Lety but they didn't have anything. They had lots of information about the German camps but nothing about Lety. When I protested that the government was taking too long over this compensation issue, I got a letter saying more than 7,000 people had applied for compensation. Then I got another one, saying more than 10,000 people. Now another one informing me that more than 15,000 people have applied, as if we are bad because we apply. That's how they treat us.

Look, I have a whole briefcase full of papers and now I have to get more. Then a commission will decide who gets compensation and who doesn't. I saw the worst under communism. Now I'm seeing the worst under democracy.

Tony Lagryn
(son of a Lety survivor)

My name is Tony Lagryn. I am 48 years old. My father and his first wife and their four children were prisoners at Lety, later at Auschwitz. My father was the only one to survive. He told me about his terrible time at Lety because after the war he tried to find one of the guards to kill him.

I was born after World War II. My mother was the second wife of my father. My father's first wife was Pavlína Lagrynová born Šmídová. She died in Auschwitz with her four children. All had been in Lety. All my father's family was in Lety including many cousins.

My grandparents, Vilém and Anna Lagryn, died at Lety in 1943. My father told me the doctors at Lety were giving the prisoners injections in their breast above the heart; when my grandfather got this injection, he died the next day. My father was there and told me these stories. Those not killed at Lety were sent to Terezín, and then to Auschwitz.

My father told me that some of the Czech police were much worse than the German Gestapo at Auschwitz. My father spent about eighteen months at Lety. He saw a Czech guard take children and put their heads into a pail of water until they died. The guards also put many children's heads into the small lake by the camp until the children died. Small children were locked outside the barracks at night in the dead of winter with no clothes on. This really amused the guards. The children howled like wolves. Many mothers went crazy trying to get out of their locked barracks to save their children. My father also told me that many times the guards would train their dogs to attack people, using prisoners in the training exercise until the dogs killed them.

Sometimes a German officer came to inspect the camp. But before he came, the Czech guards warned my father and other prisoners to say that they were living well, that they were well treated and that they had enough food to eat. When the German officer left, the Czech guards continued to beat, torture and kill the prisoners.

After the Czech guards killed prisoners, there was a special group of Romany men who had to bury the bodies of their people. They were ordered to bury the coffins standing, not laying down, so there would be more room to bury bodies. One of these men who had to bury people was a cousin of my father and he told my father in the camp what he had to do. When my father's parents died, my father told his cousin to bury his parents properly but his cousin couldn't because the guards were watching.

Only Czechs ran the camp. Only Czech police were there. I grew up hearing these stories. I remember now that my father who lived in Prague before the war knew one of the policemen in Prague that became a guard in the camp. I can't remember the name of the guard, but I remember the story. When the war ended my father came with the American army to Susice. My father got a gun from the Americans for one reason: he wanted to kill that policeman from Prague who had been so bad in Lety. My father went to Prague but didn't find the man. In the end, he stopped his search for this Prague policeman because he met my mother there. Then he was happy to be alive and didn't want to go back to prison for killing this man.

My mother was a Sinti from Rostock, Germany. On a visit to

Most she had been arrested and spent four years in Ravensbruck. She came to Prague with the Russian army and since she and my father were both Sinti in origin, they met and married.

Barbara Richterová, another survivor of Lety, knows the name of this policeman. She was a very young girl in Lety, about 16. My father was about 40 when he was there. My father was arrested in Prague and sent straight to Lety. His parents were also arrested in Prague and died at Lety. My father was born in Chumutov but lived for 35 years in Prague.

After Lety, which he said was the worst, my father was a prisoner in Auschwitz, Buchenwald, and Mauthausen. He was on a death march in Bavaria when the Americans arrived. I don't remember the name of the place, somewhere in a forest. My father and another Czech escaped from this place. On this death march there were about 20,000 people and the reason why the Germans did this march was that they were using the prisoners as a barrier against the enemy who was bombarding them. So the Germans took these prisoners and marched them as protection. When my father saw what was going on he escaped. Even the German soldiers started to escape when they saw what was going on. Of these 20,000 people only about 60 survived, according to my father. I think this death march was somewhere between Passau and Linz.

My father never told me how many people were at Lety, but he said many Romanies were there. Some of his cousins escaped from Lety and made their way to Slovakia and survived the war there. Their surnames were Bernhart and Klimt. In 1968 they escaped to West German, to Köln. Today they are all dead. Only one uncle who is 80 is alive, in Vienna in Austria, but he was not in Lety. He escaped to Slovakia before the roundup took place. Around 1947 he emigrated to Austria because his wife was an Austrian Romany.

Božena Růžičková

My father was Čeněk Růžička. My mother Aloisie Růžičková. My father cleaned and repaired kettles and pots and pans. He worked mainly in hotels in their kitchen. We lived in a wagon. I was born in a wagon. We traveled 12 months of the year, all over the country. I had three sisters and four brothers. I was born in 1924.

In 1942 my husband Antonín Růžička and I were living in Lobeč (Mělník) with my husband's sister and her husband in a house that the mayor of the village had given to us. One day the Czech police came with a truck and took all of us and several neighbors to Mladá Boleslav and put us on a train. There was a long train there for passengers. Many trucks kept arriving from the county of Mladá Boleslav, Mělník, and all these villages where Gypsies were living. In this train station the police were collecting Gypsies to put on this train. When we arrived, the train was already full of Gypsies from Jablonec.

From Mlada Boleslav the train took us to Hradec Králové where we all had to get out. We were then taken by trucks to a big hall in the center of town. We spent one or two nights there. Since we had been allowed to take a few things with us, we were able to eat.

After two days were taken by truck to the train station in Hradec Králové, then by train to Mirovice. From Mirovice we were taken by truck to Lety.

When the gate was opened, we were unloaded from the trucks. They shaved our heads, men, women and children. Then it all started.

We worked in the woods, in the stone quarry and on the farms near by. We worked on farms collecting vegetables for the owners.

In Lety we had our own clothes. They let us keep our clothes. I guess they were running out of supplies.

The guards took my earrings, my necklace and two rings, all the gold I had.

We were separated, men to the men's section, women to theirs. Children on their own.

The director of the camp gave us a speech when we arrived: "The Gate was opened to let you in; now it's closed. Don't think that you will return to someplace from here. One road brought you here, your next place will be in heaven."

In the beginning, the women could have their children with them. But a few days later all the children were separated into another block. There were several women prisoners looking after the children, but I tell you, sometimes these women were eating the food that was meant for the children, and the children would go without.

My son was a year and a half old, my daughter ten months. My son was taken to the children's barracks. My daughter was allowed to stay with me. Both my children died within a few months of arriving there. I was told they died of typhus, but I don't know. I was out working, and when I came back they were dead and already buried. I was working in the woods, in the stone quarry and also collecting crops on nearby farms.

The food was terrible, what can I tell you? The children got a very thin piece of bread and a little bit of milk. The adults got four potatoes, normally rotten inside, black; some times we got spinach, maybe it was grass because it was always full of dirt. Other times we got some red cabbage that had never been cleaned. Brown water. Once and a while we got some soup made out of white cabbage and potatoes. A piece of bread, but not every day. The portions weren't enough to keep a pig alive. The food was not fit for human beings. What can I tell you?

The camp was run only by Czech policemen. They were terrible. Once when I went to get my food in the kitchen, this guard Pešek beat me. Look what that son-of-a-bitch did to my hand. He broke all the knuckles on my left hand with his truncheon. When my hand healed, I was missing a knuckle. Look here. There's nothing but a hole where my knuckle used to be.

I was beaten many times for nothing. But I felt more sorry for the children. Close to the kitchen there was a cabbage patch. Some times the children sneaked over to get some leaves. If a guard saw them, he ran over and beat them with a stick. He just beat them and beat them and beat them. It was horrible.

Often prisoners were hung up on the execution pole, and beaten there while they hung. I don't know what happened to them. I didn't really want to know. But we never saw them again in the camp.

One man escaped from the camp and the guards shot him while he ran. When they brought him back to the camp, he was already dead. All the prisoners had to pass in front of his body. He had been shot in many places. There wasn't much left of him. We were told that anyone who tried to escape would receive the same treatment.

Some of the women prisoners had this thing with the guards. They went with them for extra food and some privileges. I knew one woman who went with the guards. She was a nice looking woman, more white than dark. I remember her name but I won't tell it to you.

This story about the children, about them being drowned in the lakes, I know it is true because when we were coming back from work these women who had just given birth would tell us that their children had been taken from them. The lake was very close. We heard things.

The German Gestapo came from time to time to talk with the director of the camp. We never knew what they spoke about.

You heard people screaming every day from the guards beating them. In every corner someone was being beaten.

One day I made my decision to escape. I had seen too much. I decided I would rather die running than stay and die there. I was tired of the beatings, the starvation, and the hard work. The last day there was this terrible guard who went from work gang to work gang telling all of us that if we ever crossed his path he would beat us to death. He was looking for people to kill.

I went to the gate and the guard asked where I was going. I told him I was going for firewood. I started collecting wood near by, but once I got a few yards away I started to run. I didn't know where I was running to. But then I recognized the same way that we had come from the train station. I was so afraid that I turned my head and saw many guards running after me, but it wasn't true. I fell down and hid under a small Christmas tree. After a few minutes I realized no one was chasing me. I walked to a small village close to the train station. I heard a voice saying that a train was leaving for Prague. I jumped on the train with no money. I went to the toilet and locked the door. By a miracle I arrived in Prague. After that I took another train, again without any money, to Turnov. Again I went to the toilet. We were near Mladá Boleslav when someone wanted to go to the toilet. The conductor came and opened the door. He asked me for my ticket. I told him I didn't have one. He kicked me out at the next station. From there I walked to my parents. It took me about six hours.

At that time my parents were still living in the wagon in Neveklovice by Mnichovo Hradište. So when I escaped I went to my parents. But I could not stay with them because the police were looking for me. It was on the Czech radio that I had escaped and described how I looked, so I could not stay with them. So my parents gave me food and I had to go live in the forest. I was living in the woods, but I can't remember how long I was there because when I escaped Lety I already had typhus. I don't know who found me in the woods and took me to the hospital in Turnov. I remember in that hospital in the hall was a Christmas tree so it must have been Christmas time. But I escaped when it was not winter time.

From Turnov I remember I was in an ambulance and I woke up in another hospital in Železný Brod. I got up after one week. In that hospital was a doctor Humhal. He was a very nice person. I had no strength. I didn't have the strength to push the button to call the doctor or the nurse. When I tried to get up, everything was spinning around and I fell down. I spent three months there in that hospital. The police were still looking for me. Finally the police called the hospital but the doctor wouldn't let me go because I still needed medical treatment. For this, the doctor was arrested. I don't know what happened to him.

After the doctor was taken away, I was taken to Gestapo headquarters in Jicin. After three months there I was taken by the German Gestapo to Prague to Pankrac prison. When I arrived, I saw my husband and a friend of my husband, Serynek. Both had escaped from Lety. We had a trial. It took all day. We were sentenced to death. I don't know what was said because they spoke only in German. But later there was a break and we got a translation of what had been going on. When I heard we got the death sentence, I felt terrible. Later the court made a change. My husband and Serynek were ordered to be guillotined, while my sentence was reduced to six years in a *zuchthaus,* and after that to be returned to a concentration camp.

From Prague I was taken by transport in an animal car for two weeks to Javor Hornyslesk in Germany. After that I was sent to Leipzig. I finally ended up in a house with only women: French, German, Russian, and Polish women.

Later a priest came to tell us we would be taken on a death march. On our walk we were watched by SS women and Russian women who collaborated with the Germans. There were only women guards, but from many different nations. When the old women could not walk anymore, a Russian guard came and shot them. This march took us about three weeks. We slept in the woods, once in a church. After the march we were taken to Lubeck to the prison. That was my last stop because after that we were liberated by the Americans. That moment was terrible because we were so happy that we cried and laughed; I cannot explain it.

Today I no longer feel so good. Today we are getting the same beatings that we got in Lety. You saw my brother today, he was beaten so badly two years ago by skinheads that he almost died. When I saw him after the beating, I could not recognize his face. There was no investigation, no court. The police and the government are supporting the skinheads. For Czechs, we Romanies have no value as human beings.

Last year I got 50,600 crowns compensation for my detention: from 7 August 1942 until 20 November 1942 (106 days); and from 8 November 1943 when I was arrested again, until 5 May 1945 (545 days). I got 50,600 crowns for 651 days.

Today I still have headaches from my experiences. I take pills every day. At night, every night, I wake up screaming. I don't remember having nightmares, but every night I wake up screaming. I know those screams come from Lety. On all the German transports, in all the German camps, I was not beaten like I was by the Czech guards in Lety. If I said the Germans were worse to me, I would be lying.

In Germany I worked in a camp cleaning feathers. One woman officer liked how I worked. She didn't beat me. She told the guards to give me more food because I was a good worker. In Lety we worked without food and were beaten for nothing. We were so hungry in Lety we could not see.

After all I have been through I don't understand why I am still alive. I am the only survivor of my family. My parents and all my brothers and sisters and their families died in Auschwitz. And now if you go for compensation for your husband who was guillotined in a Czech prison, and your children who died at Lety, they tell you that you have no rights. These people you have to deal with were never in a concentration camp.

There was a water pump but we were not allowed to use it. We had to get our water in buckets and bring it up by hand.

The food was terrible there. There were worms swimming in the soup. In the morning we got black coffee and a quarter piece of bread that had to last for two days. For lunch we had cabbage soup and in the evening only black coffee.

For the babies and younger children they made some kind of mash, but I don't think they got it very often.

There was one woman called Striberová from Bernatice who was in charge of the children in the camp. She was very nice to the children. She was also a prisoner there.

My wife saw our child twice a week. She sneaked out of her barracks. If the guards had seen her do this, they would have beaten her right away.

There was one doctor who gave us something in our mouth, some kind of liquid, against some kind of sickness. We weren't sick at that time, but he gave it to all of us. It tasted bad.

Václav Flachs was in charge of making the wooden coffins for the dead bodies. We saw dead bodies every day, especially children. We saw two or three bodies every day. These children died mostly from hunger.[4]

Whenever the guards took us to wash in the pond, they ordered us to drown each other. They had great fun watching us. We never killed each other but we had to pretend to do so to amuse the guards.

Once in a while a group of 15 to 20 people were taken to the forest to make a walk. If one of us went to the bathroom there, the guards would beat him.

Near the place where our clothes were burnt we were sent for punishment if we did something wrong. We were told to take our shoes off, then they burned our feet with a candle. They also slapped our faces many times.

Janovský's wife lived there during all the time we were there. There were no children there. If she wouldn't have given me the cake once and a while I guess I would have fallen down and starved to death. She was never mean to me, but I was not allowed to take any food back to the camp. He spoke Czech, but he was a German. She was a Czech.

Václav Flachs just looked at the guards, in their direction, and he came up and beat him. One time Mrs. Flachsová was holding her three-year-old child on her arm; in her other hand she had a cup of soup. When one of the guards saw how the baby wanted to drink the soup, he took it from the mother and threw it in the baby's face. The baby's face was burned by this hot soup.

There was one man 80 years old who used to ask the guards all the time when he was going to be sent to the front to fight. He was a white man. I don't know what happened to this man. He was still there when we left.

I remember one Gypsy called Slanicka who was in the camp for eight months. He worked sewing clothes. He was also beaten very often, but then they released him. We don't know if he bought his way out or not.

The guards many times told us that Lety wasn't hard enough for us and that we would have to go to Terezín.

Some of us wore prison clothes, but many of the Gypsies wore their own clothes that they had brought into the camp. There was one Gypsy woman from Prague who was very beautiful. Many of them really weren't dark, but they were beaten much more than us white people. I don't know why.

The Gypsies we saw in Lety behaved well. They were good people. There were no problems between the white and black prisoners.

People were also shot in Lety but they didn't die. They were shot in the arm or leg. The guards were always shooting in the air to frighten us.

My wife saw Janovský beat people all the time. She worked for him. She knew him well. All the guards beat people, including Janovský.

The hunger and the beatings, those were our worst experiences in Lety. When I was working on the road in Lety they beat me so badly I ended up in a hospital.

We were never paid for working in Lety. We were supposed to be paid, it was supposed to be a work camp. Just the opposite; they took all our things away from us. We lost a lot there.

This guard told us on our first or second day that we didn't belong in the camp and that we could go home in three weeks. But we still had to pay the 20,000 crowns. I am sure if I had not paid those 20,000 crowns we would have died in Lety.

I gave 20,000 crowns to my cousin who was not in Lety. He told me he could get it to a German lawyer in Prague who was his friend and this lawyer could get us out.[5] And that's how it happened. One day a guard came up to us and told us we could go home.

I couldn't even walk to Mirovice, I was suffering such hunger. We begged people on our way for food. The guards didn't even give us money to pay the train.

From Mirovice we took the train to Domažlice and from there another train to Osvračín. Our daughter was sick, very sick after three weeks in Lety. She had a lung infection. She was also very skinny. For three months we had to visit the doctor continuously until she recovered.

We found our home the way we had left it. We continued living as we had done before. I went back to work on the road. My wife stayed at home to look after our daughter.

We never received any compensation for our stay in Lety. Our neighbor who was in another concentration camp told us it was a waste of time to apply because we had only been there for three weeks.

My wife still has nightmares about Lety. Whenever she looks back to those times, she starts to cry. So do I. It was the worst three weeks in my life – the worst time in my life.

After we were all released, we saw the Flachs on several occasions. They were friends. Whenever his wife would talk about their time in Lety, he would yell at her and tell her to be quiet. He never wanted to talk about Lety. He never wanted to remember those times. They lost two daughters there.

In our villages around here, there are no Gypsy families. People like us very much here in the village. We sometimes see on television the problems that the Czechs have with the Gypsies in the cities, that the Gypsies don't want to work. There are very good people living in our village. All of them are working. They are very sociable families.

But Lety was so bad that if this kind of situation would be repeated today, I would kill myself, hang myself. I would never live through another Lety. Although we were only there for three weeks, these were the longest, worst, three weeks of our lives.

(1) This was the first week of the camp, before it became overcrowded.
(2) A.Š. and many former prisoners at Lety still believe the Germans built and ran the camp. See Kuchař oral history.
(3) A.Š. is about one meter fifty (less than five feet) tall.
(4) This was the first three weeks after the Gypsies started to arrive.
(5) This was a Czech lawyer in Prague 6 who spoke German. Some survivors have identified him as Dr. Beneš, others as Dr. Benda.

Marie Petrskovská

I was born on 7 August 1928 in Veltrusy, county Mělník. My mother Kateřina Studená came from Plavsko; my father was Jan Vrba from Pacov. He was a knife sharpener, fixed umbrellas, and owned a small portable fair with three merry-go-rounds. My mother didn't work because we were six children. In the winter we lived in Plavsko but in the summer we traveled in our wagon, working fairs. My siblings were Jan, Václav, Antonín, Antonie and Umberta.

I was very young and I didn't know what was going on but I remember there were trucks waiting and my father ran to buy things for our trip. We had received a message to return to Plavsko and there we found the trucks and many families, our relatives, waiting for us.

We were taken by truck to Lety that day, 3 August 1942. I remember this very well because I was thirteen years old. The Vrbas and Studenýs went with us. We were all related.

When we arrived at Lety, I saw wooden barracks. Right away the children were separated from their parents. I was a stupid child then, that's why I don't remember very much. They shaved our heads, and after that no one could tell if we were girls or boys. We all wore the same kind of clothing.

When I entered the camp, I had long black hair. My mother used to braid it. It would have been better if my mother had cut off my hair before we went to Lety. Then she could have sold it.

We had to stand in line every morning and if the prisoners weren't properly dressed they were beaten immediately. The guards didn't care if we were women or children, everyone got beaten.

I remember a young woman. She was not black. The guards tied her hands behind her back, her feet to the ground, then pulled her up on a post with a wheel and pulley until her organs collapsed. I was just leaving the children's house when I saw this. It took about twenty minutes for her to die. My parents knew her name but I can't remember it. We talked about her a lot afterwards.

Prisoners were beaten for everything they did wrong. I remember they took the clothes off of one of the women in winter, threw water on her, beat her up, took her to one of the wooden caravans where they locked her up, then opened up the windows until she froze to death.

I remember when one man stole a piece of bread from another, and it was reported to the guards. Then a German came and beat the thief to death.[1] I remember putting my hands over my ears so I couldn't hear the screams.

The food was very, very bad. It was a mixture of old water and old food. Gypsies were cooking in the kitchen but they could only cook what the guards gave them. In the morning we got black coffee and a piece of bread; for lunch pieces of carrot cooked in water; whenever we had dumplings they had a black color; in the evening we got black coffee; some people also had bread which they saved from their morning's ration. We had little tickets that we had to take to the kitchen hatch to receive our food. I remember the food always tasted very bitter.

I'll never forget the little children sitting on the stairs of the huts, all huddled up, shivering from the cold and hunger. Every morning several of them were dead. When I remember this, I want to cry.[2]

One day in the children's barracks two women came to visit us. I remember them talking to us. They weren't supposed to be there. Parents were not supposed to visit their children. The next morning I saw these two women dead on a pile of children's bodies.

I will tell you the truth now. They brought us into the camp because they thought we were Gypsies. But we weren't. We all came from mixed marriages. Only my uncle had quite black skin. The rest of us were all normal white people. All of us went to school, even when we traveled from village to village. Our parents put us in school even if it was only for three weeks.

One family was released after their relatives in Prague paid money to get them out. When they left, my father sent a note with them, hidden in their linen, asking our family in Prague to send us food. The guards found the note when the family was searched before leaving the camp. They confessed it was my father who wrote the note, so the guards put chains around his feet, and he had to wear these chains for two or three weeks. Later the guards found he could sharpen knives so he was sent to the kitchen to work for the rest of the time that we remained in the camp. My uncles Studeny and Vrba also worked in the kitchen.

I was in the group of older children that worked on farms outside the camp. We went to a farm every morning and came back every evening. Sometimes I was able to get cigarettes for my father. I was in charge of collecting potatoes. We also worked in the stone quarry. I was very afraid of the guards and often thought about escaping from the stone quarry. But I couldn't leave my brothers and sisters. I was the eldest one. The youngest, Antonín, was only three years old.

Before going to Lety I didn't like tomatoes. But when we worked on the farms, I stole tomatoes to eat. We weren't allowed to take food back to the camp, but we always tried to smuggle things in. Usually they had a control at the gate and they took everything off us.

We were taken to the pond once in a while to wash. I remember seeing a black grass snake in the pond so I wouldn't go into the lake for a long time. There were a lot of guards with us, watching us so no one would escape.

Two of my cousins escaped but the guards caught them near the forest. They put chains around their feet, tying them together. They had to walk around the camp like this for two weeks.

My mother had a baby in the camp at the same time she had typhus. I remember she had a very high temperature and no milk. The baby was always crying, screaming; there was no one to take care of her. She died after two weeks.[3]

During the typhus epidemic I went to my father's barracks and put a blanket on him. I remember Emil Studený visiting him. My mother was there when Emil turned around and told her that Jenda, my father, was dead.

The guards had him carried to a Gypsy caravan where they stored dead bodies. They threw him in there but left his head sticking out. I ran over there, crying, to hold his head. I begged my father to wake up again.

My mother was a whore. When we were released from Lety my mother took us back to Plavsko then ran away, abandoning us. If my father had not died, this never would have happened.

I don't remember any women sleeping with the guards. The women weren't abused.

A little boy stole a small piece of cabbage from a kitchen window. A guard saw him and almost beat him to death. When children's feet stuck out of their bed, guards would come in and beat their feet with the truncheons.

I remember a short little guard who used to run after us screaming, "I'll beat you, wait until I catch you, I will beat you." He yelled at us in German, holding up his stick. I called him an asshole under my breath. I remember that really well.

I never heard about children being drowned in rain barrels or in the lake, but I know several newborn babies were thrown in the latrines. My mother told me that some women who gave birth in the camp threw their own babies into the latrines.

The older children and the adults were all buried in the forest. The dead bodies were put into simple wooden coffins, then thrown into the holes in the forest. So many people died, if they hadn't buried them in mass graves in the forest there would have been no place to put them. So many people died, you can't imagine. I can't tell you a certain number. I never met the person who made the coffins. I don't know who made the coffins, a German, a Czech or a Gypsy.

I don't remember any names of the guards. I was only thirteen years old. They were Czech but some of them spoke German. The really black Gypsies were beaten all the time. The guards hated these black Gypsies.

I don't know why, but I was always afraid of the really dark Gypsy people in the camp too. I never thought I belonged to them. I was afraid of their black color. They had big swollen lips, black skin like shoes, long skirts and very dark hair. I can't help myself. They always frightened me. You can think what you like about me, but I never had contact with such people.

I remember when they built another wooden house outside of the camp. They put a fence around this new house, then we waited for what would happen to us. We waited a long time and during that time we were beaten very often. Then some men came from Prague to control us. They spoke Czech but at times they would yell, *"Schnell, schnell."* They wore civilian clothes.

The house was built for the ones who were to be released. The Studenys were separated first, then the Vrbas. All the black Gypsies were sent straight to Auschwitz.

I thought when the other families were sent to Auschwitz that we would be sent there also because our father had died. At the end we were all standing in line and the guards were going from one person to another. After they took all the people away for the transports and we were the only ones left, they looked at us. I think my little brother saved us. He was only three years old and had blond hair. One of the guards said, "Look this kid has blond hair, this family isn't Gypsy." Then they let us join our cousins. I took a deep breath and was happy that we were all released.

When we came back to Plavsko, we had nowhere to live. The house we used to live in was occupied by another family. Some of the Studenýs moved to Prague. My mother slept with us in a tent we put up in front of the house where my aunt lived. She told us we couldn't stay there. We had to move. Near these houses was a small shack where a man used to live by himself. When he died, we moved in there. My mother had to clean this place for a long time. It was full of fleas and dirt. My mother put a bed in one room; all six of us had to sleep together in one bed. We only had a table. She stayed with us for about a year, then one day she just disappeared.

Since I was the oldest, and there were a lot of berries and mushrooms in the forest, I took everyone to the forest to collect food. We had enough to see us through the summer. In the winter a social worker came and took all my brothers and sisters to a children's home. I was the only one they didn't take away. I was about fifteen. I packed my things and went to Prague to find my uncle who had been in Lety.

The wife of my uncle was in the hospital. Another woman came to take care of the children. I slept on the floor. One night my uncle tried to rape me. When this woman screamed, I grabbed my things and ran away. I went to the police station. They asked how old I was. I told them my life story. I also told the police that I had never slept with a man before, that I didn't want my uncle to rape me. They let me sleep there the night. At that time the police still dressed in black uniforms with silver helmets.

I was too old to be sent to a children's home, so they sent me to a religious welfare society where the girls had to sew, and do laundry. I stayed there until I was twenty-one years old. Then I went to Krc where I worked on a little private farm. Later in Prague when I was twenty-four years old I met my husband. We had five children.

Today I still feel those beatings in Lety. Once I was walking past a guard and I looked at him. He asked me why I was looking at him. He called me a pig and then beat me with his stick until my back bled. That's what I remember the most about Lety, those beatings, and the hunger, every day.

Sometimes I dream about my father coming toward me and the guards watching us, ready to beat us. Once I dreamed of seeing my father standing in front of me. I wanted to talk to him but he warned me with his finger that the guards were watching. I dream very often about the guards at Lety, then I wake up screaming.

Whenever I see a program on TV about concentration camps I start to cry and my son has to turn off the TV. Once there was a program about little children in a camp and I had to cover my ears with my hands and run out screaming. Maybe you think I am old and crazy today, but whenever I see something on TV that is similar to our experience in Lety I still feel it.

One year ago my brother Jan and I each received 50,000 crowns for being in Lety, but we had to share this with our other siblings who were also in Lety. After Christmas I received another 23,000 crowns just for myself.

Life today in this country is still hard. People still remind me that my father was black like a shoe. People are always saying bad things about Gypsies. I didn't do anything bad to the people who live around us, but they are very distant with us. I try to be friendly with our neighbors, but they just walk away when I want to talk to them. Sometimes they say, "Go to hell, we don't want to talk with you shits."

A neighbor once asked me where one of his chickens was. I saw it hiding and pointed it out to him. He never apologized.

(1) Probably Josef Janovský.
(2) And she did, for several minutes.
(3) Stanislava Vrbová was born on 13 November 1942 and died on 21 December.

František Kejval
(as told by his daughter)

My father worked for Heydrich at his castle by Panenské Březany.[1]

All my life I have tried to find out what happened to my father after he was sent to Lety. Three years ago I started the paperwork for compensation, but the Czech government is always asking me for another piece of paper. Now I'm told I can't have compensation until I get a certificate that my father was a political prisoner. Where do I get such a certificate?

My father, František Kejval, was born on 13 June 1913 in Lukavice. All his life he was a farm laborer. I think both of my parents worked on farms. Perhaps they traveled from farm to farm to work as was the custom in those days.

In 1941 my mother and my father lived in Panenské Březany where Heydrich lived with his wife and two sons in a small castle. My mother took care of Heydrich's cows. My father drove a horse and wagon carrying sand on the farm. I don't know what the sand was for. I believe one Sunday my father was ordered to work, but because it was a Sunday he didn't want to work. That's why he was arrested.

Probably the rules about working were stronger in this town because Heydrich resided there, so any infringement had drastic results. I was six years old when the Gestapo came to our house and beat my father. They said he refused to work so he was taken away to the work camp at Lety by Písek.

We never saw him again. My mother had to take care of me and my brother. Later I lived with my grandmother, only coming back to see my mother after the war. When I was ten years old, my mother showed me letters from my father from Lety but those letters were never saved.

My father's brother Karl who lives in Ostrava wrote to me that my father was arrested in 1941 by the Gestapo because he wouldn't fulfill the order to carry sand and other construction materials for the German Wermacht.

I gave this letter to the Defense Ministry, which is in charge of my compensation application, but now they are insisting that I get a certificate that my father was a political prisoner before they will consider paying me compensation. I don't know where to get such a certificate.

I have a letter from the State Archive in Třeboň saying that my father died in Lety, but they won't give me a certificate saying how or why. I also have this letter from the Museum in Auschwitz:

The prisoner František Kejval born in Lukavice entered the concentration camp in Auschwitz on 29 April 1942 on a transport coming from Prague. He was registered as a Czech prisoner with the number BV 33,964. On 26 June 1942 he died according to the law w/w w KL. Auschwitz.

The State Archive in Prague also wrote to me that if I went to Poland I could find information on my father in the file KT-Auschwitz no. 6 from 26 June 1942.

I have written about ten registered letters to various Czech archives and institutions but I can't get anywhere with my inquires.

My father was not a Gypsy. None of his ancestors were Gypsies. I really don't know why he was sent to Lety. I thought Lety was only for Gypsies.

(1) SS Obergruppenfuehrer Reinhard Heydrich was Hitler's viceroy for the Bohemian-Moravian Protectorate. Known as the Butcher of Prague for his ruthless orders against the Czech people, Heydrich was wounded by Czech parachutists from England on 27 May 1942 and died several days later from infection. His family was awarded the farm and castle at Panenské Břežany but at the war's end left it and escaped to Bavaria.

Marie Serynková
(as told by her son)

My mother was born on 24 February 1923 in Bednava, Rakovník. The name of her mother was Barbora Serynková; I can't remember the name of her father. He might have been called Josef Serynek. He had horses and wagons and traveled around the country with his family, repairing kettles and selling ceramic cooking pots.

My mother came from a large family but all were killed at Lety except for a brother who now lives in Germany. He changed his name for some reason but I don't know why. He changed his name in Germany but never told even my mother why he changed his name. He and my mother were the only ones of our clan to survive Lety. He is about 73 years old now. He married a German Gypsy.

My mother had many cousins in the Lety concentration camp. I remember one of them, Eva Ševčíková. She had no children because she was sterilized either in Lety or in Auschwitz. She died in winter time about 13 and a half years ago in the Plzeň hospital. She married a man she had met in one of the concentration camps but he is also dead. He died one year after her. His name was Gustav Ševčík. Her maiden name was Serynková.

My mother and her family were arrested near Písek. They were in the area with their horses and wagons traveling, looking for work. The Czech police came with a truck and took them to Lety. I don't know what happened to their horses and wagons.

My mother didn't like to talk about her experiences at Lety. She told me more about Auschwitz. She had terrible nightmares about Lety. I remember one incident, though, that happened at Lety. A Czech guard saw a small boy about four years old scavenging for potato peelings. Like every prisoner there, the small boy was dying of hunger. The guard came over, took off his belt, and wrapped it around the boy's neck. Then the guard held the boy up, a few inches off the ground, until he died.

When Czech TV showed things about German concentration

camps, my mother had to leave the room. Then her nightmares would start again and she would be very depressed for several weeks.

My mother always complained about being hungry all the time at Lety. She never got over those terrible moments of hunger. Maybe that's why she was fat for the rest of her life. She couldn't stop eating.

My mother told my wife more than me. Those two were always talking together. My wife told me that mother saw dead bodies piled up in heaps at Lety, almost mountains of them. There were many beatings at Lety and most of these bodies were the result of those beatings.

I remember my mother telling me how she stole potato peelings out of the garbage to give to her father. He had to work hard building a road for the Czechs and never got enough to eat. At night she would escape from her barracks and sneak over to the men's barracks and pass the potato peelings through the iron bars to her father.

She herself was beaten many times and never understood how she survived those beatings when other people died of them. She saw people beaten every day, killed every day.

At first she worked in the stone quarry near Lety. She said all the children had to work there carrying the stones, climbing up a hill with the stones as punishment.

People were dying every day at Lety. She told me on more than one occasion that several times during the coldest days of winter, the Czech police would call all the prisoners out, line them up, and then spray them with cold water. This was a way to make the people sick so they would die faster.

My mother caught typhus at Lety but like her beatings she was one of the few to survive. She said a lot of people died of typhus but more died of the beatings.

She said her father was electrocuted, that's how he died, but she never told me how it happened.[1]

In the summer my mother worked in the fields picking potatoes. Many of the local farmers were allowed to hire the prisoners to work for them. The prisoners didn't get any money. The camp commander got it. The prisoners didn't get anything from these farmers, not even any extra food. If you got caught stealing a potato or caught eating a raw one, you were beaten to death on the spot. But people had to steal to survive, like today in the Czech Republic. My mother also worked for private farmers picking sugar beets. But always the guards from Lety were there to watch them.

My mother always wanted to run away while she was working in the fields but she was afraid to. Anyone who tried to escape and got caught was killed, either beaten to death or shot.

Mother also had to go into the woods to collect kindling wood, and make small bundles and bring them back to ... that's where the story would end. Then she would just cry. She never told me what the wood was for, she could never finish that story, she just ended up crying.

These are my mother's papers she gave me just before she died. She was sent from Lety to Auschwitz on 20 April 1943. There they tattooed her arm with number Z-7749. On 15 April 1944 she was sent to Ravensbruck.

In 1973 my mother heard that people who spent the war in German concentration camps were being paid compensation. She wrote to the Red Cross and to our Czech government. The Red Cross confirmed she had been at Auschwitz and at Ravensbruck. The Czech Federal Ministry of Defense sent her this letter on 10 July 1973 certifying that she was a political prisoner of the Germans from 20 April 1943 until 21 April 1945, but she never got one crown of compensation.

When Václav Havel became President of the Czech Republic in January 1993, my mother wrote a personal letter to him about her compensation. His office answered that he was taking a personal interest in her case and that his office would do the maximum to help her, but she never heard from them again. She died on Christmas day 1994.

(1) See Karel Kloc story.

Karel Kloc

I was born on 2 March 1932 in Mělník. My mother's name was Božena Klocová. My father was Antonín Čermák. I have a sister Ludmila, and four brothers who have already died, Josef, Eduard, František and Albert. My father worked in a factory. My mother was a housewife. We lived in Kolín but my father had a sideline in horses so we traveled a lot in the summer in our wagon. In the winter we lived in our house. We were not Jews, or whites. To tell you the truth, we were something like Svetskys.[1] My mother and father both looked white.

One afternoon some German and Czech policemen came to our house and took the whole family away.[2] We had to walk to the police station in Kolín where already a lot of other families were gathered. At the police station German and Czech guards were watching that no one would escape.

I believe our whole family was taken to the concentration camps because of racial reasons. We children went to sleep at night, went to school in the morning. I don't know if my father did something wrong. My grandmother had already died.

We had to stay four days at the police station. There were white people, Svetskys and Gypsies all together. There were about 4,000 to 5,000 people there.[3] Later we were taken away by cars and put on a train in animal wagons and taken straight to Lety.

The children less than 14 years of age were separated from their parents. The children more than 14 were counted as adults.

They shaved our heads when we came to the camp and gave us some striped clothes to put on. On the right side of the jacket we had numbers for Gypsies and for whites.[4] We came to Lety in the summer of 1942. There were wooden barracks in the camp and a latrine for about ten people.

There were 15,000 or 16,000 people there. In the morning we got one-eighth of a loaf of bread, and a small piece of margarine. For lunch we received some potato goulash. We got nothing for supper.

I don't remember the names of any of the guards anymore, only the guard who took us away. His name was Sedláček. When we were released, they took some of the German guards away and killed them, shot them.[5] To tell you the truth, I suffered very much there. I was there from 1942 to 1944, then we went to Terezín for three months, then to Auschwitz.[6]

My parents worked in the stone quarry. There was one guard who beat my father there. When my mother saw this, she took a stick and beat this guard over the head until he fell down the hill. Then the camp director told my mother that she and her family would be the first ones on the next transport to Auschwitz. That was why we were sent to Auschwitz.

When people were not strong enough to work carrying the stones, the guards shot them or beat them with their guns on their heads until they died.

At roll call one morning I saw a German guard take a baby and with his feet on the baby's feet pulled it violently up until the baby was in pieces.[7] Most of the babies were liquidated by the guards as soon as they were born. Some were sent to Germany to be educated as Germans.[8] These children never returned to the Czech Republic; they never knew if they were Czech or German.

They took us to some showers once in a while to wash ourselves. Also, there was a pond. The guards made us go into the water and then they put electrical wires into the water, pushed the button and all of the people who were in the lake died.[9]

Before the guards pushed the button, they asked the Gypsies if they had stolen anything. When they didn't answer, they killed them. Other prisoners had to carry the dead bodies out of the lake and take them away to mass graves around the camp. I can show you exactly where the mass graves are. There were about 50 to 60 people in each mass grave.

Now there is a pig farm on the place where all the mass graves are. They had to take all the bones out of the earth to build the farm there. President Havel was there a year ago and asked why they had put a pig farm there.[10]

There was a German capo who cut the skin away from the people who had tattoos to make purses. Her name was Joklová. Then she took prisoners to the pond and made them clean the pond with a spoon, or she just shot them. She made a mark on their forehead and shot them right there in the head.[11]

There were four execution posts in the camp. They hung people there for about half a day. Sometimes they shot the people at the post and then left them lying on the ground. It was worse in summer because the flesh smelled. This is how we got sicknesses there.

There was a gas chamber in Lety. They had the liquid in big barrels. The gas came out of the showers. It was a wooden house. They told the people they would get washed, gave them towels and later gassed them.

Most of the people died of typhus. The typhus broke out because of the bad health conditions and dirt. I don't remember when it broke out. There was one German doctor there. Some of the prisoners were doctors. But what could they give to the people, an aspirin that was all. We didn't get any injections during our stay there. When we were released, we got an injection in our arm.

I was ten years old in Lety. I was with the children, so I didn't have a job. My brother was sixteen and he worked in the stone quarry. There was one capo in charge of us children. Her name was Káťa. We were about 80 children in one barrack. When we played, she used to come and put a string around our neck and towed us behind her until our tongues stuck out of our mouths. She wasn't Gypsy, she was white and spoke Czech well.

Once a German guard brought a food package for one of the children and gave it to the capo but she took it away and gave it to some man she was with in the camp. She said the children would only get diarrhea from that food package.

I can write everything down for you, I could write a big book about what I suffered there. The worst was the hunger we suffered, and then all of us got typhus. I also feel like I have very weak nerves, that something is wrong with my brain today because of my experiences at Lety.[12]

I had a dream once. It was in the morning and I was still sleeping. My wife and my nephew were already awake and told me later that I was jumping up and down and screaming, "don't shoot me, don't shoot me." One month later I had another dream, then I screamed, "why are you taking away my father?" Only after a while did I remember what I had dreamed.

There was no heating in the winter. It was very cold there. During the time I was there, a lot of people died of the cold. Sometimes there were piles of dead bodies that they took away from the barracks. It is difficult to estimate how many people died. There were mass graves, then they poured chlorine over them. They also took away many bodies to big ovens where they burned them.

The older women worked, but I don't know where. We were children, we didn't see everything.

Káťa killed a lot of people. She must have had a lot of deaths on her conscience. After the war I heard someone killed her.

Four of my cousins died in Lety. Two of them were shot, as was my grandfather. One of them was hung up. They were just taking him down, taking the rope off his neck, when we arrived. My grandfather was Antonín Čermák. My cousins were Josef and Eduard Kloc. Josef was the one they hung up. Eduard was one of the ones they shot. I don't remember the others.

I could tell you a lot about the pond. A lot of people were killed there, drowned there.

A lot of people worked in the stone quarry and in the forest. Some people ran away. When the guards caught someone, they killed him. They either hung him up or shot him.

Every day people were beaten to death in Lety. I was a witness sometimes to those beatings, those killings. I saw several with my own eyes. Most of the beatings were carried out by the capos. They beat people several times on the head until they killed them.

Today if I were in Lety I could show you where the mass graves are. The pond was our big destiny. I could show you exactly where people lay under the earth. We didn't even have peace at night. Sometimes we had to stand in line at night, men, women and children separated for three hours, standing like that. Guards walked between the people with their dogs. If a prisoner moved, the guards set the dogs on him.

From Lety we were sent by train in animal wagons to Terezín. I was two months in Terezín then they sent us back to Lety, before they sent us to Auschwitz.

Later when I was in Auschwitz I saw them put my mother and father in the gas chamber. I saw them go in alive, and later saw them bring out their bodies. The distance was only from this bed to the wall. That's how close I was to seeing their bodies. Three months before the war ended, my parents were killed. I was also on the list but survived. There was a Polish woman who cured our sicknesses. She told me I was on the list, but fortunately the Russians liberated us.

When I returned from Auschwitz, I was only bones, like a skeleton. I had spots all over my body and inside these spots, inside the flesh of my body, were fleas.

Since coming out of the concentration camps I am mentally sick. I am seeing psychiatrists all the time, getting medicine. My sister who is living in the Slovak Republic, she could tell you novels about how we suffered in the concentration camp. She lives in Lucenec. You could write to her. She has a telephone.

My nephew, as you can see, has black skin. People call him a Gypsy. He is the son of my brother who is white, but my nephew has the skin color of his mother. My nephew is afraid to go to town. Why do the people make differences? I can't understand it. Why do they put all people into one sack? My nephew is Czech, pure Czech. Two days ago he went to town and four skinheads came up to him and asked, "What are you doing here you Gypsy?" They told him if he didn't give them his money they would kill him, so he gave them everything he had. When they see someone with black skin, they beat him right away. My nephew has scars on his arm and back where skinheads beat him. Now he is an invalid. Whenever he goes out, he makes sure he is home by 5:30 p.m. You can't be out at night. The skinheads will get you. Some places in Prague like Wenceslas Square are off limits to us.

Sometimes I go and work in a little factory where my nephews work. I sharpen knives there, fix umbrellas and shoes. The two brothers of my nephews are white. Whenever people come, my dark-skinned nephew doesn't show himself. He doesn't come out because the customers would say this shop is full of Gypsies and they wouldn't come back.

My nephew has had eight operations on his inner ear. One week ago he was in Smichov for an examination and four skinheads with chains and cans of spray were there looking for Gypsies. He hid from 1:00 p.m. until 8:00 p.m. until he could escape.

Sometimes people living in our apartment building leave their shoes for me to fix. I get them fixed the same day or the next day. We have good neighbors here.[13]

Four years ago I went to Praha Dejvice and I showed them a paper I had from Auschwitz written in three languages but I never received any compensation. Not even an answer, nothing. I have never received any compensation for being in Lety. My sister hasn't either.

My nephew is afraid to send me to apply for compensation. I don't see very well. I have had an operation on my eyes. My wife is also sick. Our nephew must look after us.

Two weeks ago my nephew heard on the radio a debate. One man said: "What do you have against the Romany people? They are people like us." The other one said, "No! Here in Prague we need a pure race. We will not leave the Romanies alone until they return to the place from where they came."

Times were never as bad as they are right now. A lot of people are complaining. I cannot ever remember a time like this. But we have our roots here, where should we go? My friend told me, "I am also afraid, my skin is even darker than yours."

If the government would give me money to emigrate to Australia or England I would go immediately. But what can I do without money, where can I go?

Perhaps I could go to England or to Australia to live a happy life, how I imagine life should be. But here I have nothing.

(1) Svetsky is a Czech-Romany word meaning "sons of the world." Before World War II it had a derogatory meaning among the pure Romany, meaning a Gypsy who had lost his dark color by marrying a white person. Many of the Svetskys were associated with the circus and later many people thought Svetskys were only circus artists.

(2) The beginning of August 1942.

(3) Jiří Letov, a commissioner with the Ministry of the Interior, testified in court after World War II that 11,000 Gypsies were sent to Lety. The official camp census never listed more than 1,100 prisoners. The official camp book for prisoner registration never exceeded 700 prisoners. In 1939 a New York Times article about Gypsies in Bohemia estimated a total population of 35,000 not counting the Gypsies in Slovakia. The present-day Czech government admits that 98% of their Czech Gypsies died in the Holocaust.

(4) During his interview, Kloc appeared to mix up his recollections of Lety and Auschwitz.

(5) Probably a mix up with the German guards killed by the Russians at Auschwitz. However, two Lety guards (Bouda and Fiala) did die at Lety, supposedly of typhus. Both opposed Janovský and were very helpful and friendly to the prisoners.

(6) The camp closed 27 May 1943.
(7) There were no German guards at Lety, although there were several German Sinti capos.
(8) Also mentioned in Janosovský story.
(9) Electrocutions are also mentioned in the Nedved story.
(10) President Havel has never called for the pig farm to be removed from the former death camp site, although the farm is in contravention of the Helsinki Agreements signed by the Czech government.
(11) No other survivor has told this story.
(12) Perhaps an explanation for some of the stories in his oral history.
(13) One elderly woman in the building bluntly told us that everyone in the building wanted to get rid of the Klocs when she saw us talking to them.

Helena Růžičková
(as told by a sister)

I was not in Lety, only in Auschwitz. But my sister Helena Růžičková was in Lety. She disappeared there with her new born baby.[1]

Our parents were Arnold Bamberger and Helena Hauer. They were German Sinti. They had a wagon and traveled around the country selling horses. We were a big family. My parents had eleven children, eight daughters and three sons. My sister Helena was the oldest. She was born in 1920 in Linz, Austria. I was born in Čermná, Lanškroun in 1923.

Everyone in our family was arrested in 1943 and sent direct to Auschwitz except for Helena who had left home two years earlier to travel in the wagon with her husband. When the train arrived in Auschwitz, the Germans tried to separate us. The children were crying and wouldn't leave their parents, so the Nazis shot them all right there in the boxcar. I was the only one of our family to survive. That night I lost my one year old daughter, my husband, all of his family, and my nine brothers and sisters and all their children.

My sister Helena was the first one arrested from our family. She was married to a man by the name of Josef Růžička; they were traveling in their wagon with a large group of Romany when the Czech police found them and took them all to Lety. My sister had three children. I remember the two older ones were Helena and Josef. The girl was about two years old, the boy about four. There was a third child, about eight months old, another girl, but I don't remember her name. It might have been Marie.

I heard from a cousin who was also in Lety that my sister talked a Romany man by the name of Klimt into escaping with her children because she feared they were going to be killed. The man took the two older children but not the baby.

I heard these two children who escaped are still alive and living in the Czech Republic, or Germany, but they have changed their names because they are afraid the police are still looking for them.

After the war I met several survivors from Lety. Žofie H. was in Lety with my sister. She is still alive, living in Prague, but I don't have her address. She and others all told me how bad the Czech police were, how people died of the beatings at Lety, how all the children under the age of two were always murdered, usually with their mothers. I always wanted to know what had happened to my sister, but when I found out I wished I hadn't asked. The details were gruesome. I won't tell them to you.

It's no better today in the Czech Republic. In fact, it's worse than in the Hitler days. Then we knew how they were going to kill us. But today you don't know when they are going to get you, or how they are going to kill you. I don't go out, ever. You must live with whites to be protected. If you're living with only Romanies, they can kill you at anytime.

There was a couple in Breclav who missed their bus so they went to have a coffee and on the way the skinheads found them and the couple was beaten so badly that the Romany man lost his eye.

This is public Nazism. This is what happens when we go outside. The Czech public is separating us like the Nazis did at Auschwitz. They are separating us and killing us.

I have never received one crown of compensation for the time I spent in Auschwitz or for losing all my family there. Look at the boxes of pills on my kitchen table. I am a sick woman, I don't have any money, yet I can't get compensation from this government.

I am sick because of what happened at the concentration camp. I can't sleep. I always have nightmares. Where is the justice? The government tells me I can't apply for the compensation of my husband because I was not officially married to him. Now I tell you something. At that time there was not one Romany family in Czechoslovakia who was legally married. We had our Romany weddings. For us that was all we needed. We had no papers from the Czechs so today they tell us we have no rights. Can you imagine how many Romany died in concentration camps and their spouses today cannot get any compensation because we did not have a piece of paper? We had children from that marriage. Isn't that better than a piece of paper?

Despite what the Czechs say, we are human beings. Human beings died in these camps, not animals. But they treated us like animals then, and they are treating us like animals now. There is no compassion in these white Czechs.

In 1995, after fifty years, this government offered me 50,000 crowns ($1,400) for being in Auschwitz. I am a sick woman, I need money but I refused their offer. Who can give me back my child, my husband, my parents, my brothers and sisters, my uncles and aunts and cousins? This was the price they put on all of that suffering. I told them no.

At Auschwitz they made medical experiments with my body. Do they think after fifty years they can make me forget, by offering me 50,000 crowns?

(1) In Dr. Bohin's book of patients at Lety, it was recorded that Helena Růžičková, born Bamberger, died at Lety on 9 January 1943.

K. V.

I'm sorry. I don't think I can help you. I don't remember anything about Lety. I was only six years old when I was there. My mother died in Lety, so I don't remember much about her either. No, I don't know what she died of.

How did I survive? I don't know. Another woman took care of me. I remember leaving. I was the last one. The guards took me to an orphanage in Nová Bystřice. I don't know why I was the only one left at Lety. When the last prisoners were set free, I was all alone.

I lived in the orphanage until I was fifteen. Then I went to a vocational school until I was eighteen. I became a miner and worked in Duchcov. I retired this year at the age of sixty. I don't know why my family was sent to Lety. Lety was for Gypsies. I don't think we were Gypsies.

Yes, I got compensation, 100,000 crowns. But it took me two years to get it. I had to prove that my father died in Auschwitz and that my mother died in Lety, and that I was there with her. I had no problem getting a certificate from the Germans, but the archive in the Czech Republic didn't have their papers in order. I had to hound them for two years to get a certificate. Back and forth, back and forth. I almost gave up but in the end I did it for my mother. The Czechs killed her. I made them give me something for her death. I upset them a lot by pestering them for that certificate.

Marie Šlehoferová

I was born on 9 August 1926 in Rokycany. My parents were Barbora Franzová and Josef Šlehofer. My father worked the fairgrounds selling clothes and many other things. He had a horse and wagon and traveled around the country to these fairs. Later he bought a small delivery van. We lived in Švihov near Klatovy in a house in the village. My parents died when I was very young, my mother from typhus, my father from leukemia. I was brought up by an aunt.

The Czech police from Klatovy came one day and collected us and all our relatives and took us to a yard in the police station where we had to wait the whole day without food or water. In the late afternoon a bus came and took us to Lety. There were about twenty of us, all Šlehofers.[1] The police gave us no reason whatsoever for our arrest or deportation to Lety. That was in the month of June 1942. I was eighteen years old.

We arrived in the evening at Lety. There was still light. The first thing they did upon on our arrival was to cut our hair, shave us. We didn't get any clothes, we kept the clothes we had on. Later they became rags and were falling off us. We were the first ones in the camp. It was a small camp with wooden buildings around a small central yard. Later, thousands of Gypsies were brought to the camp. They shared their clothes with us because we didn't have anything. My relatives knew many of the prisoners who later arrived at the camp.

The first morning in camp we had to clean all the buildings. There had been prisoners there before. My job was watching the kids. There were three barracks for kids and in each barrack there were at least 100 children. There were always two women watching a hundred kids. The children were not allowed to have contact with their parents. The children of my relatives were not in my barracks but in another.

Most of the prisoners worked in the stone quarry. The women had to work in the fields. The guards never asked people what profession they had. No matter what you had done in life, you were sent either to the stone quarry or to the fields.

All the guards were Czech. There were no Germans in the camp. One of the guards went to town to get me a pair of shoes. He was kind to me. I had no shoes when I arrived in the camp. He came from Slověnice. I looked for him after the war but I couldn't find him. I don't remember his name now.

There were bad guards, as bad as possible. I was hit once on the side of my face with a truncheon and had a wound there for a long time. I was hit for no reason at all. There was never a reason why they hit you.

There were big holes in the forest covered over with white lime. We were not allowed to go there, but later I heard from Mr. Serynek, another prisoner, that these holes contained the dead bodies of prisoners who had been murdered. These holes were very near to the camp, less than half a kilometer away. Often I took the children on walks to the lake; we were not allowed to go to the forest.

I remember an old man who they bound in iron clamps so he couldn't move. He was hung in an open Gypsy wagon and the iron was on his feet. I don't know what happened to him later. I also remember a pregnant woman the guards closed up in a small building. We never saw her again.

When the kids had to go to the toilet they were sent to the forest. Two children I knew ran away but the guards shot them. They were still alive when the guards caught them but I never saw them again either.

We had terrible food, only cabbage, potatoes and the peelings. When the women came back from the fields, they tried to smuggle in some food, a few potatoes from the field. Sometimes the guards searched them at the gate and took whatever they found. The kids were always hungry. You should have seen the eyes of those kids begging for food. An uncle of mine smuggled in a loaf of bread for me. I gave it all to the kids. When I saw their eyes, begging for food, I had to give them everything I had.

There was one German policeman in the camp. He was the only good man.[2]

One of the Gypsy women gave me a gold ring because I smuggled in some bread for her children. When the Gypsy women came back from the fieldwork they had to pass through the gate and sometimes there were controls and the guards took the food from them that they were trying to smuggle in. There were lots of tears because they wanted to give this food to their kids.

I was in Lety for six or seven weeks[3] before the husband of my cousin got us out. Finally they found out, that it was a mistake, that we weren't suppose to be in there. About fifteen of us were released because of his efforts. When they set my family free, the guards forgot about me. When I finally found out that they were leaving, I began crying and finally they let me go as well. After they released us, we had to wait for a bus in the village of Lety to take us to the train station. We were so hungry we stole bread. I had nothing to wear. I was dirty like a pig. We had no money at all. We went home then by train.

When we arrived home my uncle who had horses and cattle discovered another farmer had been given them while he was in Lety. He never got his animals back. The police in Klatovy never apologized to us.

The guards tried to keep one of my uncles in Lety. He was from Husinec. There were other Šlehofers in the camp that I didn't know. They were all released because this relative went to all these offices in Prague pleading our case. It turned out that the police in Klatovy had made a mistake. After the war I went to the mayor in Klatovy and asked for a document that I got detained and sent to Lety. He told me there were no more records and he couldn't give me a certificate.

Marie Stiebrová from Bernartice near Klatovy was also in Lety with me and was also released with us.

We were very lucky the day they released us because that same day many buses came to Lety to take hundreds of Gypsies to Auschwitz.

There were no illnesses while I was at Lety, nor any doctors. I never heard of people dying from typhus. There were mass graves while I was at Lety but all the people were killed. They didn't die of diseases. I was so afraid of the guards I never spoke to them. I never knew their names.

I saw beatings every day. It was terrible. Some of the guards were so bad, I could only believe they were not regular policemen, that they had been sent to Lety as punishment. They had uniforms but they were so bad they couldn't have been normal police. Normal police wouldn't have done those things.

There was a Gypsy called Istvan. The guards heard him speak Romany so they beat him up, really badly, then took him away. I never saw him again either.

The kids always wanted to see their parents but they were not allowed to have contact. Sometimes they could catch a glimpse of their mother through the fence. It was a huge camp. Most of the kids spoke Czech, but some only spoke Romany.

Two kids of Václav Flachs died in Lety. I remember that. I got to know the family after the war.

We were lucky. None of my relatives died at Lety.

I tried to apply for compensation but the archive at Třeboň told me there were no documents about me being in Lety. None of the Šlehofers got any compensation. My husband was five years in Dachau but he got no compensation either. He listened to a foreign radio program once and the neighbors informed on him. That's why he was sent to Dachau.

Last year the government announced a new compensation plan for concentration camp survivors but I was in a health spa and when I got out I only had four days to apply before the deadline.

I tried to get some documents but everyone at the offices in Třeboň State Archive told me I had no right. The minimum compensation was 2,000 crowns ($60) and I couldn't even get that.

(1) According to archive records, there were forty Šlehofers in Lety.
(2) Later, after the interview, she said the only good man in the camp was Janovský, the director. Since he dressed in a black uniform and insisted his men salute him in the German style, this may be the person she is referring to here.
(3) Třeboň archive wrote that she had been in Lety from 2 August 1942 until 22 August 1942.

K. P.

I was still a child when I was in Lety. I don't remember much. My father was taken directly to Buchenwald, and my mother straight to Auschwitz. Only we children were taken to Lety.

I remember a green truck came to pick us up one day. We were living in Sedlice near Vysoké Mýto. My oldest brother Josef was sent to Buchenwald with my father. The four remaining brothers were sent to Lety:

My two sisters were already married. I don't know what happened to them. They were taken to a concentration camp and never returned.

After I was born, we moved to that village where I later went to primary school. My father had his own small carpentry shop; he made all kinds of furniture, stools, tables, things like that. My mother was a housewife.

In the late evening some Germans guards came to pick us up; they were wearing special helmets and speaking German. They took the whole family to Pardubice with a green truck. They took us to a big house where they separated us.

This house in Pardubice was a collecting camp where people were brought from all over. After my parents were sent away, my brothers and I were sent by truck straight to Lety. I was seven years old at that time. I don't know why we were taken away. Maybe it was because of my father. He might have done something against the Germans. I don't know. My father had a little radio with earphones; he listened to this in secret; we were never allowed in the room when he had his radio on.[1]

Once we were separated from our parents we knew bad things would happen to us. The first thing I saw upon arriving at Lety was small wooden houses and one big house that was for us children.

They shaved our heads and gave us some black clothes, pants and jackets and some tie-up shoes. They burned all of our personal clothes. There were ten children sleeping in each bed.

In the morning we got black coffee and a piece of bread; for lunch some kind of soup, and in the evening black coffee and a piece of bread. This continued for all the time I was there. I was in Lety for more than a year.

The guards in Lety behaved terribly. We were beaten all the time. We had to do training exercises even in winter time. They always wanted us to do something. They didn't want us to live. They tortured the children psychologically by chasing them with their truncheons, threatening to kill us. The guards didn't want anyone to live. There was no food there. People died every day.

All of the guards were bad. All of them were the same. They were there to liquidate us. I would be lying to you if I told you the names of any guards. I really don't remember.

There were some German and Czech capos there. The director of the camp was a German.[2] He had a house, a villa, outside of the camp. He gave all the orders, and the Czech guards carried them out. All the guards were Czech.

I saw people beaten to death every day; it was normal in Lety. All the guards had dogs and wore guns. I remember one child who was shot right in the head.

Most of the time the children were locked up in their barracks. The guards let us out only when they wanted to; we couldn't run around in the camp just like that.

The hygienic conditions were very bad. People got sick from the latrines because everything was so dirty.

As I told you, I couldn't see that much because we were locked up. When they took us out, we had to walk in a column and fulfill the orders of the guards.

My two older brothers worked in the stone quarry. They left in the morning and came back at night. I can remember the lake by the camp, but we were never taken there. We had to wash ourselves in the communal bathroom. Every morning we could wash ourselves in some sinks.

We lived in just a simple wooden house without heating. In winter time it was so cold that you woke up in the morning and found three or four children lying around frozen to death. People, especially the children, also died of hunger.

I heard from older children that the dead bodies were thrown into a big hole in the ground, somewhere in the forest. After having liquid chlorine poured on them, the bodies were covered with a layer of earth until more dead bodies were thrown over these.

The older boys also told me that the women in charge of giving food to the children poured some poison over their portions so many children died. These women who looked after the children were very bad. The rest of the guards were all men.

I don't know if any of the women went with the guards, we boys were only interested in how we could escape. Some of the older boys tried, but the guards always found out. The guards had small hammers which they used to knock on the fence every day. If they heard a different sound, they knew there was a hole in the fence. It was difficult to escape.

When they liquidated the camp, we went into the warehouse and saw all the food and clothes. Everyone took what he wanted. The guards had all of this during the time they worked there; they had everything.

There were so many transports coming and going with prisoners to other concentration camps, that people were not correctly registered, some not registered at all. All my details in the camp records were false; I saw these records not long ago. The people running the camp must not have wanted anyone to know how many were in the camp, how many died there. The Germans must have done this, the Czechs never acted like this.[3]

I had typhus at Lety. Almost all of us had typhus at Lety.

There were two doctors that saved us. Without them we wouldn't have survived. When we children had typhus, we went to see the doctors a lot. They gave us an injection into our breast. Later they disinfected the children's house; no one was allowed to go outside. I don't remember the names of the doctors, but they saved us.

If President Havel said that only 327 people died at Lety, that is the biggest lie I have ever heard.[4] People died every day at Lety, every day. From hunger, beatings, sicknesses, typhus.

The Gypsies and the Czechs got along well at Lety. Lety wasn't a Gypsy camp. It was a mixed camp. Everybody was there. There were as many white people in Lety as Gypsies.[5]

It's crazy to think the Germans would close Lety because it was so cruel. Sure there were beatings and deaths every day but my brother told me how cruel the Germans were at Buchenwald; the prisoners had to carry rocks there too, and the Germans would let the dogs loose to snap at their heels, bite them, bite out pieces of flesh. I can't believe the Germans closed Lety because the Czechs were making a mess out of it.

I remember when the camp was liquidated. No one was there. We took some food and clothes and went away with the Russians. The four of us went with Russian tanks to Letice near Krásná Hora. Then we walked home.[6]

My eldest brother was away for five years. My father returned but later died of an illness caught in the concentration camp. My mother returned two years after the war. I don't know from where she came.

In the 1950s at work I told someone about the concentration camp in Lety. For this I was arrested and taken away to Jachymov. I went to work, told the truth and the StB arrested me.[7] I was four and a half years in Jachymov from 1954 to 1959. In that time if someone didn't work or was punished he was sent right away to a communist labor camp. And now these assholes in our new government don't want to confess what happened in Jachymov. There were 30 or 40 work camps around there, mainly mines. Jachymov and Lety were the same.

The government office in Prague said that I was in Jachymov for only 32 days. Therefore, I wasn't due any compensation. They told me I wasn't the first and wouldn't be the last to ask for compensation. They told me all the records were destroyed. I was there for more than four years and they say I was there for only 32 days. That's the kind of government we have today.

Only the Czechs ran Jáchymov. There were no Russians there except some Russian engineers who administered the mines. But they were nice.

The Czech guards at Jáchymov beat us just like they did at Lety. When you have more time, I can tell you the names of all the guards at Jachymov. I remember them all really well. I will write some information down about Jáchymov and send them to you. I'll help you.

I have here a small booklet where every work camp I was sent to has the day I entered and the day I left. Look at all the official stamps and seals. But when I sent a copy of this official booklet to the authorities proving I was in Jáchymov and that I was due 15 crowns per day extra on my pension because I was in these labor camps, they told me it was not proof enough. They said my booklet could have been forged. A lawyer in town told me I would never get any compensation because it was too much work for our new government because too many people were in those camps. I am supposed to get 15 crowns per day more on my pension but they refuse. I tried to fight my case in court; I received a letter from Děčín; they told me that all the records at Jáchymov had been burned.

I thought about escaping from this country in 1968; I have relatives all over the world, but then I told myself I wanted to stay at home where I was born, where I still feel good despite these corrupt politicians we have today. I will continue to criticize this government because they are wrong. They are all bad. They are liars. They are covering up the past just like the Communists. They don't want justice. They just want to cover up.

The Czechs killed their own people, in Lety and in Jáchymov. My father said the Czechs used to be nice and helpful people, but the Communists changed them. The system changed them.

I applied three times for compensation for my father being at Buchenwald; I have the receipts from the registered letters I sent from the post office. But I have never received a reply from our government.

The StB, the Czech security police, had me kicked out of work 17 times during my life; they accused me of slandering Czech society in an unmoral way. I suffered a lot because I said only the truth. I'm lucky they didn't kill me. The StB was just like the Gestapo. They didn't need a piece of paper to kill anyone. The StB always burned my records wherever I worked. Today I can't get much of a pension because there is no record that I ever worked.

I feel that President Havel is an opportunist. He does everything to get an advantage for himself. I think all politicians are sons-of-bitches and now that Havel's one of them, he's no different.

(1) During the Protectorate (1939-1945) it was against the law to listen to foreign radio broadcasts. The punishment could be death.
(2) The director of the camp was Josef Janovský, a Czech police captain. He dressed like a German officer, spoke German and made his guards salute him in German way.
(3) From the Lety records in the Třeboň State Archives, the arrival lists prepared by the municipal police departments that sent prisoners did not correspond with the number of prisoners listed as inmates in the camp. This cover-up was carried out by the Lety administration of Janovský and Matějka.
(4) At the Lety memorial service (May 1995), President Havel said that only 327 inmates died at Lety, all from typhus.
(5) From August 1940 until the spring of 1942 Lety was a discipline camp for "work-shy" people. From May 1942 until May 1943 mainly Gypsies were sent to Lety although many were from mixed marriages and appeared to be white. Some political prisoners and some Jews were also held at Lety.
(6) According to the documents in Třeboň State Archive, Lety was closed in May 1943; some prisoners were kept to burn the buildings and clean up the camp but by August 1943 no one was in residence at the camp. However, several residents of Lety and Orlík have told me that there was some kind of camp at Lety until 1945, until the Russians arrived.
(7) Secret police of communist Czechoslovakia.

Adéla Studená

I was born on 21 May 1930 in Plavsko in our family home. My parents were Václav Studený and Anna Nespěšná. My parents had eleven children: Václav, Jan, Antonín, Josef, Jiří, Emil, Terezie, Kateřina, Marie, and one daughter who died as a baby.

We were living in the countryside working outside most of the time. We didn't travel like other Gypsies, we had our own fields. My parents also sold clothes and textiles in the markets of other cities. My father traveled to these markets with two horses and a nice caravan where the back opened up into a shop.

My parents were very wise people. All of us went to school; all of us knew how to read and write.

■ Prisoners' huts at Lety. Over eighty prisoners were sometimes crammed into each hut.. *Photo from collection of Marie Bártová – repro archive AVČR, ič. 95173.*

I was two years old when my eldest sister Terezie died at the age of twenty-seven. Her daughter was three years old so she grew up with us like another sister. Her name was Marie. My brother Emil and I are the only survivors of our family today.

We were living in Plavsko when the Czech police arrived on 3 August 1942 and arrested us: Emil, Josef, Marie, Kateřina, my parents, my grandparents and me. The others were all living somewhere else. I was only twelve years old.

It was four o'clock in the morning when the police knocked on the door. We were only given a few minutes to dress. We could only take a few clothes. They put us in trucks, then took us to the train station in Jindřichův Hradec. There were lots of Gypsies rounded up there. I don't remember how we got to Písek because I was crying all the way. I only know it was by train. In Písek there were more trucks waiting to take us straight to Lety.

My first shock came when we arrived at Lety and I saw all these dogs and guards. All the things we had they took away from us. Everything was taken to a special room in the camp. The first day they took the children away from their parents, to live in separate barracks. All the children under the age of fourteen were separated from their parents. Then they cut off all our hair, the hair of the children; boys and girls were separated and also my parents were separated. I remember on the right side were the men, on the left side the women and in between was a house where the kids were separated by sex.

After the separation, the big tragedy began. We suffered hunger, then came the cold, then the beatings. There was a Czech guard, his name was Havel, and he was the one who beat me the worst. One day it was so cold I found some coal and was taking it to our barracks when he caught me. He found the coal on me and beat me with it. Until this day I have problems with my ears, hearing, because Havel beat me around the head with those lumps of coal. The guards were always beating us for no reason at all; just because they felt like it, or because they were in a bad mood.

All the Czech guards were bad, but the worst were Havel and Sabernoha, and the director Janovský. Later Blahynka carried on Janovský's work, and things got a bit better. Hejduk I also remember as a bad person. He had a red mole in the center of his forehead.

Dr. Bohin was half Jewish and a doctor at the state consulate. He was punished and brought to Lety instead of Auschwitz. He was a very, very nice person. Sometimes he was allowed to go home; he liked me very much and he always brought food back from Prague for me and my niece. He had a big sympathy for us because we could read and write. He also brought back for us "hot injections" of calcium.

Around Christmas we were told that everyone would be given an injection so we wouldn't get typhus. But for most of the prisoners just the opposite happened.[1] I heard that the shots might have been to give us typhus. Many who had an injection got a high fever and then passed out. I woke up on the floor two days after this injection which was given to us just above the heart. These injections were given while Dr. Bohin was there but he wasn't involved. Some doctors arrived just to give these injections, then left the same day. The only person I knew who didn't have typhus in Lety was my father who got an anti-typhus injection when he was a soldier in the First World War.

Everyone in our family, everyone in the camp, was beaten. The guards didn't make any differences between blacks, whites or Svetskys. They beat us all. Some were hung up while they were beaten. Some people also had to stand on their toes with their arms out for two hours. There were many beatings and many tortures but I personally never saw anyone beaten to death. I never heard about kids being drowned in the lake. I remember only three women who gave birth at Lety; my mother helped deliver these children, but all three died. I think the mothers had no milk because they were starving, the sanitary conditions were too bad, or the mothers were too weak to look after children. I think this is why they died.

As trucks brought new prisoners to the camp, the dark skinned Gypsies were immediately separated from the Svetskys and taken right away to Auschwitz. Only the white skinned Gypsies, the Svetskys, were kept in the camp. When typhus broke out these transports were stopped until the disease was cleared up. Then the transports started again.

Everybody was sleeping normally, five to a bed, until typhus broke out. Then everyone was sleeping everywhere, on the floor, all over the place to get away from other people.

Behind the lake were some small hills where the people worked, collecting stones. My mother went there for two or three months to work.

I can remember my father working as the chauffeur to take the dead bodies for burial at Mirovice. He had two horses and a wagon to carry the dead bodies in their coffins. I don't know why these people died. On the way back he'd ask villagers on the road to give him food so most days he was able to bring us something extra.

When typhus broke out they buried the bodies in the forest. I think about 400 people died in the camp from typhus, these were the people buried in the woods.

Our camp food wasn't enough to keep us alive. For supper we had mashed carrots in water. In the morning we had just black coffee without anything and a quarter of a slice of bread, 50 grams. At mid-day if you were in camp you got some potatoes in water. Those out working got only supper. The worst thing at Lety was the hunger, trying to survive each day.

Once a month the guard Maxa, who was a good guard, took us to the lake where we all had to take off our clothes to wash.

There was one guard who was a real human being, Mr. Bouda. My mother loved him. He was very Catholic like her, a very, very nice person. He was a tall man with a big nose and brown hair. He talked a lot with my mother, we all loved him. Havel and Hejduk should have died, not Bouda.[2] The worse you are the better luck you have.

There were three prostitutes that they brought into the camp. They must have done some crime in Prague. Their names were: Marta, Věra and Růžena. They were wild, nice girls from Prague, but at the camp they got their heads shaved. Věra worked in the camp as a tailor. Before typhus broke out, around Christmas, they were set free.

Later three German Gypsies were brought to the camp from Auschwitz. They were capos but also prisoners. I remember the names of two of them: Rudolf and Frýda. A few months later we were shown photos of Frýda lying dead on a floor, shot to death. The three of them tried to escape from the camp; the guards caught them but shot only Frýda. I don't know what happened to the other two. I don't remember these capos beating other Gypsies. Maybe they were ordered to beat us, that's why they escaped.

Every evening we had to stand in line with our arms at our sides. Once when my mother didn't have one of her arms down, Hejduk came up and slapped her face until she fell down. If I met Hejduk on the street today I would slap his face as hard as I could.

My mother was a wonderful cook so she worked in the kitchen cooking for the guards. She was a very fine, classy, attractive woman. Next to the kitchen was a wooden hatch and in the evening my father would whistle and she would pass out whatever she had been able to steal, dumplings, potatoes, meat. I never heard about the guards abusing the women in the camp.

The only member of our family who died in Lety was Kateřina's husband. I believe he died of typhus.

After the typhus epidemic, a provisional hut was built with showers. All the sick people were taken there and washed, then put in new barracks. Near the hut was a van where the guard Havrda disinfected our clothes. Havrda was a nice man. But I don't think he is alive today because he was about fifty years old when he was in the camp.

We were about three or four months in that provisional hut being looked after by Dr. Bohin. Then in May they told us they were letting us go home because we were not pure blooded Gypsies. Some of the people had to stay as workers to clean up the camp and burn the barracks. My brother Emil had to stay with Martin Čermák and several others to do this work.

After we left the camp we walked to the train station in Mirovice. People along the way were giving us food. We were afraid to go home so we went to Varvažov. My brothers and father got jobs in the forest and I went to school there until I was fifteen. We lived in a small wooden hut near the woods.

Later the Gestapo came and took my father and Emil away and put them in jail for six months in Klatovy. After the Americans bombarded the jail, my father and brother were able to escape. They joined us back at the hut and we hide out there until the end of the war.

When the war ended we all went to Prague to live. I got married. Had children.

I never knew, I never heard, that my father accused Janovský of war crimes. Perhaps my brother Emil can tell you something. He is five years older. He would have been 21 years old in 1945. I knew that Janovský had been brought to trial but I never knew my father was involved. I never heard the outcome.[3]

We lived a very peaceful and calm life after the war. My father never had any problems with the police. My mother died on the 4th of October of 1967, father on the 6th of January of 1968.

As a survivor, I advised Mr. Bárta about making his film of Lety. A guard gave these photos of the camp to my brother Antonín. He gave them to Mr. Bárta.

I believe Mr. Bárta started his film, DON'T FORGET THIS LITTLE GIRL, with a view of the lake because it was the only thing left of the camp. There was nothing else, no barracks, no buildings, no tombstones, only the lake.

I know he showed the truncheon as a symbol of the crimes that took place in the camp. All the guards had truncheons, we were all beaten with them.

Several of the guards took photos of the prisoners and of the camp, I remember that. But I can't remember which of the guards took those photos. I remember that my brother Antonín brought me one of the photos after the war when Mr. Bárta was making the film; it was of me when I was in the camp. I was twelve. But I never saw the film.

I was very angry at the memorial service last year (1995) because the Slovak Gypsies acted like they had been in Lety, but they weren't. They were allowed to speak, to bring flowers and place them on the monument while the survivors stood on the side, shunned. These Slovaks came to fight for their rights, but they should also learn their duties.

I have been living in this house for twenty-one years and always I have been treated very well by my neighbors; they know I am living a civilized life. I have never had any experience with discrimination here. My children always had a good education. My children never had problems getting jobs. I know there are people living in the Czech Republic who hate Gypsies, really hate Gypsies, but there are others who love us. I believe that a lot of Gypsies give reasons to the Czechs to dislike them. Some of the Gypsies behave horribly, especially those new-comers from Slovakia.

The communists helped our people get a better standard of living. I appreciate what they did for us. But some Gypsies brought from Slovakia had a hard time making such a quick change. People have to understand this. Some people can't change their customs overnight.

I believe this present government isn't doing enough to solve our problems. Today there is discrimination, there are big problems with the skinheads. Gypsies and skinheads are attacking one another. The government could do more to solve these problems. I think President Havel is a wonderful person, a man with a good heart, but as a politician I don't think he could hold this job in another country. He is a big symbol but he isn't prepared to do a good job. He's not a politician. It's a dirty business. He shouldn't be in it. But I appreciated seeing him at Lety last year, standing in the rain, speaking to us.

(1) At his trial in 1945, the camp commander Josef Janovský told the court that the injections did kill a lot of the prisoners, especially the children and the old people. He offered no explanation for this tragedy.

(2) Josef Bouda was one of two guards who died at Lety. The other was Fiala. Fiala was treated in hospital for typhus but still died. Bouda had protested in writing about the conditions at Lety. Many survivors felt he was murdered. He was never treated in hospital; he just disappeared one day after being threatened by his colleague Josef Hejduk. Bouda's cause of death was listed as typhus.

(3) After World War II, an investigation was made about Lety. Several survivors had protested as did several guards. The investigation centered on Janovský, Hejduk; Luňáček, Pešek, Černý, Baloun and several others. After the communist takeover of the government in 1948 this investigation ceased. Only Luňáček was given a reprimand. Almost immediately the communists started up their own labor camps such as Jáchymov where several Lety guards were employed, and some former Lety inmates were again interned.

Robert Růžička
(brother and father of Lety prisoners)

I was born on 25 July 1910 in Horní Počernice, Prague 9. My father Jan Růžička and my mother Filomena Růžičková were also born in the Prague area. My father was a circus artist, a high flier on the trapeze with the Kludský circus. My mother was a housewife; she had eight children. All my brothers and sisters had three or four children, but all of them died in the concentration camps. I was the only survivor. We were Svetskys.[1]

I was twenty-seven years old when my father died in 1937 in Lysá. He was about sixty-five years old. I was living in Příbram when the Czech police came looking for me. It was the summer of 1942 and I had heard that all my relatives had been arrested and taken to Lety. All the Gypsies were talking about the Czech police looking for us. I escaped by living in my friends' basements and cellars in the winter. In the summer I lived in the forest. When the Czech and the German police came into the woods looking for me, I hid in the tops of the trees.

I lived this way for two years, always running. When I lived with people, they gave me food, when I lived in the forest I stole. I could always find eggs or chickens on farms. I cooked in the woods. Sometimes I met refugees in the forest, partisans, and Gypsies. I fought with the partisans for one or two months, then they went to another forest and we parted.

I never went near Lety although I had heard that all my family was there. I heard bad things about Lety. I was afraid to go near there. The people who hid me were Czech people. They weren't Gypsies. I knew them from before. They were very good to me, but I'm too old to remember their names. I have trouble remembering even the members of my own family. But these were very good people, I trusted them. They saved my life. They had been friends of my parents.

I never had any close calls. I was very careful. I watched all the people. I was very strong in those days. I could climb all the trees.

When the war was over, I came out of the woods and got a job working at the uranium mines in Příbram. I never worked underground, only in the yards, doing all kinds of things. There were prisoners working there in the mines but I had an apartment in the city and the people treated me well. I had no problems in Příbram with anyone. I had good neighbors.

In 1949 I moved to Březová Hora and built a small house. I was married to Jana Čermáková, a circus artist. We had five girls and two boys. Several of my children have married circus artists and one of my daughters performed as a dancer in the United States. Most of my children have carried on our family tradition as artists.

Under the communists I worked as a laborer but I never had to go into the mines. I didn't have a bad life under the communists. I was never involved in politics. I didn't have a bad life. I lived my own life with my family. We never had any problems. I came home from work. My wife was always cooking, looking after the kids. After supper I worked on our home. I always wanted my kids to have a better life than I had and today they are all very successful. They have their own homes, their own businesses.

I listen to the radio today and I hear stories about Gypsies and how there are problems. The Slovakian Gypsies have invaded our country and are stealing and giving all of us a bad name. If they would work instead of steal, we wouldn't have these problems. I never had any problems. But I always worked. I hear that many of these Gypsies are on social welfare because they can't get jobs. That may be true. I don't know. I live the same way as I have lived all my life. I seldom leave the house but when I go into town I have Czech friends and Gypsy friends. I have no problems.

My wife died seventeen years ago. The most important thing for me today is to pray every night before I go to sleep. I want to see my wife again; I want to lie down in the coffin with her. There's no more happiness for me in these days. I had a good family, but the best years of my life are over. I now want to be with my wife again.

(1) Gypsies who had intermarried with Czechs.

R. B.
(Gypsy fugitive during World War II)

I was born in our wagon on 14 October 1922 in Ústí nad Orlicí (Lanškroun). My father raised horses, bought and sold them. He also made loans to people, keeping their horses until they paid him back. Sometimes he didn't get paid and had to keep the horses. He also went door to door sharpening knives and scissors. All our life we spent in the wagons, traveling to different places.[1]

I had three sisters and four brothers. My parents and all my brothers and sisters with their spouses and children died in Auschwitz except for one.

My husband was originally from Slovakia so I was with him there when the Czech police arrested my family in Moravia in the summer of 1942. My husband had already heard of many arrests so he talked me into going to Slovakia. Many Romany families we knew such as Ondráš, Pafner, Buriánský had already been arrested. So we were afraid and went to Slovakia with our horses and wagon.

I knew that the family Weinreich was arrested and sent to some place in Bohemia. This family was related to my husband whose surname was Weinreich. Later I heard they were in Lety where most of them died. We were all Sinti. We used to be all over Germany and Bohemia but now we are no more except for about 16 families who have escaped to Germany, and a few scattered around the Czech lands.

The Slovaks were very nice to us. They knew very well that we had escaped from the Czechs so they helped us. We were selling our things, cloth, clothes, horses, nobody bothered us. We traveled from Bratislava to Trnava, Nitra, Topoľčany, Piešťany. My husband originally came from Topoľčany, but we traveled the whole country without problems. We always slept in our wagons at night. We parked near the woods and cooked our dinner outside. No one bothered us. There were four or five families with us all the time, four or five wagons. We were all related.

At the end of 1945 we came back to the Czech lands. One of my brothers survived Auschwitz. He was twelve years old but so skinny I didn't recognize him. We found him in Zábřeh by Olomouc and he told us what had happened to our clan. I also found a sister-in-law had survived but lost her husband, her daughter, her parents and all her brothers and sisters.

Zábřeh by Olomouc became a center for Romanies returning from the war. It became our information center. There we found out what happened to all our people. Everyone in Moravia who had lost contact with their families during the war took their wagons and headed for Zábřeh.

My uncle also returned from Auschwitz to Zábřeh. He took care of my brother until we arrived. Every Sinti who survived made his way to Zábřeh. But very few of our people survived.

We were very leery of the Czechs after the war. We no longer trusted them. Sometimes there were fights but normally we couldn't say anything, we had to be quiet. Otherwise, we would be arrested. What could we do? We wanted to claw out their eyes, seek revenge against these people who had taken our loved ones away but what could we do? When someone told a Czech they were worse than Hitler, that Gypsy was arrested and their family broken up again. We couldn't read or write, we couldn't make a formal complaint.

All we have left are our photos. Every night I light a candle for my parents. Now the newspapers say we can ask for compensation but when I go to the office they say I don't have a right to compensation because I was over eighteen when my parents died. I have no right to compensation although I lost all my family.

When anyone in our clan dies, he is taken to Zábřeh. It is our last resting place for our family. If someone dies in Germany their body is brought back to Zábřeh, no matter how many years they have lived away. Zábřeh is where our ancestors came from. Their bodies are there, so our bodies must be there. I live now in Prague but when I die my body will be taken to Zábřeh. Life was not easy there but we will always return.

Most of our clan is in Germany today. There is no discrimination there. Everyone can get a job. We can live like human beings there. But some of us can't afford to live.

If you are white, you can also survive in the Czech Republic. But if you are dark you have no chance. It is like 1933 in Germany. The people here support these kind of things against us like the German public did against the Jews. It is very sad what is happening today in the Czech Republic. The white people want to renew the fascist system like in the 1930s. We know how many people died as a result of that system. I am sure they want to have a pure race again. But this time it's in the Czech Republic, not Germany.[2]

My grandson was beaten two weeks ago on his way to school by skinheads. His nose was broken. Seven of them attacked him. He is fourteen years old. His parents went to the police after taking him to the hospital. But no one was arrested. The police just laughed at us.

We do not want to leave this country because our ancestors are buried here. This was their home. This is our home. We will never leave, that is why they are killing us. They want us to leave but some of us will never leave. We are determined to be buried here with our ancestors.

Our children today have lost their original language and their traditions.[3] If the communists hadn't taken our wagons and horses in the 1950s we would still be traveling.

Gisela Burianska was in Lety. She was 74 when she died a few months ago. It's a pity you didn't interview her. She told my sister-in-law how her sister and baby were murdered in Lety. Gisela had five daughters but I don't know where they live today. They all married non-Romanies. They don't want to suffer like Gypsies anymore.

(1) At this point her nephew, visiting from Germany, interrupted the interview, saying: "Tell them the truth. Tell them the truth about Gypsies – how you taught us to steal. How we weren't a real Gypsy unless we stole."

She replied: "What are you talking about? Everybody steals, not just Gypsies."
(2) "Now you're telling the truth," her nephew said.
(3) Her nephew interrupted again, exclaiming that too many Gypsies were still stealing, still following the old ways.

Ladislav Stokinger

I had no father. My mother's name was Růžena Stokingerová. I was born in Prague on 3 March 1930. I had two sisters, Josepha and Marie who died recently. My brothers were Karel, Jiří, and Jan. My mother died in Lety from typhus. Her second husband Hynek Vrba was sent to another concentration camp and died there. Before the concentration camps, he worked in the forest as lumberjack or hauling out logs with a horse.

The Czech police came to our house sometime in the summer of 1942. They caught us at home in Plavsko and sent us to Budweis. All the people were collected there before being sent to Lety. We were taken by train to Mirovice and then by truck to Lety, arriving there on 3 August.

Before we arrived, there was a work camp at Lety for some criminals, some delinquents. My first day at the camp, the guards beat me. I was twelve years old.

There were two big barracks for kids and little wooden cottages for four or five people each. I don't know how many prisoners were in Lety, but there were a lot.

There were Czech policemen but the commander was German. In the end there were capos from Poland.

The food was nothing but water from cooking red cabbage. Sometimes a piece of bread. That's why we died of typhus. We had nothing to eat.

I was in the barracks with the kids. I got some kind of clothes but not working clothes because I was only twelve. We had to work on the tomato harvest. The rows were a kilometer long. There was a long line of kids picking these tomatoes. I can't tell you how many were working there because my only desire was to escape. That's all I ever thought about.

The guards beat everybody. Whoever came in their way they beat with their truncheons. There was such a hunger there that whenever any prisoner saw a rat they killed it and ate it on the spot. The guards also hung up inmates on a post and let them hang there until they died. Only a very few survived the execution post.

Many times an inmate would tell the guards that a person stole a piece of bread from him. Then the guards would hang that person until he was dead.

The first chance I saw that I could get away I took off. About half a year after being in Lety, I ran away with Josef Vrba and we took the train to Prague. We went without a ticket. Nobody ever noticed us. We had no shoes but no one paid any attention. Josef was my age and was from Prague so we went there. He had an uncle by the name of Kocek. His uncle told someone about us so we were taken to a children's home. We were there for three months before the police came and took us back to Lety. They were always Czech police who got us. They were worse than the Germans.

My mother was still alive when I got back to the camp but they wouldn't let me see her. I was put into a Gypsy wagon in chains with Josef. We couldn't move. Every time a guard came by the wagon he would beat us. We were held down with iron balls. Every time one of us had to go to the toilet the other had to come along. We were kept for half a year in this wagon in chains.

I saw guards beat people to death every day. Later these Polish capos made prisoners do knee bends holding out their arms with a wooden stick on top of their hands. If they drop the stick, the guards beat them.

Štěrba was the deputy commander, a small man from Písek. He was a bad one. He managed all of this. He was always beating people, beating them to death. There were many bad guards. I remember Baloun. He had a red nose and went around the barracks beating people. Hovorka was another bad one.

There were some girls sent from Prague who had to sew. The guards went and made love with them when they wanted, I think in barracks no. 6 or barracks no. 4. I believe those girls died there in Lety. These girls weren't Gypsies. We thought they were prostitutes. They had to go every night with the guards.

I didn't see the guards kill any kids. The dying was so quick. I was standing there once and I had four dead bodies around me just like that.

There was a woman called Maria Turinová. She lost nine kids at Lety. They said they died of typhus. But those kids looked like the kids you see now on TV from Africa. I think they starved to death.

There was a Gypsy there called Serynek who was a doctor.

A German woman rescued me. She was sent there as a punishment and was in charge of all the women. She went with the women like a capo to the stone quarry. She spoke Czech but I can't remember her name. Whenever she had the chance, she brought me some food when I was in the wagon in chains.

Once three German officials came to Lety. All the prisoners had to stand in a row. These Germans selected people for the transport. These Germans took me and my sister aside and we weren't sent on the transport. They put their hands on the back of our necks to find something there about our race. I don't know what we had that was different from the Gypsies.

Poelderl was in charge of the dead bodies. He was a prisoner but he was allowed to go by horse to get wood and carry the dead bodies away. His wife was cooking for the commander and the policemen. His wife's name was Vanda. Poelderl's name was Jan, Honza.

There was a lake and Poelderl carried the dead bodies to the forest by the corner of the lake and buried them there in mass graves. I never heard of a gas chamber at Lety.

The women who were in charge of the kids were these circus people. They ate all the food that was for the kids and the kids had no food. The women went for walks with the kids. They were never afraid that the kids would run away.

No one cared when someone was sick in the camp. I never saw any doctors.

There were many Gypsy wagons there because the Gypsies were sent there with all their things. Half the wagons were used to store dead bodies until they could be buried, the other half were used as punishment cells where prisoners were put in ball and chain.

My father was a circus man but my mother was no Gypsy. My

stepfather traveled around the country sharpening knives and scissors. In 1939 there was a new law to stop people from traveling so from that time on he worked in the woods. He was executed in another concentration camp in 1942. He was detained before we were sent to Lety. Before we went to Lety we got his clothes back with a note saying he had been executed.

The prisoners worked in the stone quarry and in the forest. My mother mainly worked in the stone quarry.

I was lucky. There were others who got beaten to death.

I was never told why we were sent to Lety. We weren't Gypsies.

When the camp was closed, all the kids without parents were sent to their hometown or to an orphanage. My younger brother Karel was sent to an orphanage while I was sent to my hometown of Plavsko where a farmer adopted me.

In the end there were more than a hundred prisoners who were sent home. Moláček, Vrba, Studený, Dubský.

The guards did very bad things at Lety, but they were never punished for that after the war.

The only problem I had after the war was cursing the communists. For that they put me in jail for sixteen years. I was sent to Ostrov, then to a uranium mine called Jachymov. There I found this Sterba as a guard again. This labor camp in Jáchymov was worse than Lety. If there had not been Russian commanders in Jachymov, the Czechs would have killed all of us. The camp was called Nikolaj and this was almost an extermination camp. The Czech guards could kill prisoners only when they tried to escape. So the guards would take the prisoner's cap and thrown it on the fence, then order the prisoner to retrieve it. When he did, they shot him.

Jehovah's Witnesses had to stand all night naked between the wire fences. Various people were there, conscientious objectors, all kinds of people. When there was any kind of suspicion they let you stand outside in the yard in very light clothing and you had to wait there, three or four hours until they found you were innocent. Again, it was our people who did this to us, Czech guards.

In Jachymov some of the prisoners attacked a guard and threw him down a mine shaft then escaped. So the guards took other prisoners and shot them, seven or eight. For three days we had to parade around these bodies, spitting on the prisoners. We were only kept two years in one camp, then we were sent to another camp.

I was in so many camps, I can't remember all the names. But I can remember all of the commanders.

I was detained in 1949 and was one of the first prisoners in Jáchymov. I was in Příbram in the uranium mines there too, and in many other prisons.

I tried to escape the country in 1949 and was caught at the border. That began my journey to all these camps.

In 1961 I was released from my last camp, then I went to work in the forest.

I tried to get compensation for being in Lety, for my mother dying in Lety while I was a minor, but I got nothing. I wrote and got a certificate that I was in Lety but they wouldn't count the time I was away from the camp when I escaped. Here you see it! The government sent me a letter saying I didn't qualify for compensation because I was in Lety for less than three months. At least the communists gave me 10,000 crowns for being in jail for sixteen years. They also increased my pension by 1,200 crowns. But for Lety I got nothing.

Today it is a battle for food again. The government increases your pension by 400 crowns but at the same time they put up the water bill by 800 crowns.

I will never forget Lety. I was there as a boy so I tried to take it as a piece of fun but it was bad, very bad. I tried not to let it enter my head, but the time there was bad. The worst thing for me was that the guards were Czech. The Czechs were doing these bad things to their own people. If the other prisoners had not given me some food, I would have died too. The worst people in Lety were the Czech guards. The worst in Jachymov were the Slovak guards.

Marie Vrbová

My father, Josef Vrba, was a fisherman. He worked on the carp ponds. My grandfather was the miller in Pacov. We were living in

Plavsko, county Jindřichův Hradec, when we were arrested on 3 August 1942.

About midnight the Czech police arrived with a big truck. There were five or six of them. The police told us we were under arrest and that they were taking us to a labor camp called Lety by Písek. We were thirteen people, living in our house: my grandparents, my parents, and also my brother Josef and two sisters Antonie and Eva, my cousin Karl, and his brothers Jan, Jiří, and his sisters Marie and Josefa and their mother.

My grandfather, Karl's mother, and my sisters Antonie and Eva all died in Lety from typhus according to the guards, but I don't believe it. We were always being beaten with truncheons. People were beaten so badly that there were always deaths. You never knew when someone would be killed. You went out to work in the morning. When you can back you heard people were dead. Our people weren't sick, but when we came back from work several more would be dead. You don't get typhus and die that quickly do you?

It was the beatings and the hangings that killed most of the people. If somebody tried to escape and the guards caught them, there was an execution post where people were hung by their hands until they died. Men, women, children, it made no difference. They got no food, no water, they just hung there with their hands tied behind their backs, strung up until they died.

When we arrived at Lety our heads were shaved. Our clothes were taken from us and we got some bad clothes with stripes. At first I thought it was going to be a nice camp. There were ducks on the lake. But later we had to wash in that lake where people were drowned, after the guards ate all the ducks.

I remember when we were standing in a long line for breakfast, how many times my mother and father were beaten because they gave us children their breakfast, their bread. My father was supposed to have some privileges because in the camp he was the shoemaker for the guards. But they still beat him, just like everyone else.

The guards used their dogs, big black German shepherds, to make us run out of the camp in the morning to work, and also at night to get us back in quickly.

My mother used to work in the room with the doctor. She had to clean this room. She saw many children, and older men and women, get these injections straight into their heart. After that, these people were taken to another place to die. Then the guards removed their gold teeth and had the prisoners take their bodies to a big pit.

I can't believe there is a pig farm there today. You must be lying to me. Only animals would do such a thing. Do you know how many bodies are buried at Lety? Thousands. You must be lying to me. No human being would build a pig farm where so many people are buried. We never heard of a memorial service there. We never received a letter.

The guards were very bad to us at Lety. There were only Czech guards so we couldn't understand why they were so bad to their own people. We weren't Gypsies. I know they called it a Gypsy camp, but we weren't Gypsies. Look at our skin. We are white. Why were we sent to Lety?

I remember a guard by the name of Hejduk. My mother told me he was in charge of the guards. If he didn't like someone he sent them to Auschwitz on the next transport, or had them beaten to death. He was the worst man in the camp, that's why I've never forgotten his name.

The food was terrible. We got some red cabbage or beets, but both were covered in dirt, in mud. The water was always brown. There was a small lake, a pond, that was where we got our drinking water. But many times we didn't even have that to drink. We were always hungry, always thirsty.

Karl and I were both sick so my mother went for water. She pleaded with the policemen to let her get some water from the lake for us. For this he beat her. She got a bad beating just because she wanted water for us. We thought she was going to die. She couldn't move for two weeks. A Jewish doctor saved my mother. He was a prisoner too, but he helped save many people. He later lived in Votice but he died several years ago. He tried to do his best to find medicine for my mother.

When the guards discovered that a woman was pregnant, they took her away. We never saw those women again. They certainly never survived Lety. I heard they were rabbits for experiments but whatever, we never saw them again.

The children and the old people were the ones who died the most. Those were the people who suffered the most. The Czech commander didn't want kids or old people in the camp.

My mother told me that there was a special room with a big glass window to kill people. These people were locked up there with no water. They were crammed in like sardines. Most of them suffocated in that room. If you survived, you were beaten to death.

There were just too many people in the camp, the guards wanted to get rid of them. The extra food they didn't have to give to the dead prisoners, the guards took home to their own families. We always saw them leaving the camp with food under their jackets. The guards also took watches, money, anything of value from the prisoners.

Perhaps the worst thing that happened at Lety was how the guards abused the women. Whenever a new transport brought new prisoners, the men, women, and children were separated. The women were then separated for a second time, putting all the good-looking women in one block for the guards to use. When the guards had enough of these special women, they killed them. This is what my mother told me. I am not lying. I know what my mother told me. You can't imagine the many different kinds of horrors that happened at Lety.

We hardly ever saw my mother in the camp. My uncle and aunt died early, shortly after we arrived. We were all alone for such a long time. It was terrible.

Please, I can't get over what you told me about a pig farm being there. Please tell me it's not true. You can't build a pig farm where so many people are buried.[1]

Nobody can give back the lives of our families, at least they could let them rest in peace. How can they rest in peace with a pig farm over them?

I got 23,000 crowns compensation. It took me two years to get this. They sent me back and forth from office to office always wanting more documentation, more information. And what, for what? They made us beg for our compensation. I shouldn't have taken it. But I thought my children, my grandchildren, would benefit.

Today I would like to find these guards and do the same thing to them that they did to our people. Where is justice? There is no justice in this country.

My poor mother, she died four years ago. She could have told you so much more. I was so young in Lety. Today you can't speak about Lety because no one believes you. It took my mother five years to recover from her nightmares. She always remembered the first day when we all arrived together. She was always crying for my two sisters who died there. It was terrible for my mother the rest of her life.

I visited the Terezín concentration camp after the war as a tourist. When I got there, I started to shake, I could not walk. I don't know what happened to my body. The people I was with took me outside. I couldn't breathe. It reminded me so much of Lety. When I visited the Terezín camp, I had this feeling when I entered the gate that it would be locked forever behind me. I had to run away. This was about 1948.

In 1970 some friends invited me to visit Auschwitz, but I couldn't go. Never again do I want to go near such a camp. You can't believe what happened at Lety, what happened to my relatives. I can't even watch these things on TV. Just the mention of a program on a concentration camp makes me break out into a sweat. I can't sleep that night. I was just a child at Lety. Think about what my poor mother went through.

When we had to get papers for our compensation, the Germans were very good. They had their papers in order and attended to us very quickly. We did not suffer waiting. But here in the Czech Republic it was humiliating to ask for our papers and to wait and to be treated as if we were robbing the state of all their gold. I tell you it was terrible trying to get some compensation from the Czechs.

My mother planted two small trees at Lety for my two sisters who died there. About 1950 she went there and planted two fir trees, the kind you have for Christmas. I don't know if they are still there. If what you say about the pig farm is true, I suppose they are gone. Oh my God!

You know I still have bad dreams about carrying those stones at Lety. Can you imagine, I am 62 years old and I still have bad dreams about carrying those stones. Going out the gate in the morning to work in the quarry and coming back at night. I still see that gate. I still feel the weight of those stones.

I don't want to talk about Lety anymore. Why didn't you come here four years ago when my mother was still alive?

(1) She broke into tears at this point, and sobbed for several minutes.

V. V.

You want to know about Lety? Let me tell you, I will never forget the day my grandmother pleaded with me to bring her some water from the rain barrel; she was lying on top of this pile of dead bodies, dying. She called my name but I couldn't go to her. The guards would have beaten me to death. That's what I can tell you about Lety. There were dead bodies all over the place. You couldn't walk without stepping over dead bodies.

Me? I was born on 9 January 1927 in Vidhostice (Louny). My parents were Arnoštka and Bohuslav Šmíd. My father worked in Přeštice cutting wood in the forest, and my mother was a housewife because there were nine of us, nine children. Today the only ones alive are: Václav, Arnoštka, Helena and me.

When we were arrested in 1942, we were living in Nezdice by Přeštice. On a Saturday morning the Czech police came to pick me up while I was working as a kid in a factory. They didn't even let me change my clothes. They were Czech policemen from Přeštice. They took me to Přeštice where my whole family (parents, grandparents, brothers and sisters) were waiting for me; they had been picked up earlier. I can remember that three other families were also there. All of us slept that night in the town's sports hall. In the morning the police put us on a train in pig wagons and took us directly to Lety. The other families with us were all our cousins.

I remember simple wooden houses that were built in a square, with simple beds inside. In front of the gate were some big houses for the guards. Even today I don't know why we were taken there. No one has ever told me. My mother was Slovak. My father sometimes used to trade with horses. When we entered, I saw a sign over the gate: Gypsy Camp.

The first day we had to stand in line to get shaved, then separated. There were many white prisoners in the camp, not just Gypsies. There were also many dark Gypsies. We called them Gypsies of the Forest. Their women all wore long skirts. They were mean people; they always beat the white prisoners. I never found out why we were there. We weren't Gypsies or Svetskys.

We wore used clothes from the Czech army. We always had fleas. I was always picking them off my clothes.

I worked in the stone quarry. My father worked next to the kitchen making coffins. I remember after they ran out of coffins they put people in mass graves in the forest.

In the morning we got only black coffee and a small piece of bread; at midday some potatoes, or soup with pieces of cabbage swimming in water; they didn't even wash the cabbage that came from the field. Many times there were worms and dirt in our food. For supper we got only coffee or some watery soup. Food that arrived from relatives was taken by the guards, unpacked and thrown into big cooking pots and mixed up and then we got this to eat. Only men worked in the kitchen. The hunger was terrible.

Sometimes women were taken to the toilets to clean out the pits then carry the baskets full of their shit to the fields. A lot of women and children were killed in those toilets, thrown into those pits.

We were all beaten. I was beaten on my back and couldn't walk for fourteen days. People were beaten to death. Some prisoners came and took away the dead bodies every day. They took them away on little wagons to the mass graves in the forest, or to Mirovice and buried them next to the wall, also in mass graves.

All of my brothers and sisters were small children in Lety. We were not working because we were so young. Once I escaped with two boys but after crawling through a hole in the fence I got scared and went back. The two boys were caught a week later and brought back to the camp in chains. They were kept for two days in a small hut. A lot of people tried to escape. They all had to pay for that when they got caught.

The young women told me they didn't get their monthly periods in Lety; I heard that something was put into the food. They never told me they were molested.

Most of the children were always covered in blue bruises from the daily beatings. I remember children eating their own skins they got so hungry. People smuggled in lettuce from the fields; we also ate worms we were so hungry. I wasn't in the camp very long, but my experience was terrible.[1]

Sometimes Germans came to the camp but I don't know what they did there. All the guards in the camp were Czech. There was a very short guard who hit me on the back. He was always smoking a pipe. He slipped on the ice once when I was walking by and he attacked me as if it was my fault. Life wasn't very important there. You killed or got killed. I only remember the name Hejduk, but I can't tell you why.

It was very cold in the winter time; I can't remember any heat in our wooden barracks. We only received some blankets to sleep in.

There were some doctors living in a house by the guards but I don't remember their names. My parents knew more about the camp but they don't live anymore.

Women who gave birth to their babies, all of these babies died after a short time. I don't know why. Most of the deaths that I remember were children.

We were sent to the lake to wash ourselves when the weather was nice. If the weather was bad, we didn't get to wash.

In the fall I was taken with other kids my age to Čimelice to work on a farm and sleep in the hay. Life was better outside the camp. We got more to eat. The farmers cooked for us, we had enough food when we worked for them. The farmers' wives were very good to us.

When we returned to camp, I got typhus. There were two big rain barrels and by drinking the water from those barrels we all got typhus. During the typhus epidemic we children were thrown out of our beds; some children were taken away and I never saw them again. After I got typhus, I was unconscious for a long time. I can't remember anything about the camp from that time on.

I had little blue spots over my whole body; the doctor put some orange cream on my body that healed the sickness.

I had horrible dreams when I was in the hospital. I saw myself with a burned red neck and face; after I was released from Lety I had no more nightmares. I never look at TV if there is violence. I have seen enough violence in my life.

My paternal uncle Josef Šmíd paid a high amount of money for us to be released from the camp. I remember when we received the letter saying we were going to be released; I was in the hospital suffering from typhus.

When I was released from the hospital, I went by train to Přeštice. There I went straight to the police station; I wanted to register that I was again a resident of Příbram. The police threw me out with my papers saying they didn't want to get typhus from me.

I went to a friend's house and stayed there for a while until I started to work on a farm. I had to look after 17 cows every day. After three months my parents and brothers and sisters returned from Lety. My paternal grandmother died in Lety and also some cousins.

Our life started again in our home where we lived before we were taken to Lety. Everything had to be bought again, starting with the furniture because it was all sold when we were taken to Lety.

I once read a book about Lety. Many of the families had their names in that book. On the first page was a photo of my father. Some woman two kilometers from here had the book. She was a pure Gypsy.

My father might have been a Svetsky. My paternal grandfather used to make horse bridles. In the summer they always traveled in a horse and wagon. My parents also traveled in the summer. All of us were born in different places because our parents were traveling. My father died about fifteen years ago; my mother twelve years ago.

I thought I would get some compensation for being in Lety; I was in Lety from 3 August 1942 until 12 March 1943. I applied in 1995, but until now (May 1996) I have received nothing. The Ministry of Defense sends me postcards from time to time telling me to be patient.

I don't know any Lety survivors, only my own family. We shouldn't have been in Lety. I don't know why we were there. My uncle got us out, but I never learned how much he paid.

(1) She cried at this point, and for several minutes we had to wait before continuing the oral history.

Karel Vrba

I cannot remember a lot, but I will tell you what I know. I was born on 3 April 1913, in Zbelitov, county Písek. My mother was Karolína Havlíčková, my father Vojtěch Vrba.

At that time there was a lot of unemployment. We lived in a small village called Plavsko, working in the fields. We never traveled. My parents didn't have any horses, no wagon. All of us, all my brothers and sisters, knew how to read and write. We all went to school. My sisters were Tereza, Anna and Karolína; my brothers were Josef, Hynek, Antonín and Jan. Josef and Hynek died in Dachau. Antonín died only a few years ago. Jan is in a hospital now in Jihlava. He can't talk anymore.

The Czech police came to pick us up one morning about eleven o'clock.[1] The police took us to České Budějovice by trucks that were waiting outside. We were allowed to take only a few clothes with us and some linen. The rest of our things we had to leave in Plavsko.

The families Pelder and Dubský were already in the trucks waiting for us. My grandmother and grandfather were also arrested with us.[2]

In České Budějovice we had to wait a short time before being taken directly to Mirovice. There were some other families already waiting at the train station. In Mirovice there were other trucks waiting to take us to Lety.

We were arrested for racial reasons. My mother and father were both white, but the Czech police thought we were Gypsies. We were never Gypsies, and that is why later we were released because there in Lety they found out that we were not Gypsies.

The first thing I saw at Lety was a camp of wooden huts full of people. I had never seen such a thing before.

We immediately were separated, the children from the parents. That's why my little daughter died; she was only six months old. Two weeks after we arrived, I was told she died of typhus.[3] My father also died of typhus in Lety a short time after we got there.[4]

We wore old army surplus clothes. Everything we brought into camp was put in storage. There was a lot of dirt in the camp.

For lunch we usually got red cabbage cooked in water. For breakfast black coffee; for supper the same thing we had for lunch. Sometimes we got a few potatoes.

There was a German director of the camp.[5] All the guards were Czech. I remember Hejduk. He was a very bad man.

There were two former Gypsy wagons used to store dead bodies. I can remember that at least four or five dead children were brought to these wagons every day. Older people were brought to these wagons every day too.

The bodies were taken to Mirovice to be buried until there was no more room, then they were buried in mass graves in the forest behind the camp. Most of the people died because of hunger. The little children ate anything they could find. That's probably how they got typhus.

I can't remember anyone who got beaten to death by the guards. They were guards from the Protectorate; they did their job; I never saw anyone beaten to death.

There was no torture, no one was hung up. It was a collecting camp where people were brought from other camps or released. Most of the women worked at the stone quarry; others built the road going around the camp. Some men worked in the forest cutting trees.

I was working three weeks in the kitchen until I got typhus. There were no women in the kitchen. All the cooks were men. The women were in charge of taking care of the children. There was a small manufacturing hall. I was in charge of making shoes. The women sewed. It was a small business there.

Before the typhus epidemic broke out, we were all taken to the lake to wash. We stopped going there because the typhus broke out. Nothing happened at the latrines.

We didn't have a good time at the camp, but I can't remember any cruelty there. No women were abused there. I am positive that no women had to sleep with the guards. Most of the guards were old men. I can't remember any young guards there.[6] The guards treated us nicely. They didn't hit anyone.

Some prisoners in the camp had money but there was nothing to buy. I don't know anyone who bought their way out. All those who managed to leave were released because they didn't belong there, they weren't Gypsies.

Nobody escaped from the camp, I can't remember anyone who

ever even tried. The guards would have shot them right away. Two German capos were brought from another camp to Lety. These two tried to escape but the guards caught them and shot them.

My wife had beautiful long hair but they shaved it off after typhus broke out. They told us we could get typhus from fleas so everyone had to have their heads shaved during the epidemic.

Having typhus was my worst experience at Lety. Everyone in our family got typhus in Lety. My father died of it. I remember Dr. Bohin. He saved my life. I was lying there sick and he said to my wife, "I will try to find something to help him." He was a Jew. He gave me an injection into the bottom of my foot and saved me. He was the only doctor there. He tried to help everyone but there were too many prisoners. He couldn't save us all. He cured a lot of people. I don't know how. He had no medicine, so I don't know how the poor man saved so many of us. He came to the camp just before typhus broke out. He was our savior. I never saw him after Lety. I know he lived in Prague because some of my relatives used to see him there. The father and mother of my wife used to go and see him in Prague. I believe he had a big funeral with a lot of people in attendance. Everyone loved him.

My wife told me afterwards that during the six weeks of my illness I did not speak a word. I said nothing. Even today I can remember nothing of that time. My wife got typhus shortly before I got it but she was cured after a short time. They say the cure takes about six weeks.

I remember Bohuslav Šmíd. He made the coffins. I don't remember how many people died, but it was a lot. Most of the people who died in Lety were people who lived in the forests. They weren't from any villages. Their deaths weren't registered anywhere. Bohuslav couldn't make the coffins fast enough after typhus broke out. He only had a few pieces of wood anyway. In the end they buried everyone in the forest without coffins.

There were three prostitutes brought from Prague to the camp. They were in charge of the sewing. Later one of them married a guard from Mirovice.

Near the end another director was brought from Hodonín. After he arrived, life in Lety changed. He brought food for the children for Christmas.

It is easy for the government today to say that not so many people died in Lety because no one knew they were there. Many, many Gypsies were in Lety, people who lived in the forests, people who were never registered anywhere. They were brought to the camp without anyone knowing about them. They all died in Lety. If the government says only 327 died in Lety, they are not telling the truth. I remember four and five people sleeping in one bed. Thousands were there. Most of them were buried in the woods.

I remember that the newborn babies seldom lived. Their life was very short after birth. Their births weren't registered; the guards could do with them what they wanted.

I had a cousin Jan Vrba die in Lety, also from typhus.

I never had any bad dreams after I got out of Lety. I think about Lety often these days, in the evening, but I've never had any nightmares.

When we left Lety our clothes were given back to us. But when we got back to Plavsko we had to borrow knifes and forks to eat. We had nothing. We found nothing inside our home. Everything had been stolen.

When I was released from the camp, I worked two years in Pribras drying peat for fuel. We moved here from Plavsko in 1947. We built this home here. We live a very quiet life here, but in the big cities I hear there are problems with racism. My son has dark skin, but he has no problems here. White people should show more respect to Gypsies. We all have clean homes. The skinheads think they can rule the world because they have shaved heads and follow a racial policy.

I have a photo of us at Lety. A guard took this of us when we were released. I don't remember his name, but I received this photo in 1987 from my brother Jan.

We arrived in Lety on the 10 August 1942 and we were there until the 23 May 1943. Two months ago I received 23,000 crowns for being in Lety. I asked for compensation for my wife but I got nothing.

The memorial that is now at Lety, they should have put it there a long time ago. People are talking a lot about Auschwitz and Dachau today because so many were killed there. No one wants to remember a little Gypsy camp in the Czech Republic.

(1) It was 3 August 1942.
(2) Josef Vrba born in 1862 was sent from Lety to Auschwitz on 2 December 1942. There is no record about his wife.
(3) Františka Vrbová died on 21 August 1942, eighteen days after they arrived in camp. The first reported case of typhus at Lety did not occur until December.
(4) Vojtěch Vrba died on 21 January 1943 at the height of the typhus epidemic in Lety. He was seventy-three years old.
(5) The commander of the camp was Josef Janovský, a Czech police captain. He liked to speak German, tried to make his men learn German, and insisted on being saluted in the German manner.
(6) The average age of the 91 guards at Lety was 35 years old.

Terezie Hubená

I was born eighty-eight years ago in Písek on 29 November 1908. My parents were Vojtěch Vrba[1] and Karolína Havlíčková.[2] I don't remember what my father did, what was his profession. I had one brother, Antonín.[3] He went to Lety with my parents, but I never saw him there. I don't know what happened to him. I hope he is still alive.

My husband was working in a factory in Ledenice when the Czech police came to our home to arrest him.[4] They didn't say why they wanted him. A day later they returned and arrested me and my five children. They took us straight to Lety.

I remember that first day in the camp very well, because the first thing they did was cut our hair.[5] They even cut the hair of my six-week-old son, Honza. He was my youngest. His name was Honza, Jan. He was in good health, he had never been ill a day in his life, but eight days after arriving in Lety he was dead.[6] They told me he died of typhus.[7]

My job at the camp was to look after the children. They weren't supposed to play or laugh. The guards gave me very strict orders about keeping the children quiet. But how can you have so many children and not let them play and laugh? The guards beat me many times with the truncheon because of this. How many times? I cannot count that far.

I don't remember the names of any of the guards. That was too long ago. I remember the director of the camp. He was always telling us: "One road brought you here, the next one takes you to heaven."

The food was awful. We only got red cabbage with dirt. They boiled it in some brown water. It was tasteless. We gave better food to our pigs.

I tried to save some bread and a bit of water for the children but when the guards saw me giving this to them I got another beating. The beatings were terrible in the camp. The guards beat you for every little thing. When you stood in line for breakfast you could not move or speak. One word, the slightest movement, and the guards were on top of you, beating you, sometimes to death.

While I was at Lety I got a letter from the Czech police in České Budějovice to inform me that they had hanged my husband. No reason was given. I didn't tell our children until after the war was over. I don't know why he was hanged. I've never been able to find out.

Lety was supposed to be a camp for Gypsies, but we weren't Gypsies. We were all white, everyone in my family. Why we were sent to Lety, I don't know. Perhaps it was my fault. I made linen tablecloths in those days and went door to door selling them like the Gypsies. We had to make some extra money. We had five children. I guess someone told the police we lived like Gypsies, that I made my living working like a Gypsy. That's the only reason I can think of, why they sent us to Lety.

My daughters (Karolína, Zdenka, Milada, Antonie) all survived Lety. My mother too.[8] My father and my son Honza died there.[9] I don't know what my father died of. I seldom saw him there. He was an old man already but he was in good health. They never told me what he died of. I just heard they threw him in the mass grave, a big pit they had behind the camp.

The guards did many cruel things to people in Lety. They had this execution post in the camp. Sometimes we had to watch while they hung a person up. They would tie his hands behind his back, then haul him up with a cable as they turned a wheel. Not many people survived the execution post.

Were women abused at Lety? I don't want to talk about it.

My children had to work in the fields, in nearby farms, collecting sugar beets. I think they got some extra food that way. It wasn't given to them. They had to steal it. I don't know if they were ever beaten. We don't talk about Lety at home. We never talk about those times.

I got typhus in Lety. They sent me to a hospital in Písek.[10] My daughters and my mother never got typhus. I was the only one.

My worst experience in Lety was seeing the children die of starvation. I had to look after them but there was nothing I could do for them. If someone complained, they were killed.

How do I live? I get a pension, 4,500 crowns a month. I never got any compensation for being in Lety. Is there such a thing? I never heard about it.

Of course, I have nightmares about Lety. I'm eighty-eight years old but there are some things you never forget. My memory isn't very good these days. I can't even remember who our president is. Havel? See, I knew, but sometimes I can't remember right away. Except for Lety. That's a place I will never forget. But I don't want to talk about it anymore. Those are bad memories. I was there with all my children. Poor Honza.

(1) Born 31 October 1879 in Horní Pěna (Jindřichův Hradec).
(2) Born 23 November 1879 in Nicov (Prachatice).
(3) Born 25 May 1906 Radobytce (Písek). Sent from Lety to Auschwitz on 4 May 1943.
(4) County České Budějovice.
(5) 3 August 1942.
(6) Jan Hubený was born 30 June 1942 and died in the Lety camp on 16 August 1942.
(7) No case of typhus had been reported yet; the first case of typhus according to the official report was 13 December 1942.
(8) They were set free on 27 May 1943 with the last 150 prisoners because they were white.
(9) Vojtěch Vrba died in the Lety camp on 21 January 1943.
(10) She was sent to Písek hospital on 7 March 1943, and later released with her mother and daughters from the Lety camp on 27 May 1943.

V. R.

I don't really want to talk to you. I don't want to talk about those times. I have a bad heart. I'll tell you a few things but you can't record what I am going to say. You can't come into my home. We can talk here, out in the street.

I was born in 1927. My parents were Čeněk and Františka. I had fourteen brothers and sisters. My parents and eleven of my brothers and sisters died in Lety.

I was twelve years old when I was in Lety. I remember the director of the camp. He was a police captain. He was a son-of-a--bitch. No, I don't remember his name but he and the guards were all sons-of-a-bitch. There were no Germans there, just those Czech sons-of-a-bitch.

The food was only for the guards. They had everything: meat, butter, eggs, bread. The food for the prisoners they kept in a warehouse. They gave us so little that I remember once they had to destroy some of the food in the warehouse because it got bad from being there too long. People died of hunger in Lety, especially the children. There was food. We just didn't get it.

Jesus Maria, there was never a moment when someone wasn't being beaten. People were beaten so badly they died. Every day.

New born babies seldom survived. I don't know why. I don't think there was any food for new born babies. The mothers weren't allowed to have them because they had to work. If the treatment had been better, I'm sure not so many people would have died.

We all had to wash together in the lake, completely nude: men, women and children. That wasn't our custom. Some people were more upset about that than about not getting enough to eat.

The director of the camp was such a son-of-a-bitch that I heard someone shot him after the war. No, I don't remember his name, but I'm sure someone shot him.

Another bastard was Pešck. He was the guard in charge of the kitchen. He beat a lot of people, a lot of people died of his beatings.

I had to work in the stone quarry. It was very hard work. I was only a child. We didn't have enough food to work so hard. Even the women and the young girls had to work in the stone quarry. No matter how hard you worked, you were still beaten.

I was in Lety eighteen months. Later I was sent to Auschwitz and then Buchenwald. In 1995, I got 73,000 crowns for being in the German camps. For Lety I got nothing. I was told that Lety wasn't a concentration camp so I had no right to claim anything for being there.

Under communism we had some peace. It wasn't a good life but they didn't beat us, they didn't allow anyone to kill us. But now under this new government we are being terrorized by the skinheads and no one is doing anything about it. In fact, I know this government is supporting all these attacks, supporting the skinheads to get rid of us. These things never happened before, except in Lety.

Antonín Vintr

I was born 30 March 1934 in Žebrák (Beroun). My father was Antonín Vintr, born in April 1913. He raised and sold horses. We were all born in the wagon; the wagon was our home for most of the year.

My mother Josefa Vintrová was born 8 July 1916 in Kralice na Hané (Prostějov) in Moravia.

My mother's parents had horses too and traveled around the country sharpening knives and scissors and selling horses. Her father raised horses and made most of his living selling these wonderful animals.

My eldest brother Karl was born in 1933, my sister Karolina in 1938 and my other brother Arnost in 1941.

We were with our wagons near Prague in Janonice when the Czech police came and arrested our whole clan in August 1942, including all our grandparents, aunts, uncles and cousins, about fifty members of our clan.

When the police arrived to arrest us, I remember my father went to the wagon and got his billfold that was full of paper money. He tried to bribe the police not to arrest our family. The police asked where my father got so much money; my father showed them his license that he had to travel and work, he said he was a business man who sold horses, textiles; he showed the police many rugs and tapestries we had to sell. My father told the police we had a home in Kyšice near Prague where we lived during the winter; he told them we only traveled in the warm months. But they arrested us and from just our wagon, they took a half kilo of gold mainly in coins, rings and earrings.

We were taken by bus from Prague directly to Lety, to the camp. The police took from my parents four horses and two wagons. I don't know what they did with them.

My mother's cousins, the Janosovskýs, had to drive to Lety with their horses and wagons accompanied by the police. Their wagons were put inside the camp and used to store dead bodies until they could be buried or burned.

We arrived in Lety on 5 August 1942 and were held there until 27 May 1943.

Our first day in Lety we were all separated, the men to their barracks, the children to theirs, the woman to another one.

I remember the first night we children cried for our parents until the guards threatened to kill us.

My father was a very strong man. He was white, as white as any Czech. No one could believe he was a Gypsy. In the morning we all had to line up for roll call. An announcement was made that anyone who could speak German was ordered to step forward. My mother could speak German fluently, but my father couldn't. Then they asked people with professions to step forward. My father could cook so he stepped forward. From that day on, he was the camp cook while my mother helped the doctor who spoke German. He was Jew from Auschwitz who volunteered to work at Lety to save his life.

All the prisoners had striped clothes but my parents didn't. My father was dressed in white pants, white jacket and white hat.

After two months the Czech police brought a German officer to Lety. He was the first German we had ever seen in the camp. All the white Gypsies which meant all my family were pulled aside. All the dark Gypsies were loaded onto trucks and taken to the train station in Mirovice. We heard later that they had been taken by train to a concentration camp in Poland.

Although my father had privileges in the camp because he was the cook for the guards, I wasn't allowed to live with him. I lived with my grandfather in his barracks.

The guards had wooden clubs about a meter long, thicker than a child's arm. They used these clubs or their truncheons to beat people. Every day I saw dead bodies being carried through the camp on stretchers after these beatings.

My uncle, Karl Janošovský, had the job of stacking up these dead bodies, until they could be carried by other Gypsies to the pit.

My father told a Czech policeman in the camp, please I need a favor. Can you find my gold and my money that the police took? If you can find this, I will give you half. The policeman told my father to forget about his gold, that the Germans already had it.

There were many children in the camp. We were always hungry. Many times we children escaped from the camp to eat grass. Although my father was a cook, there were also three other cooks so he could not steal food all the time because the other cooks also were taking food for their families. My father kept us alive but he couldn't keep us from getting hungry.

Look, I tell you one thing. About the beatings. There in that camp if you moved your eyes to the left or to the right, the guards might beat you for that. Many times I saw people beaten to death for no reason. The guards liked to beat the prisoner's feet because if you fell down they had the right to beat you to death.

My cousin Antonín Janošovský who was sixteen years old worked in the camp warehouse. He was stealing cans of food for us. The police caught him. They beat him until he couldn't stand anymore, then they tied his hands behind his back and with a wheel and pulley, hauled him up in the air where he hung for a whole day and a whole night until breakfast. I took him water in the morning before the guards came but they caught me. They beat me so badly that I could not walk for four days. My whole body was black and blue. If my father had not been the cook, they would have beaten me to death.

I never saw my cousin again until after the war. He told me my mother somehow saved him. This is probably why she was sent to Auschwitz despite my father's privileges. But my mother was also the only one in the family with dark skin. From Auschwitz my mother was sent to Buchenwald where she was released in May 1945.

As a child I wanted to go everywhere in the camp at Lety, seeing everything, listening to everything. So I saw a lot of things in the camp that other people didn't see because they had to work. I didn't really have a job in the camp because my father was a cook. All of us children had protection because my father cooked for the guards. The only job I had at Lety was to feed the guard dogs in the morning. Then I was free to run everywhere. That's why I saw so much at Lety, perhaps more than anyone else.

I don't remember the names of the guards, but I remember one of the guards, one of the worst. He had a mole in the center of his forehead. But to tell you the truth, I don't want to remember him. I might have nightmares again. Can I recognize the guards in this photo?

Oh my God, oh my God! That's the doctor my mother worked for; he liked my mother. And next to him is Janovský, the camp commander. His word was law. He was the worst! He shot the most people! He was always shooting someone!

I'm sorry I spit on your photo. I couldn't help myself. I'm sorry I'm crying. I guess I've ruined your photo with my spit and my tears. But really, that man Janovský, he was the worst man in the camp. The guard with the mole was bad,[1] but Janovský was the devil himself.

But all the guards were bad. They were afraid to lose their jobs so they always tried to out do each other in killing prisoners. It was as if they got a bonus for the number of people they killed. Everyone wanted to kill more than the other. In this way, all the guards were bad. There were no good guards in Lety.

Some guards abused the Romany women. But normally they didn't have to beat them for sex. More often than not, the women went voluntarily with the guards to protect their children, to get privileges for their families. We children, we talked about this a lot among ourselves; we couldn't understand it at that age. Our Romany culture, our traditions didn't allow our women to act this way. But now I can understand why they did these things.

I remember the guard with the mole in the center of his forehead, every morning at roll call he would go out on a balcony and point out a young woman or a young man and the guards would bring this person to his office. Those young people, we never saw again.

We had several German Gypsies in the camp who cooperated with the guards. To survive they took orders from the guards to beat us, their Czech cousins. The guards liked to see Gypsies killing

Gypsies. It was fun for them. Sometimes a Czech Gypsy would stand up to a German Gypsy, telling him he wasn't as strong as a Czech Gypsy. Then the guards would come over and shoot the Czech Gypsy right there on the spot.

When a woman was pregnant in the camp, she was not allowed to keep her baby after it was born. Some times the new born babies were drowned in the latrines, sometimes in the rain barrels, or they were just thrown alive into the pit with the dead bodies.

No family was allowed to keep a child under the age of two. All those children were taken to the pit as soon as the family arrived in the camp.

When families arrived with too many children, some were taken away right away and never seen again. The guards had a special place in the woods where they would take these children. Sometimes I followed them, hiding behind the trees so the guards wouldn't see me. In back of the camp, deep in the woods, there was a small place that not many people knew about. In this place there was a vehicle, a military or police transport van without windows. Children were sent there supposedly to clean the inside. The guards called it their "portable kitchen." But really it was a gas chamber.[2] Afterwards, the bodies of the children were burned in a big brick fireplace that had been made next to this van.

Although I did not suffer like others in the camp, and all my immediate family survived, I had nightmares about Lety for a very long time. Nightmares mainly about the beatings. My grandmother was killed in Lety, beaten to death. Many, many cousins, aunts and uncles died in Lety because of the beatings. How many times have I had nightmares about Lety? Hundreds of times. I know only one thing, from all these nightmares and all these bad memories, I got sick. Despite our privileges in Lety, I spent 15 years in a psychiatric clinic after the war.

Before we were arrested and sent to Lety, I used to read and write Czech. But in this camp I forgot how to read and write. After World War II, I went back to school but only for one year. No matter how hard the teachers tried to help me, I could not learn to read or write again. From the school I was sent to the psychiatric clinic because they said I was sick. In 1956 the doctors told my parents I was only 50% normal. In 1963 the doctors reversed their decision and shortly after that I got married to a Polish girl. But I know I am still sick. For more than thirty years I have been taking medicines.

Lety destroyed my life. To this day I don't know how to read or write. I am completely illiterate. My parents used to read things for me, but my mother died in 1988 and my father in 1991. Now when I get mail my brother-in-law must come over and read it to me.

What is happening today in our country? To be honest, any Romany who stays in this country today is an idiot. I am white, I can pass for a Czech, but those who are dark are stupid to stay here. Too many Czechs are trying to kill us, and the police are helping them. Five years ago I lived in Austria. If I knew what was going to happen after the Velvet Revolution, I never would have come back here.

The Czechs have always hated us, before the war, during the Hitler times, during the communist times, even today in this democracy we are hated.

There is only one place in this country where Romanies are safe. If you go to old town here in Prague and go to Perlova Street, you will see the Romany prostitutes with the police all around because the police are paid by the hookers to protect them. The police have a business with them. But these are the only Romany safe in this country. This is the only place in the Czech Republic where Romanies are protected from the skinheads.

In my opinion it is something terrible, something you can't imagine what is happening in this country. I am white so I don't have problems, but my nephew has a dark girlfriend and they are afraid to go out at night. My nephew rented a flat here but when he moved in with his girlfriend the landlord kicked them out because she is dark. He threatened them with the skinheads so they left. But it is not only the skinheads but the normal Czechs that turn you away from restaurants, that prevent you from getting jobs. It is worse than World War II. Now with freedom, people are getting kicked out of apartments. I know a woman with six children now living in the park. You can't imagine what is happening in this country.

But to be honest, there are no real Romanies left today. The young Romanies have forgotten our traditions, our culture in their struggle to survive. My mother was not allowed to wash the women's clothes with the men's; where you made your food, you were not allowed to dry your clothes. These were some of the old traditions.

I am prepared to go to church and before the priest swear that everything I have told you is the truth. Let God be my witness

(1) Josef Hejduk.
(2) A skinhead I interviewed in Mirovice also told this same story. He told me he heard it from the Mirovice cobbler who repaired the boots of the Lety guards. The skinhead used exactly the same words "portable kitchen" when referring to the gas chamber inside the military van.

Alžběta Lagronová

My name is Alžběta Lagronová. I'm 69 years old. I was born on 14 September 1926 in Rychnov nad Kněznou by Hradec Králové. My maiden name was Richter. My parents were Robert Čermák and Maria Richterová. They never married but they had eleven children. All of us were at Lety, including my grandparents, except one sister who was sent directly to Auschwitz. Today my brother Eduard and I are the only ones still alive.

We were arrested in 1942 when I was sixteen. It was May or June. I remember this because it was warm. We were arrested by the Czech police from Pacov. We were living in a small village by Pacov called Tymova Ves. There was no warning the police were coming. It was a big surprise for us. We were sleeping in our wagons. It was about five or six in the morning. The police had a big truck. We asked them where they were taking us. They told us they were taking us to work, we had to work. About an hour later we arrived at this big gate. I didn't see anybody open it, it opened by itself. I didn't know the other Romanies in the truck, there were about 30 of us.

The first thing they did with us was to cut off all our hair. We looked like skinheads. The whole camp was filled with Romany people from all over Bohemia.

A few days later the police took some Romany men and brought our horses and wagons to the camp at Lety. We had beautiful wagons filled with furniture and blankets. We had wonderful horses too. I don't know what they did with the horses, but when the men came back to Lety with our wagons, they stripped the wagons then used the wagon to store dead bodies until they could be buried.

In that camp was a room for a doctor to see people. The Czech police who were taking care of us made us stand in line and one by one until we all got injections just above the heart. After this injection we started to feel like we were drunk. We were very weak, then very sleepy for about six weeks. People started to die very quickly after these injections. I had a high fever for six weeks. Those of us who survived walked funny for a long time.

I remember the worst of the guards, they were real fascists. All the guards were Czech, they were worse than any German. Not everybody was bad, but the worst were Hejduk, Černý from Prague, Baloun, Havrda from Prague, Maxa and Pešek. These men were the worst, but many of the guards molested the women.

Janovský the commander was a very bad man, molesting many of the women, and giving orders to hang people all the time. He was living there with his wife outside the camp. But from his home he watched the prisoners with his binoculars and if we made just one step out of line he called the guards and they hung us up. I never saw Janovský personally kill anyone with his hands, but I saw Hejduk kill many people.

I had to make the fire in Hejduk's office every morning while he went through the camp looking for victims. He was a killer. He picked up young girls and young boys and he took them to his office to beat them. On many occasions these kids covered me in blood. When he saw I got blood on me he sent me out. Later I had to come back in after an hour to wash up all the blood. I never saw those young people again.[1]

Hejduk told me that I was not suppose to say anything about this. If I did he would take his gun and shoot me. He was about 30-35 at that time. Pešek was also young as was Černý. Černý was like 24 or 26.

The Czech police lived directly behind the camp in a wooden house. They slept there. The director had his own house separate from the guards.

Shortly after we arrived at the camp, a typhus epidemic broke out. Because of the epidemic no one could leave the camp. Nearby was the village of Mirovice and no one could go there, not even the guards. 50 or 60 people were dying everyday from typhus.

There was a carpenter's shop in the camp making make-shift coffins as fast as they could. Behind the camp was a forest and in the forest the prisoners had to make big holes for many coffins at a time.

My father had to work digging these holes for the bodies. He also had to throw lime into the coffins before the lid was put on.

About thirty children were also dying every day. We got the typhus from hunger. We were really hungry there. People were so hungry they were looking for mice to eat. We probably got typhus this way.

Our whole family got typhus but only my sister Františka Richterová died in Lety from typhus. My brother Josef escaped from Lety, but when the police found him they sent him directly to Auschwitz where he was shot. My niece Barbara Richter escaped with him. They caught her in Prague and sent her directly to Auschwitz as punishment. But she survived the war.

My brother Eduard Richter also escaped from Lety and was captured by the dogs and sent to Auschwitz. He too survived and came back after WW II. Another sister, Marie, was arrested in Cimechy with her husband Jan Růžička and their two year old daughter. They never went to Lety, but were sent directly to Auschwitz. He is still alive living in Třebíč. He can tell you many things, He's about 70 years old today. My brother Eduard and sister Marie came back from Auschwitz but both were very sick with bad lungs and both died shortly after returning from Auschwitz, she about 1947 and Eduard about five or six years after.

A lot of people tried to escape from Lety because the guards were so horrible. I saw Czech guards kill children and adults by sticking their heads in water until they died. There was a wooden rain barrel with very dirty water and the guards drowned them in that rain barrel. When my brother Eduard and my niece Barbara Richter saw this, they escaped.

Nearby the camp was a lake where the guards also drowned people. Twice a week we had to go to this lake to clean ourselves.

The lake was small so we were all touching each other. It was impossible to wash because you couldn't move there were so many people in the lake.

Jesus Maria, they beat us too. They tied our hands together and they hung us up for three or four hours at a time. Why? They just liked to do it, to see us suffer.

How many Romany were at Lety? There were so many people we were always touching people when we walked; big families, many, many people. I don't want to lie. I can't estimate a number. I can just say that Lety was a small city. We were sleeping in wooden barracks with five people in one bed, there was no place to squeeze in another person.

About six months after we were there, a German officer from Prague arrived. He was the only German I ever saw at the camp.[2] The Czech police called all the prisoners out to make lines to take people to the Písek train station to be on the transport to Auschwitz. They told us where we were going.

The camp was like a small city full of Romany people and every day there were transports to the Písek train station. The trucks came everyday bringing people to the camp and taking people to the train to Auschwitz. The camp was so full they could not take them away in trucks fast enough. Trucks took them away every day.

The director told us that we would be going to Auschwitz. It was no secret. He told us that we would take a train from Písek. but there were too many of us to go all at once. It took months, over a year to send everyone to Auschwitz.

When this German arrived, he brought to the camp four Romany men and two Romany women from Auschwitz. These Romany were wearing black clothes with a black triangle patch on their sleeve. They were capos from Auschwitz. They had truncheons like the Czech guards. They were German Sinti. They were brought to Lety because of their experience at Auschwitz. These Romanies treated us in the same way as the Czech guards. There was a kitchen where we had to pick up our soup of potatoes and carrots at lunch time but we were afraid to pick up our food because these German Romanies standing there frightened us with their clubs.

The Czech guards gave these capos their orders. We asked the capos why they did these things to us, their brothers. They said, we have to, otherwise we will be shot if we do not follow orders. They told us the Germans at Auschwitz were not as bad as the Czech guards at Lety. From that time on many of us prayed to be sent to Auschwitz.

After 13 months in Lety my mother and I and the rest of our family except my father were free to go home because we had typhus. They sent us home because we were sick and they thought we were going to die and they had no more room to bury people. Jesus Maria. They didn't want to send us to Auschwitz because we had typhus.

Before we left, I heard someone screaming. I saw a small boy about five years old, very skinny; his parents had already been sent to Auschwitz so I took this boy to our barracks. When the police came to make an inspection I hid him under my blankets telling him to be quiet.

When we got to leave the camp I took the boy with me. The Czech commander of the camp stopped me. He asked who the boy was. I said he was mine. He told me I didn't bring any child with me to the camp. He took the boy away from me. I don't know what happened to him.[3]

My father had to stay there with about fifteen other prisoners to destroy the camp, burn up all the buildings. When everything was destroyed and burned, my father joined us in Týmova Ves where we were waiting. We had no wagons, no horses, so we were living in tents we made out of blankets. After working for some time in the fields for nearby farmers, many families put their money together and we bought a small house.

I went back to Lety about ten years ago with my husband in our car. In the forest behind the camp, which was now a pig farm, I found a tall wooden cross someone had made and left there. I could tell a Romany had made it.

My husband and I spent two days there in that forest walking around because I knew where all the bodies were buried. We slept in a tent we had brought. During the day we put candles where I thought the graves were. My husband took a knife and made a hole for the candles. We stayed there until the candles burned out.

I was sick when I saw there was a pig farm where the camp used to be. It is exactly in the same place where the barracks used to be.

We saw other Romany there in the forest but we didn't talk to them. Everybody wanted to be alone with their own sad thoughts.

When we were going home we passed through Mirovice and went to the restaurant to buy coffee. There were some old Czechs there so I asked them why the pig farm was built where our people died. I told them I had been there and many people had died there so why were they desecrating the place with a pig farm. They didn't answer me. They just shrugged their shoulders.

I also asked the old Czech men in the restaurant if anyone of them knew the guards Hejduk, Pešek, and Černý and they said yes, they knew them. They said they used to come to this restaurant on their days off to drink beer, but they no longer lived in the village. They thought they were living in Prague.

I am certain that Černý, Pešek and Hejduk must still be alive. I don't understand why they have never been brought to trial. They killed people, they tortured people. It was their personal decision, they weren't under orders to do those things. I can't understand why nothing has happened to them. These men were Czechs; why were doing this kind of thing to citizens of their own country? The Germans weren't there to make them do these things to us. Is there no justice? I can recognize them for sure. I can testify. Of course, I am afraid someone will kill me. I am afraid they will have sons. But I am sure I can recognize them even at midnight. I would like to see them. I would like to tell them something.

When I heard about you getting the Czech government to put up a monument at Lety, I wrote asking about compensation for being a prisoner there. I was told recently that I might get something if I could prove I was in Lety. I went to the state archive in Třeboň where you found your information. They gave me a certificate saying that I was in that camp. I sent the certificate six months ago to the Ministry of Defense, but I never received an answer.

I think there are still many survivors from Lety. I know some are in Prague, some in Plzeň. I know their names but not their addresses. I have a cousin in Příbram who survived Lety. She must be about 69 now. I'm sure she's still alive. I lost contact with everyone because we moved to Slovakia after the war. We came back two years ago after the split. I was in Brno and now I am here in this town, but I don't like it. It's like 1939 all over again.

Fascism has returned. The Czechs are killing the Romany again. Skinheads? We used to call them Hitler Youth. It is absolutely the same today in the Czech Republic what Hitler was doing in 1939. New citizenship laws, skinheads, beatings, killings. In the market in Brno I saw the skinheads attacking the Romany who were selling fruit and vegetables outside. The skinheads came and beat them up and broke their teeth. These skinheads don't say anything, they just come with chains and balls with spikes and beat them up. I saw one Romany lose three or four teeth to these new Hitler Youth this summer in Brno.

(1) In 1998 Alžběta told CBS News researchers: "Hejduk beat these boys with his own hands. He wore leather gloves. I saw the blood coming out of their ears and mouth. Other prisoners had to carry the boys away. I had to mop up the blood and teeth afterwards. I never saw any of those boys again." This statement was translated by PhDr. Vladimíra Žáková as Alžběta spoke to the American television researchers.

(2) From court documents and the testimony of Lety guards, this man has been identified as Dr. Stuchlík, a Czech who was in charge of all the work camps in the Protectorate.

(3) See oral history of K.V.

Eduard Čermák
(son of a Lety survivor)

My father, Martin Čermák, was born on 28 November 1911 in Hodolany (Olomouc), Moravia. His family, the Čermáks, were well-known horse dealers for centuries. People came from Poland, Hungary, Austria and even Germany to buy horses from them. Our family is still remembered in Moravia for their horses.

My mother Anna was the daughter of František Chadraba and Anežka born Richterová.

My parents and their five children were living in an apartment in Prague in 1940 when they were arrested on 3 August and sent to Lety. They lived near the local police station in Prague 4, but a policeman there didn't like them. My parents were well off and even had a farm where they had their horses not far from their apartment. They knew the police were rounding up vagabonds for a work camp in South Bohemia, mainly arresting Gypsies. Our clan didn't hide because they all had jobs and owned their own homes. But the Prague police still arrested them. The Czechs have always hated Gypsies, no matter how hard we worked.

My father was the first prisoner to arrive at Lety before the camp was even built. He and fifteen other prisoners were housed in a hotel in Mirovice until the camp was finished. The police escorted my father with several of his horses and one of his wagons from Prague to Lety. During the construction of the camp, the police used our horses and wagon to haul lumber. After the camp was opened, the horses were used to haul water, while our wagon was used to store dead bodies until they could be buried or burned.

I was not at Lety. I was not born until 1944. But our whole clan was there, including my aunts, uncles, grandparents and my five brothers and sisters whom I never saw. Although my parents survived Lety, their five other children died in Auschwitz.

Before being sent to Lety my father had a son with another woman. His name was Jan Richter. He and his mother ended up at Lety too, but he survived. He lives in Prague today but he might not remember anything. He was only three years old when he was in the camp.

My father once found Jan among the bodies of the dead prisoners. He had been sick from hunger and had passed out. The guards thought he was dead. When my father came back from work, he heard someone crying in one of the piles of the dead. It was my brother Jan.

What did my father do in the camp at Lety? His most important job was building the gas chamber. He used to talk to me a lot about it because he and the other men knew what it was going to be used for so they worked very slowly when they were building it. It was an underground bunker behind the lake where the forest begins. The guards teased them about it, that it was going to be the "permanent kitchen." Deep in the woods there was a "portable kitchen," a metal van that was used to gas children when there were too many in the camp. Their bodies were burned in a fireplace nearby. After my father and his work crew finally finished the gas chamber, some men came and put in the pipes. But the camp was closed before the gas was installed.

My father told me many times that Lety was established to exterminate our people. In the pond there are many bodies. They drowned many of the children there.

How many people died at Lety? All the Gypsy wagons were full of dead bodies, every day. Our wagon was there. It was always full according to my father. There were piles and piles of bodies.

My father told me that they got rid of the bodies, many of them, by burning.

When prisoners arrived, the guards were always looking for gold. If you had gold in your teeth and wouldn't give it to the guards, you were the first to die.

My father's children were starving so he stole some bread for them. The guards caught him and beat him so badly about the head that he had no hair left. My father told me that Czech police did this to him, not the Gestapo, not the Germans. Only Czech guards were at Lety.

The Czechs treated our people just like animals, worse than animals. When a woman gave birth in Lety, her child was taken directly to the latrine and dropped in the shit hole. Most children below the age of two were drowned either in the lake or in the rain barrels. If archaeologists ever do a study at Lety their hairs will stand up on end. No one will believe the number of bodies there.

Beatings? Everybody was beaten at Lety, even the children. If you helped another person, this was a reason to be beaten. My father used to say that he was so rich in beatings that he had enough to buy Wenceslas Square.

Hejduk is a guard I remember my father talking about, him and Komárek. Hejduk I remember because he was in charge of the worst policemen, the ones that punished you if you got caught trying to escape. If you looked at this man in a way he didn't like, he called you back and beat you.

My father also talked about Komárek because he was the one who yanked out my father's gold teeth. Komárek was the one who liked gold. His hobby was gold, so if you gave him some you could have privileges. This Komárek was also in charge of the work gang in the woods and later in the stone quarry.

During morning roll call, some of the old men had to be held up by the young men, they were that weak. In the woods the old men hid while the young men collected their quota for them.

My mother worked in the stone quarry, carrying baskets of stones to my brothers and sisters who hammered the stones smaller so they could be used on the new road the prisoners had to build.

Hunger? Everybody was hungry at Lety. In the morning many people went to work in the woods in gangs of eighty to a hundred people. Five or six men always snuck away from the group to steal from the local farms: chickens, vegetables, especially dogs. They cooked these things in the woods and then brought them to the people; all this food was shared among lots of people so each one got only a very small helping; this extra food saved many people. But if a guard found a small piece of food on you, you got a terrible beating and no food at the next meal.

Hangings? I don't want to talk any more about these things. If I talk any more, I will get goose bumps. But there were many hangings on the execution post.

There was also a place in the barracks, my father said it was called the rest lounge, where prisoners were taken who got mad at each other. The guards encouraged fights between the prisoners; they wanted them to kill each other; this was another way of getting rid of the Romanies.

I can't talk about this anymore, remembering these stories is making me cry.[1]

In 1943 a new director came to run the camp. He saw my father, and my father saw him. They knew each other from Moravia. He asked my father why he was there; he wasn't supposed to be there, only Gypsies who didn't have jobs. The new director told my father he would set him free right away, but my father said he couldn't leave without his family. When they were preparing the last transport to Auschwitz, the director told my father to take his family and leave, they were free. My father's five children were already in Auschwitz, but he left with the rest of the clan, about 20 people. The new director of the camp (I can't remember his name[2]) used to go to school with my father in Moravia. They knew each other very well. That is why my father survived Lety. Otherwise they would have killed him when the camp was closed because he knew everything. He was the first prisoner to enter Lety, and the last to leave.

After Lety, my father was never normal again. He smoked too much. He had nightmares every night. Many times he woke up screaming in the night. His screams woke up my mother; she had to calm him until morning. I tried to help him but he just sent me back to bed. For the rest of his life he had these nightmares.

After the war, when you went to apply for a job in Czechoslovakia, people asked where you worked during the war. If you told them you were in a concentration camp, they said you must be bad and they wouldn't hire you. To get his job in the railroad station, my father had to pay the boss to hire him. That's how the Czechs treated you after the war when they knew you were from a concentration camp.

My father worked in this railroad station in Prague for 38 years, putting the wagons together. He had many diplomas for his good work, but he told me there was no reward good enough to compensate for what he went through at Lety. He told me I had to work harder than the whites just to make them think I was their equal. I tried working for the whites but I couldn't take it. That's why I work on my own. I have my bus and my feather cleaning machine. I don't make a fortune, but I don't have to work for the whites, I don't have to listen to their racist remarks.

After the war my father found this policeman in Prague who had sent our family to Lety. One night my father put a gun in this policeman's mouth. The policeman begged my father not to kill him because he had children. My father told him that he had lost five children in Auschwitz. My father wanted to pull the trigger but couldn't. That's the real difference between a Gypsy and a Czech. We still respect life.

About fifteen years ago in Bohdalec, Prague 10, there was a central heating plant where the government burned books and papers on the people who were in concentration camps. I got a call one day from some men who were unloading a box car. My father had worked in that railroad yard for 38 years. The men knew my father had been in a concentration camp, so they called me. I went down to have a look. I found a book on Lety and Terezín. There were photos of the prisoners at Lety. I saw the box cars full of these papers and books. The police were taking these papers and books from the box cars and putting them in trucks to be taken to the heating plant. I saw this with my own eyes. I stole this book that was written in Czech about Lety.

I showed this book to Robert Tříska and he recognized his parents and brothers and sisters and all his family who were at Lety. Over the years the children of the Lety survivors have come to my home and taken the pages that pertained to their family. It was about two inches thick with about 300 pages. Half of this book were pictures. The rest contained the names of the families. When people heard I had this book, they came to my place to read it. I lent it to Robert Tříska, but when he died, I never got it back.

My uncle Jan Čermák made the wooden cross that you found on the ground there at Lety. We made it in Prague and took it all the way to Lety in a truck. An old carpenter in Prague 4 made this cross for us. He wasn't a Romany but he understood and didn't charge us very much.

In 1986 we put this cross up near the mass grave. The cross was about 4 meters tall. In the center of the cross we put a crown of barbed wire.

When we were putting up the cross, a forester came and said we couldn't put it there without permission. My uncle beat this man up. He told him he didn't know what had happened there in World War II. This forester called the police. My uncle also wanted to beat up the police. I was the only person there with my uncle. After I explained how our relatives had been murdered at Lety the police let my uncle go.

We put the cross near the grave of my grandmother, Anna Čermáková. Over the years my uncle and my father showed me where all the graves were. I know where everything was in Lety: the barracks, the gas chamber, the mass graves.

Today, the situation is just as bad in the Czech Republic. There is no democracy for Romanies. We are poorer than we used to be. Even today if you don't give money to protect yourselves, forget about it. You can have money, big cars, houses, but you don't have any rights because you are dark, you are a Gypsy. You might not be poor, but you are not free because you are dark.

I would like you to come to the different places where I work and listen to what the people have to say. Anna, an old woman, about 75 years old, brought me her pillows to clean the other day. She talked about President Havel. She told me that during the war she worked for his parents, cleaning and cooking for them. She said that everyone who worked for them was so afraid of them that they feared even to touch the door handle. They were afraid to do something wrong because the Havels were such good friends of the Nazis. I told her I hoped it would be better one day for us Gypsies because Havel is our president. But this was her answer. Everyone in the Havel family was a fascist, so she didn't think President Havel could be any different. There were many meetings of the Gestapo in their home, many parties with Czech people who were cooperating with the Germans. This woman told me Havel doesn't know anything about democracy. He doesn't know what it means to be poor and hungry and to live in terrible social conditions, how it feels to be discriminated against. He has no idea what racism is. He was born a privileged man and is still a privileged man.

A friend of mine had a car accident. He got two years in jail for this, although it wasn't his fault. Now he wants to go to Yugoslavia but he can't get a passport because he was in jail. Mr. Havel was in prison but he can still get a passport, he can still go to the United States for his vacation. And let me tell you, while he was in prison he got many privileges, special food, special treatment. My son was arrested about the same time as Havel in 1984 and ended up in the next cell. My son had to clean Havel's cell. So even in prison Havel had privileges. No one cleaned my son's cell. Havel's wife could come to the prison and spend two or three days there in Vinařice. But my son wasn't allowed any visitors; his wife couldn't stay with him. In this country if you have money, you can do anything.

If President Masaryk knew what was happening in this country today he would wake up and his body would shake. He would see the corruption in the government, the blackmail, the killings, and he would ask, "What kind of democracy is this?"

Of course, what I am telling you is all to no avail. Our government is covering up, lying about all this kind of thing, especially about what happened in Lety. This government is no different from the previous government, the communist government, when it comes to respecting the dead at Lety.

The Czechs have a big monument in Lidice for their war dead. That's because they want to have a monument against the Germans. But we get no proper monument because we weren't killed by the Germans. We were killed by the Czechs.

(1) There was a several minute pause at this point while Eduard wept so hard he shook. After drying his face and moustache on his handkerchief, he continued without any prompting.
(2) Štefan Blahynka from Hodonín.

A. N.

I don't really want to talk about Lety. I've already spoken about it to a Czech historian from Brno.[1] I don't think there is any more left to tell you. I'm also afraid that all this information will be published and something could happen to me.

All right, come in, but you'll see I have very little to say. I don't really remember a lot about Lety. I was three and a half years in concentration camps, only five months in Lety. The book by the Brno historian contains my information about Auschwitz.

My aunt Božena Vrbová could have told you more. After the war she was in Prague and met the director of the camp, Janovský. She met him at "255", the organization of political prisoners. She had to get a certificate for compensation that she was in Lety. Janovský and two other guards helped her. They were her witnesses. They remembered she was one of the sewing women in the camp. She had no contact with the guards so I'm surprised they remembered her.[2]

I was born 16 June 1923 in Spytihněv (Moravia). My parents lived in Prague where they owned a small shop. I had four siblings but none of them was in Lety. I was sent to the concentration camp because my husband was half Gypsy so they took me with him.

My husband and I lived in Mezilesí (Pacov). He was a bricklayer with a full time job when we were arrested. His parents were arrested with us. They lived in Nová Ves; they were selling horses and textiles. Half the Gypsies I knew escaped to Slovakia before they could be picked up. All the Richters in Brno today came back from Slovakia after the war.

We already knew one week before the police came that we were going to be taken away with other families in our village to a work camp. We didn't know we were going to a concentration camp. The police took us by trucks to Tábor and from there by train to Mirovice. In the train there were a lot of families that had been picked up from many different counties.

The first things I saw at Lety were the wooden barracks surrounded by a wire fence. People were sleeping six, sometimes ten, in one bed; we were spread out among all the different barracks. They shaved our hair when we came into the camp.

The cook from the previous labor camp wasn't there anymore, so Mrs. Poelderlová and I worked in the guards' kitchen, cooking their meals for them. There was a house where Czech prisoners used to live, so I slept there with three other women. One of them was B.R. She and another woman, K. L. worked as cleaning women for the guards. We didn't have too much contact with the other prisoners. The guards used to lock our door in the evening and unlock it in the morning. The guards kept us away from everyone especially when the typhus epidemic broke out. Matějka was another guard. I don't remember which cleaning lady he went out with. Janovský's wife only was there once or twice a week. So he had his own cleaning lady too.

I was separated from my husband. He worked on the road gang and was sent away for some weeks at a time. I was pregnant when I arrived in the camp.

Since we only cooked for the guards, we didn't have to wear prison clothes; we wore normal dresses. We were allowed to keep the clothes we brought to camp. I ate what the guards ate. We had white coffee with bread; good soup, meat twice a week. We also had fresh vegetables every day because there was a garden near the guard's house. The prisoners had to pick the vegetables and bring them to our kitchen. In the evening we had goulash with cabbage and dumplings. Our food was separate from the prisoners'; they had their own kitchen. One of the guards used to go to Čimelice to buy food every day for us, especially milk.

We used to cook for about 15 to 20 guards every day; some

guards worked outside the camp with the work gangs so we didn't cook for them. Most of the guards lived in the camp. During the time I was there the guards didn't change. All the guards were Czech; there were no Germans in the camp except the three Sinti capos. I don't know if anyone in the camp was working with the Germans but they were never in the camp while I was there.[3]

The men who came from Prague to organize the transports to Auschwitz were also Czechs. There were never any Germans at Lety while I was there. No German Gestapo came by either. No Germans at all.

During my time in the camp there were two transports to Auschwitz. I remember one of these transports very well because the guards knocked on our door to come into the kitchen very early to cook for them. We had to serve twenty-five extra guards that morning. After breakfast they got up and loaded four big trucks with dark-skinned Gypsies, men and women, and took them away to the train station. The guards left the children of these prisoners in the camp. All the children ran to the gate calling for their parents. It was a terrible scene, also for the guards. Our guards had to go with these transport guards to take these Gypsies to the train station. When our guards came back, they told me they had never seen anything like this before; at the station everyone was crying and screaming for their children. For those first transports they kept the old people and the small children in the camp.

Later another transport came and took the old people and the young children to Auschwitz, direct to the gas chambers.

The situation inside the Lety camp was terrible. It was very dirty; the latrines were never cleaned, only the shit taken by buckets to the garden by the prisoners. There were not enough toilets for everyone so the children just went on the ground, all over the camp. I think this is why the typhus came.

I don't remember anyone being killed in the latrines, but the prisoners were beaten very often. Four Gypsy Sintis were sent from Dachau and these behaved very badly, even killing children. They beat everyone they saw, anyone who came in their way. One of them was called Robert. Another one was very young, almost a boy. The young capo refused to beat the children so the other two punished him by making him extend his arms straight out and then with a large stone on top of both hands he had to do deep knee bends without bending his arms or letting the stones fall. Whenever the stones fell, they beat him. He was one of their own German brothers but they treated him terribly. Three of them stayed in the camp. I don't know what happened to the fourth.

The guards beat the people also during the night, whenever they wanted. Havrda came from outside the camp to check on the people to see if they had fleas and lice. Some of the prisoners had money that our guards didn't take away from them so they paid Havrda to bring them cigarettes or food. Robert once saw one of the women receive some food from Havrda so he went to her, took every thing away from her, and then beat her until she couldn't get up. She was sick for a long time but she didn't die. These two capos were terrible killers.

I remember a beautiful woman, A.I., who worked in the sewing room and later was with B. R. working in the kitchen. She ended up in Auschwitz with her two children. I saw her there. Her two children were sent to the gas chambers after she was sent on a transport, I don't know where. I was sent to Ravensbruck, then Leipzig. I lost my only child to the gas chambers too.

I remember the name Hejduk but I don't remember where he worked. Matějka was the first man under Janovský. He spent most of the time in the office. He didn't go into the camp very often.

I don't remember any of our guards being bad or beating the prisoners, just one. He was very bad, he beat everyone but I can't remember his name. He was short, the shortest of all the guards. He was very cruel. The first day when we all arrived well-dressed he said, "Come on beauties," and he took us behind a shed where a prisoner shaved off all our body hair.

People were not allowed to go to the lake by themselves to wash. There was a very clean lady who many times washed her hands at the water pump. Whenever the short guard saw this, he came up and beat her right away, telling her she cleaned herself too much. Whenever the women had to carry the shit away from the latrines and wanted to wash their hands, they automatically got beaten.

The women who had babies in the camp usually lost them. I don't remember hearing that the babies were murdered. They just didn't survive because the conditions were so bad. In Auschwitz all babies born there were drowned right away, and then thrown behind the gate.

Whenever anyone escaped and was caught, the guards put their feet in chains and locked them up in a shack. After the two German capos tried to escape and were caught, they were put in chains too.

Our guards, especially Luňáček, got very upset about the German capos beating the people, but they couldn't say anything against the capos otherwise the Gestapo might have taken our guards away.

Janovský seldom went to the camp. He was an old man at that time; I don't know anything about him beating people. I didn't see what happened in the camp because I was in the kitchen all day then locked up at night. I never saw much in the camp.

Deaths in the camp? There were dead bodies every day in Lety. I can't tell you how many; they took the bodies away every day in wagons. In the beginning the dead bodies were taken to Mirovice; later they just threw them in some mass graves in the forest. Most died of typhus but also from hunger; the food they received was worse than the food given to the pigs. With that kind of food they had to die, get diseases.

Because my girlfriend and I lived near to the gate, we weren't controlled like the other prisoners. I used to work in the kitchen under the supervision of the guard Luňáček. He was a good man, a very good guard.[4] My girlfriend and I used to tease him that we were going to run away, and one day we did.[5]

We walked over to Mirovice, then took the train in Prague. My aunt who was also a prisoner in the camp had some money hidden in a thermos. She gave it to me for the train tickets. Alena Nováková, I think, was the girl I escaped with. She was half Gypsy.

I escaped because I wanted to be free; the first days in the camp were tough, we had to work long hours, but the guards never bothered us. We just wanted to be free. The guards knew I was pregnant. If the cleaning woman slept with the guards, I don't know. But each guard had his own cleaning woman and they were with them a lot.

I went to Prague to see my mother and my sister. They gave me a wig so no one could recognize me. I wanted to join the partisans.

When the Gestapo in Prague caught my girlfriend who had

escaped with me, I went straight to Prostějov. The Gestapo forced her to tell them where we had stayed. Then the Gestapo arrested my sister. In their office they beat her but in the beginning she didn't tell them where I was.

Shortly after my baby was born in the hospital at Prostějov, my sister told the Gestapo where I was. She finally told them because they threatened to send her to Auschwitz.

The Gestapo came to Prostějov; in the hospital they locked me up in the infection center with my little girl. I stayed in the hospital for four weeks then the Gestapo came to pick me up and took me to the criminal office in Prostějov. There I spent a couple of days there and then they took me to the train with my baby and we went straight to Auschwitz.

I was three and a half years in concentration camps. I was in Lety for five months from April 1942 until September.

My baby died in Auschwitz. Life in Lety was much better than life in Auschwitz. In Auschwitz there were seven or eight hundred people in one barrack. The cruelness in Auschwitz was horrible. When the men went out in work gangs, 15 or 20 would be killed in the fields every day.

My worst experience in Lety was when the short guard hit me with his stick five times on my back because I didn't stand in line in the morning when they were counting us like he wanted me to do. I was hit so hard I could hardly walk after I was beaten. Every day this guard beat people. He was the worst.

I never had any nightmares about Lety but I did about the other camps. I always dreamed that someone was always walking behind me. I always felt someone behind me. In my dreams I remember the children, the circumstances.

After the war my girlfriend and I met some of the Lety guards in Prague. We asked them why they didn't catch us when we escaped from Lety. They told us they went to the forest and had a nap for two hours instead of looking for us.

The Lety guards were really nice men.

---

(1) Prof. Ctibor Nečas who interviewed her about Auschwitz, but not about her experiences in Lety. Necas published over 50 interviews with Gypsy Holocaust survivors but only about their times at Auschwitz. Necas contends that only 360 Gyp-

sies died at Lety, all from typhus. The Czech government use him and his books as their cover-up of Lety.
(2) All the sewing women in the camp slept with the guards.
(3) She was in Lety from 11 August 1942 until 9 December 1942.
(4) After the war, Luňáček was the only guard found guilty of misconduct at Lety. He received only a reprimand.
(5) They escaped on 9 December 1942.

Helena Richtrová

My father Čeněk Chadraba was born 30 May 1903 in Bohusovice, five kilometers from Terezín. Františka Šulcová, my mother, was born in Cerny Dunajec, Novy Targ, Poland, on 10 October 1900. My parents worked the markets, selling baskets that they wove at home in Jeníkov (Čáslav). We lived there with my father's brother and his family. Together we had a small farm with chickens, a cow, some horses. We were living in a normal house. We weren't travelers like other Gypsies. My father had a license to sell in the markets. All our papers were in order.

I was born 6 April 1936 in Slovakia (Nové Mesto nad Váhom) when my mother was on her way to Poland to see her family. She hadn't seen them in more than 18 years. She stopped at a farm along the way. The people were very kind to take her in. They were so kind they offered to take care of me while my mother went to Poland. They wanted to adopt me but my mother said she couldn't give me up. In the end, my mother never got to Poland and never saw her parents again.

I had six sisters and two brothers. We arrived in Lety on 6 August 1942. We were arrested by the Czech police. They came with a truck and we had to take everything we owned with us, including all our cooking utensils, clothes, etc. I was only six years old so I don't remember how we went to Lety. I just remember the truck and then we were in the camp.

When we arrived, they took all our clothes. We had to take them off, then they shaved our heads bare. We received another set of clothes and wooden shoes. They took everything from our parents:

watches, rings, chains, earrings, all our money. We had to give them everything. I remember when I was released from the camp, I had nothing. I was almost naked. They made us bring all our belongings to the camp but we had to live there with nothing.

All of us were sent to Lety together except for my eldest sister, Žofie, who was in Prague with our Chadraba relatives. When she returned, she found that we had all been arrested and taken to Lety. She came on her own to Lety because she wanted to be with us, but the guards wouldn't let her in. Instead she was arrested and sent straight to Auschwitz on the next transport.

My mother always said that the old people who died first in Lety were looking after us. They had their hands over our heads to protect us. It was a miracle that no one in our immediate family died in Lety. My father had many relatives die in Lety. There was stomach typhus in the camp; my mother and one of my sisters had it but they didn't die. There was a lot of illness, different kinds of illness, but the beatings killed most of the people.

At breakfast we had to stand in line but if someone didn't stand straight, the beatings started right away. My mother was badly beaten once because she didn't stand straight in the breakfast line.

My husband was also in Lety. His name was Stanislav Richter. I didn't know he was there. I never saw him there. I met him after he got out of Auschwitz. He told me he saw some terrible things at Lety, but he would never talk about these things. But every year as long as he lived, he went back to Lety on the 1st of November to pay his respects, to remember his sister and his other relatives who died there.

My husband worked as a helper in the kitchen. Once he tried to escape with a friend and the police caught them. They were chained together in a wagon and beaten very badly. When he could walk again, he was sent to Mauthausen.

I was in a block with other children. My father was with the men, my mother with the women. We were very hungry. We never got enough to eat. I remember we were so hungry that when we had a chance to work in the woods we would grab handfuls of grass to eat.

But there were worse things than hunger at Lety. My aunt told me about a woman whose four children were burned to death at

Lety by the guards. The mother was forced to watch this but could not take it and threw herself into the fire to die with them. She was a beautiful woman. I don't know why the guards did this to her. But all the survivors I know still remember, still talk about this story.

My cousin Václav Weinreich from Teplice used to interview people about Lety but he died five years ago. He was a German Gypsy. He had some photos of the people in Lety. His wife is dead but his children live in Teplice. He was never in a concentration camp but he wrote many things about what happened to his Romany relatives in Lety and other camps. But no one was interested in what a Gypsy had to say about a Czech concentration camp. He never got anything published.

The doctors in Lety made some experiments with my sister Julie. She got some injections from them. After the war she had a baby boy who was born with the eyes of a rabbit. He had bad vision all his life and his mother always believed it was because of the experiments in Lety. The doctors made many experiments with the women in Lety. My sisters always told me about this, how doctors made experiments with their bodies.

In 1979 I went to Lety with my husband. We were shocked by what we saw. On the site of the concentration camp was a pig farm. We walked on the other side of the farm into the woods and we saw there a herd of cows grazing where our people had been buried. On the ground among the cows I saw many bones that had come to the surface. These cows were crapping on the bones of our people.

When my husband saw this, he was very upset because his sister had died in Lety. Her bones were there. So my father wrote a letter to the Antifascist Union about putting up a memorial there but he never got a reply. So he had made a marble plaque and he put it up in the cemetery in Mirovice. He did this just before he died. He was so upset by seeing those bones, the bones of his people just lying on the surface of the ground, that he got sick. He was only 53 years old when he died. I think he got so upset seeing that no one cared about how many people had died at Lety that it killed him. Human beings died at Lety. They weren't animals.

Today there are people who say that very few people died at Lety. But as a child I saw dead bodies carried to the pit every day.

Every day people died at Lety. They were thrown into the pit and covered over with lime. Every day. Every day.

When there is a program on TV about concentration camps, I have to get up and leave. I still cry when that word is mentioned. But what is happening in this country today is like being in a concentration camp. There are racial attacks every day. Our people can't get an education. People are always talking bad about us. There is terrible discrimination against the Romany in this country.

I cannot understand the terrible things that are still happening to us today. I have two children, a son and a daughter. My daughter is white with green eyes and leads a normal life. My son is dark with brown eyes and can't get a job. He has used my phone many times to answer ads for jobs; many times he was told over the phone that the job was still open but when he arrived the position was always filled. He is a tiler. It took him three years to learn his profession. During the communist times he had a good job. But now with democracy he can't work because of the color of his skin. My daughter is lucky. She is white. She has a good job. She has a normal life. This is something you just can't imagine until you have to live like this. My son just doesn't know what to do now. His whole life is in turmoil because of the color of his skin.

Emil Khiel

(Lety guard, as told by his son)

My father was a guard and a night watchman at Lety concentration camp. About a year ago Czech TV called us and said my father was the only guard still alive. They wanted to bring a TV crew to Rychnov and interview him.[1]

When my father heard this he collapsed. He's been in bed ever since. He lies there with his mouth open but he can't speak. He doesn't speak to any of us. He doesn't read, he doesn't watch television. He just lies there with his mouth open staring at the ceiling. He can't even put on his own pants.

The doctor told us on several occasions that my father was about to die. Over the New Year's holiday we almost lost him.

My father was born in Užhorod, capital of the Carpathian Ukraine that had been part of the Hungarian Kingdom before World War I. His father was from Prague but when he couldn't find a job he migrated to Užhorod. Emil learned a civilian profession, but when he couldn't obtain steady work he became a policeman. After the annexation of Carpatho-Ukraine by Hungary in 1939, the family had to leave so they returned to my grandfather's birthplace.

After registering in Prague, the Land Office (county office) gave my father a job as a policeman at Lety. The Germans didn't send my father to Lety, the Czechs did.

In 1947 there was an investigation about Lety and my father had to write a report about being there. I still have a copy of his one page report. This is what it says:

I was transferred to Lety in September 1940 just after the camp first opened. I was there until the camp closed for good in May 1943.

There were about 200 prisoners and 30 guards in the camp. Everyone was of Czech nationality.

At Lety I was in charge of guarding a work gang that was building a highway. I had to watch these prisoners and make them work as hard as possible. I also served as a night watchman at Lety.

The camp commander was Josef Janovský, a police captain. Janovský was a hard man and gave me orders to do inhuman things to the prisoners. I refused to obey these orders. Instead, I tried to take care of them, and sabotage the orders of Janovský.

After Lety I was transferred to the Terezín concentration camp. There I worked in the fortifications (guarding political prisoners). When the war ended I helped disarm the Germans, then I joined the revolutionary movement and helped with the expulsion of the Czech-Germans.

My wartime activities were all for the benefit of the Czech people.

My father never talked about his experiences at Lety. I only know something about them from my mother. She told me he had a very hard time there and that immediately after Lety was closed my father had to seek psychiatric help in a clinic. My mother said this was because of what happened at Lety.

When the war ended my father joined the revolutionary movement, then around 1949 he returned to Rychnov to work as a policemen. In 1955 there was a purge of the police force by the communists and my father lost his job. He then became a worker until he retired in 1972.

After Lety my father was unable or unwilling to socialize. He never had friends, and only stayed with the family. My mother blamed all of this on Lety. But he was not a bad man. When we cursed Gypsies at home, he always told us not to, saying they only need a strong hand and someone to tell them how to work. He told us he got along well with the Gypsies at Lety. He never had any problems.

My father has a sister in Prague. Perhaps she knows more than I do. I do know that our family was from Prague. My father once told me that his ancestors were English, that they had originally come from England and that he had "blue blood" in his veins.

I know our name sounds German but my father couldn't speak German at all. He could speak a bit of English, some Russian and was fluent in Hungarian, because of his stay in Užhorod.

I know my father didn't do anything wrong at Lety, otherwise the communists would have arrested him after they took over. They were always looking for fascists.[2]

I'm sorry you didn't come here two years ago when my father was in better health. I'm sure he would have enjoyed talking to you. No one else has ever been by to talk to my father about Lety.

How do we get on with the Gypsies today? Ask my wife.[3]

My son wants to read your book when it's finished. My wife told him he shouldn't. I'm sure there was some dirt at Lety.

(1) Editor's note: I gave Czech TV the list of the guards at Lety on the understanding they would find the guards for me and we would interview them together as part of an expose on the Czech government's cover-up of Lety. I have found four Lety guards still living but Czech TV dropped the project after government pressure.
(2) We asked for Khiel's address at Rotter's pub in Rychnov. A man who said he had been drummed out of the police force after the dissidents took over in 1989 immediately gave it to us. He knew Emil well, but when he found out we wanted to interview Khiel about his war record, the man said, "I know who you are." From that moment on we couldn't get anything out of him. He said to stop asking questions, it was too dangerous, that no one in town would tell us about Emil. He then told us Emil was dead; he had been a Jew and had died in a concentration camp. At the pub

next to Khiel's home the bartender told us that he had never heard of that surname in Rychnov, despite three generations of Khiel's still living next door.

(3) She said: "When a Gypsy works everything is all right, but when I have to work for him (my work pays for his unemployment benefits), I feel angry, resentment, a grudge."

Josef Janovský
(court examination of the accused on 20 September 1945)

I do not feel that I am guilty. I confess that I was the camp director in Lety and for that reason I was entrusted with the administration of the whole camp from the 1st of June 1940 until the 20th of January 1943. Thirty-two guards who supervised the work gangs were also under my direction. The civilian staff who administered the camp and kept everything in order were sent to me by the Land Office. At the beginning, this camp was meant for people who had been in prison before, for people who didn't want to work, and for people who were considered dangerous for the public good and public safety, and later for notorious vagabonds.

Sometime in the autumn of 1941, the camp was changed into a prisoner-work and rehabilitation camp. (sentence missing......) From the 1st of March 1942 the camp was changed to be a Gypsy camp which I presume was working until May 1943. I worked in the Gypsy camp only until the 20th of January 1943 when I was recalled from directing the camp because of the contamination of typhus and Mr. Blahynka was named as my successor. After a short sickness, in March 1943, I began work in another rehabilitation camp as an economic administrator. In this camp, a man by the name of Šmíd was the Gestapo director. Further administration of the camp was organized by guards who were directed by the higher ranking sergeants (word missing). From this camp I was released early and transferred to Prague countryside north.

■ The Gypsy children of Lety upon their arrival in August 1942.
Within weeks most had died of starvation or were drowned
by the guards in the pond or in buckets of water.
Photo from collection of Marie Bártová – repro archive AVČR, ič. 95179.

(Court examination of the accused on 17 January 1946)

I hereby claim that I am not guilty as written in paragraphs 15 and 16, and I have the following to add:

On the 20th of January of 1943, I was recalled from the position as camp director [of Lety] and presented myself to the presidium of the Home Office to the director of the council division for Lety, Cecha. In April I was entrusted as the director of the agricultural work camp in Planá nad Lužnicí. I was recalled [from Lety] because of the outbreak of typhus and the number of deaths; I was recalled from Planá because the camp director and Gestapo man Šmíd fought with me because I did not execute all of his orders.

The outbreak of the typhus epidemic at the disciplinary camp in Lety was not my fault. I always intended to uphold the health conditions, but I was not supported by the health division of the Land Office in Prague.

The disciplinary working camps [in Czechoslovakia] had been established on the basis of SL. nar. 72/39 [a governmental decree] from the 2nd of March 1939 and Sl. nar 188/39 from the 28th of April 1939 although it [these laws] excluded the purpose of the camp.[1]

I hereby attach copies of these laws and statues which gives the legal basis for why these camps were made by the Home Office and Land Office in Prague.

I, the accused, served under the Land Office in Prague, Department 22, and the Home Office, Department VS; those in charge at the Land Office were the head consul Svoboda and Dr. Kuchař; those in charge at the Home Office were the head consul Dr. Seidl and the head commissioner Stuchlík.[2]

I received my instructions from above by telephone or in writing from the board of directors. According to the laws [mentioned above], the reason for the continuation of the camp in the winter of 1940/41 was that the equipment, supplies and food stores would not be stolen. For that purpose one group of workers stayed in the camp. This group was then replaced after two months so that each group had two months of free time which I myself arranged. For the prolongation of the camp I received this order from the Land Office with detailed conditions on how to continue.

On the basis of the governmental order mentioned above, the

Home Office, Department 2, and the Land Office, Department 22, brought out an economic directive, order from the Land Office in Prague, Department 22, from 31 May 1941, number 212/7 from 1941 and a further order number 201/74 from 1939 from 5 July 1940 regarding the adjustment of the norms regarding prisoners' rights. I followed these instructions to the letter, and also the instructions for heating [the camp].

I contest that I detained or held back on purpose the coal for heating. I was responsible for everything so I had to plan it [the supplies] carefully. The houses were badly built, made out of thin wooden walls, so it was almost impossible to heat these [buildings] properly.

The prisoners were ordered to work correctly according to the instructions pronounced in the governmental orders which are enclosed. I correctly followed my instructions and did not exceed them.

At the beginning [of the camp] the work was directed exclusively to building a road [highway 19]; later in the forest and on agriculture. As long as the prisoners were in the camp, everything was in order.

After the Gypsies arrived in the camp, their clothes and linen were taken away from them and some of the clothing considered useless was destroyed or burned. The rest of the clothes had to be put into a warehouse and because at the beginning there were no work clothes for women I used the excess clothes from these Gypsies. Therefore, it happened that the linen and shoes were used mainly for clothes and shoes for the children and women.

Dr. Pikna was the first to take charge of the medical care in the camp; after a short period of time he was taken away by the Gestapo.[3] Later his position was take over by Dr. Čížek from the health department of the Land Office in Prague, and after his departure a contract was given to Dr. Kopecky from Mirovice. This doctor was suppose to come everyday to the camp to inspect the prisoners. Examinations and treatment were carried out by Dr. Kopecký under his direct responsibility and knowledge. I can confirm that if he had not fallen ill, the health situation in the camp would not have deteriorated. Afterwards I arranged a contract with Dr. Neuwirth a well-recommended man from Stary Sedlo, county Písek, whom

I had to ask three times if he would take over this position in the camp. Dr. Kopecký lives in Mirovice, county Písek.

As in all punishment and prisoner camps, the treatment had to be strict so that everything would be in order and I gave the orders for the punishments according to the camp regulations; I didn't shoot, and I also didn't tell the guards to treat the prisoners in a brutal way. I disclaim any torturing, and I especially disclaim hanging prisoners on the execution post, or beating them in freezing weather. I did not force my subjects through beatings and several kinds of punishments to a higher work rate in the interest of Germany, nor did I threaten them with a concentration camp.

Finished and signed at 11:15 a.m.

(1) Janovský is basing his defense on a governmental decree brought into law thirteen days before Germany invaded.
(2) Janovský's defense makes it clear that Czech government officials in Prague ordered him to do what he did, not German officials.
(3) Dr. Pikna was appointed to this post by Prague, but later it was discovered he was involved with subversive elements in Brno. He spent the entire war in Germany in the same concentration camp as Jean Paul Sartre.

František Kánský
(Lety guard testifying at Janovský's investigation)

I was born on 15 January 1910. From 20 September 1940 until the 18 May 1943, I served as the head of a labor gang and a guard of the discipline camp, later known as the Gypsy camp, at Lety by Mirovice, county Písek. From the police force, there were 35 colleagues. As director of the camp there was staff captain Josef Janovský who before lived in Jílové by Prague, now at a place I don't know.

The inmates and Gypsies were put to work on building a highway. Janovský told us to force them to a higher work output. When I and my colleagues sabotaged this order, we got threatened by the director Janovský who said that we were sabotaging his orders. At various meetings that were organized by Janovský we were asked questions by him: *whoever doesn't like this profession should say so – what do you want better? Whoever does not fulfill his duties properly and sabotages my orders, I will send him to where there is no way back. The Empire's army has no better conditions, so what do you want? Is this your bread?*

By these kind of threats used against me and the other police, we were continuously in fear of him, that Janovský would fulfill these threats against us. Janovský continuously told me and the others to force the inmates and the Gypsies to work at a higher labor output, to beat them with the truncheon, and because these orders made me feel awful, disgusted me, I didn't comply with his commands; I was several times called after work to his office where he threatened to write a bad report about me. But somehow I escaped the claws of this disgusting man. Apart from the above-mentioned, Janovský ordered us to bind inmates and Gypsies that broke the rules, even for banalities, to the post in the yard where they were hung up. But today I don't remember the names of these people.

Janovský ordered the inmate "Valek" to be tied up on a bench (rest of sentence missing....) Inmates that were obviously underfed became weak and in fact sometimes ill; they were treated not by a normal doctor but by a camp doctor. When Janovský found inmates being treated, he and Václav Baloun who was from the former police station Kdyně beat the patient with truncheons just to expel the inmate from the doctor's place. This method was used by Janovský most times with Baloun, and sometimes the consequence was that really ill inmates died the next day (viz inmate Šebek). That means they should have been treated by the doctor and not at all by these disgusting men beating them. Since it is a long time since I left this camp I don't remember precisely individual cases. But these things were done by these men daily. If it is necessary, certainly all my colleagues that were in this camp with me as well as the inmates and persons from the surrounding villages like Lety and Staré Sedlo will give the same information about these disgusting deeds that were ordered on us by Janovský and realized by himself there. Whenever we got into contact with the villagers we complained about Janovský. The list of the policemen who were sent to work in this camp in Lety is certainly still available at the State Office in Prague.

The Imperial Salute of lifting up the right arm was not made in the beginning in any of the police stations. But Janovský ordered us to salute this way by his own will in order to be able to boast that he was collaborating with the Germans. When there were visits to the camp he wanted us to speak and salute in only the German way, although this was at this time nowhere else carried out.

In August 1942 Gypsies were brought to this camp in Lety, men, women, children, and although in this camp there was only room for about 40 more people, the director as far as I know let them bring there 1,100 Gypsies so that the camp was overflowing. The Gypsies were led to work on the highway near the camp and we on our own had to go with them according to the command of Janovský and show them how to work with a shovel.

The working time in the summer months was from 6 a.m. until 6 p.m. When the Gypsies came back to the camp they had no water to wash.

For these one thousand Gypsies there were only two toilets. Every Sunday during the 32 months that I was in the camp we had to go in the late morning to work with the Gypsies so that the work for the Empire went on quickly. The Gypsies couldn't dress because of a lack of work clothing that was taken from them on the command of Janovský and so they had only rags on their bodies. The food that the Gypsies and the inmates were suppose to get was not given to them.

Because of Janovský's commands, it was his fault that in December 1942 there was an outbreak of para-typhoid fever, spotted and stomach typhus and other infectious disease among the Gypsies. Step by step these disease were transferred to us policemen because we had to serve in this camp continuously even in the times of these disease. The camp had to be quarantined and as far as I remember about 12 of my colleagues were infected. I don't remember anymore their names any more, but two died. This was all the fault of Janovský which can be confirmed by other colleagues who had been in this camp with me.

Signed: 25 June 1945 in Nový Bydžov, 5 p.m.
(document no. 8 of Janovský file)

Václav Studený[1]
(Lety survivor testifying before the court in 1945)

The witness states in evidence:

At the time when I came to the camp the living accommodations there were terrible. In one room could only be accommodated six people, but normally we were ten. In the women's rooms it was even worse. The women were squeezed together so much that they couldn't even lie down comfortably, they were forced to sit up. The treatment of these prisoners was horrible. For every little thing we did we were beaten with fists, sticks or truncheons. I myself saw Janovský beat people, mainly slapping their faces very hard. The torturing of the prisoners was carried out only by groups of guards on the order of Janovský as their director. We were forced to call Janovský "director," we were totally subjected to him.

I can remember that there were ten guards: Havel and other people. Havel in reality wasn't a guard but he wore a guard's uniform; he was totally devoted to Janovský and he was also one of the most brutal guards in the camp. Once one of the prisoners called Sulc went to the village to beg for bread; when they found out about this in the camp, the guard Luňáček beat Sulc in such a brutal way and tortured him for so long that Šulc fainted and had black bruises from the beatings, the punches in his face. The guard Luňáček tormented him by threatening to shoot him and pointed his pistol at his head when he went to sleep.

I can remember another case when a prisoner called Ryslavy who was in charge of tending Janovský's geese was accused by a farmer that he took his pocket watch away from him. This farmer was baling hay in the field when he lost his watch and he suspected that Ryslavy who at that time was tending the geese had stolen it from him. Only after some time later did the farmer find out that Ryšlavý didn't steal the watch because the farmer found it in the hay; it had fallen out of his pocket while he was baling. Because of the farmer's complaint, and I think on the direct order of Janovský, the guards devoted to Janovský beat Ryšlavý in such a very brutal way with their fists and truncheons that his face was covered with so many bruises you couldn't recognize him. His face was still swollen after a few weeks. I can remember that at that time, the guards beat him for two days and a lot of guards took turns in this torturing. I can find out the address of Ryšlavý; I know that he is living in Prague and I will give it to the local national committee.

I also saw how the guards beat the Gypsies that were building the road and this is how they were forced to perform at a higher work rate. I also saw that on the order of the accused Janovský, the guards had to tie up two women on the execution post for two hours. They tied their hands behind them, then pulled them up on the execution post feet first so that these women touched the ground with the ends of their fingers. This was a horrible punishment because the ones who were hung up for a long time couldn't bear it and lost consciousness. From the ones who suffered this I heard that they fainted from being tied up. And when the guards received the order to take away these people they poured buckets of cold water on the prisoners and this is how the suffering of the prisoners was even worse. This hanging up was a normal punishment in the camp. The other prisoners were not allowed to watch; whenever someone stopped to look and was interested in the punishment he obtained the same punishment like the one who was hanging up. When he showed concern for the one being punished the guards detained him.

I know that all these hard punishments were executed in the camp on the direct order of Janovský because everything the prisoners did was right away told to him. Anyone who did something wrong had to report to Janovský who then pronounced the kind of punishment for the prisoner. The usual punishments were: beating the prisoners many times on their backs, hanging them up on the execution post, putting their feet in balls and chains, and punching them in a brutal way in the face and such. From the moment Janovský was recalled from his function as director of the camp, and was replaced by his successor, all these brutal punishments given to us were stopped.

In the same way that many of the guards were devoted to Janovský, so was the doctor Neuwirth allied to him also. When this doctor examined us he looked at us from a distance, of about four meters. He only walked by us and didn't even take any notice that we were there. It also happened that he passed by the sick in this way, and in the end he only saw half of the people and then he left and didn't even look, not even from a distance, at the other half of the ill people. It also occurred that he did not consider some people very ill; when this happened the ill people were beaten very brutally by Janovský and his guards, and Janovský (missing word) these people who were not considered as ill and the bad food that they gave to us.

I also saw a lot of people whose sickness was perceptible on first sight. They were so sick that they couldn't even take care of their own physical needs, peeing in their own pants. It's possible that some of the ill people that were not considered as sick by the doctor, Janovský or his guards, were tortured and after a while they died. The conditions in the camp got worse and worse; after that people died daily from very normal things. We weren't surprised that so many people were dying in the camp. I think also that because of this treatment that the people who were really ill were not considered sick and that at the place where they were examined they were also punished and tortured by not receiving food, so that this circumstance contributed to the outbreak of typhus, para-typhus and other illnesses and that the number of deaths kept increasing.

Another reason why the typhus infections and other illnesses spread in the camp was because our nutrition was very poor. Even though the prisoners in the camp were to receive a lot of food, as I said before, such as flour, fat, eggs, bacon, sugar, biscuits, cookies, oranges, lemons, and other fruit, we didn't receive any of these things. There was also a big garden near the camp where they planted big quantities of tomatoes, cauliflower, cucumbers, kohlrabi, cabbage, carrots, and others. From all that, we only received carrots, and the tail ends of the other vegetables.

All this was taken away like the supplies from the warehouse and fats and other things and also supplies that were taken away from us and with the things we hadn't seen before, and used by the Janovský family who also gave a small amount to the guards but only to the ones that were devoted to Janovský.

Our usual food in the morning was black bitter coffee with a piece of bread; for lunch there was soup in which they threw in the tail ends of cabbage heads and such, and perhaps also dirty worms, it was all quite dirty and thrown into the soup as it was picked. Besides that there were potatoes which were mixed with green lettuce or with carrots. The head lettuce was cooked and mixed with the potatoes. For supper we had again the same soup we had at mid-day, the same old crap.

Under Janovský we received sweet dumplings about three times (while we were in the camp). During the time I was in the camp while Janovský was the director, Janovský's wife with his daughter lived in the camp continuously, excluding the days they went to Prague to visit someone. When Janovský's wife was not present, Janovský ate together with the guards, otherwise his wife herself cooked for him. I also know that the whole Janovský family lived from the food that was meant for the prisoners. Janovský's wife cooked very well and she baked a lot of cookies, and made many different kinds of good meals. I know this from a Gypsy servant who Janovský liked very much and with whom Janovský took the cinema. She always had with her some baked sweet cookies and also many times I received from her some pieces. I know that this was a very expensive sweet pastry.

That Janovský took for himself different things from the camp supplies I also know from his wife who once on the request of the guards cooked some dumplings out of wholemeal flour for them; for that purpose she wanted to take something away from our full sack of wholemeal flower, and Janovský protested that she shouldn't touch the flour, that it was his flour.

Janovský also had rabbits, geese, and pigs to which he gave the leftovers from his own kitchen and from the camp kitchen. Many times I took away something good I found in the garbage that was brought from Janovský's kitchen and was suppose to be for the rabbits and I ate it. This garbage was much better than what Janovský gave to the prisoners as normal food. It also happened that the milk meant for the prisoners in the camp, especially for the children, went sour and was not used for the benefit of the children in making cottage cheese or something else, but a lot of one liter milk pitchers were poured into the pig troughs which belonged to Janovský. Janovský got the meat from these pigs instead of the prisoners. The prisoners in the camp were suffering such hunger that the ones who had good stomachs ate potato peelings from the buckets for the pigs. This undernourishment also contributed to contagious infections.

The children also didn't receive sufficient food; they received regularly also the same that we got but sometimes on a special occasion they received better food in the evening and what they received and was considered to be better food was normally rotten and not good enough to be used, for example sometimes the eggs.

All this was in the time when Janovský was the director of the camp. When the other director came, the conditions changed absolutely and the children received what was due to them. Also from the time when the new director entered the camp, not only the sanitary conditions improved but mainly the nutrition and the medical examinations and the overall treatment of the people. The Gypsies who came to the camp had a lot of things like clothes, linen, different supplies, harmonicas, radios and other things. One well-built Gypsy wore a beautiful long fur coat and this was taken away from him when he entered the camp. Also I and my family were told that we would go to work and therefore we took with us a lot of things, all of our clothes, linen, goods (curtains, sweaters, women's underwear, and such). All of this was taken away from us as it was from the other Gypsies with the pretense that these things would be taken to the warehouse but we never saw them again. In this way, they took away from me things valued at 18,000 crowns.

I also heard that the workers who worked on the labor gangs received from Janovský things from the ones that were taken away from us, and people told us that Janovský in this way paid the workers, that he didn't have to give them cash. But what he did with the cash that was meant for the construction, I've never heard. The accused Janovský would have continued to raise hell for a long time in the camp if a group of guards hadn't come forward and made the point that this behavior of Janovský had to stop. These guards came to us prisoners and asked us about different things that occurred in the camp; they also asked me. At the beginning I didn't want to tell them anything because I was afraid that they would tell it to Janovský and that they would torture me more. But they assured me that nothing would happen to me. I told them what

I knew. This happened when the sergeant Strnad found out that Janovský took away by car several full boxes of eggs that were meant for the prisoners. From the group of guards that disclosed Janovský's behavior were the sergeant Strnad, and Hucek and Kolařík, whose actual addresses I think you can get from headquarters of the SNB in Prague.

> This Statement made before the investigating magistrate on 6 October 1945 in Jílové.

(1) Václav Studený was the only Gypsy to testify in court to the crimes committed by the guards in Lety. Gypsies seldom seek justice in a white man's court. Gypsies believe either in revenge with the knife or in silence. Silence they believe is their best weapon. Maybe that is why it has taken fifty-three years for them to tell their side of the story about Lety.

František Kuchař
(testifying at Janovský's investigation)

I know the accused because I was his direct superior since I was in charge of the department for labor/discipline camps. I was there until 18 February 1942 at the state office as a special advisor, so that what happened there later on, I don't know. I can not talk about the accusations of Dr. Kopecký because it is concerning Gypsies.[1]

As far as I know, the concentration of Gypsies was done on the order of the Empire and I know that the camp was so filled up that it could not fulfill its function. About bad treatment, the intentions and running of the camp, I can not speak either, and I say the same as Dr. Stuchlík that there were special rules given by the Ministry of the Interior and the State Office. Referring to the rules, given out by these institutions, the statements of the accused are correct. Whether he behaved correctly according to these rules, I don't know, but until this time as far as I remember there were no complaints about him.

> Signed on 21 March 1946 in Prague.

(1) Lety was not made an official camp for Gypsies until the spring of 1942.

František Kuchař
(Director of the Protectorate labor-discipline camps in 1942-1943, as told by his widow)

My husband died in 1979. He would have been 85 years old this year (1996). If you want to know something about the war, I don't know much. Yes, my husband was working in the Land Office, but behind the scenes he joined a secret group who smuggled false identity cards to the partisans. These were identity cards of people who had already died; the resistance fighters were grateful to have them when they were stopped by the police. My husband was never awarded anything for this heroic act. He always said this was his personal patriotic duty.

During the war my husband was in charge of the labor-discipline camps. This was his first real job. He was 31 years old at this time. He couldn't tell me a lot of details about his work because it was a state secret. I do know he went to visit these camps often and always told the guards what they must not do with the prisoners. These prisoners were mainly Gypsies, not Czechs.[1]

My husband always tried to make it easier for the prisoners so that they wouldn't face any harm.

I know there was a camp in Chroustovice for young prostitutes who had been working on the streets, some even from the age of twelve. At this camp they were taken care of by nuns who had been expelled from the Sudetenland by the Germans. These weren't Gypsy prostitutes, but Czech.

I don't remember any of my husband's colleagues. I don't remember the names you said such as Stuchlík or Svoboda or Janovský.

I don't think that the prisoners had a bad life because they had Czech guards. It was much better than in German camps. My husband never collaborated with Germans because there were none in the department where he worked. The Germans of course controlled our country during the war, but they never got involved in the internal camps such as the ones my husband ran.

Yes, my husband visited Lety often. It was a camp for Gypsies. There were not only men prisoners, but women as well. They had to work building a highway or working in the forest. The housing for the prisoners was very good like on a military base.

After the war my husband worked for thirty years in the Ministry of Transport. I learned my English 55 years ago but I seldom have a chance to practise it. But I prefer to tell you about my husband in Czech. My English isn't that good. But tell me, how did you get my address?[2]

I appreciate that you are doing this research. There are very few people who study things that happened so long ago. I wish you a lot of success.

(1) Although Gypsy families arrived in the Czech lands as early as the 15th century, they were not granted citizenship until the 19560s. Although Gypsies as the second largest minority were suppose to have citizenship when Czechoslovakia was made a country after World War I, President Masaryk vetoed the proposal.
(2) Out of the Prague telephone book.

Josef Koudelka
(Lety guard testifying at Janovský's investigation)

I was transferred in the year 1940 from the police to the staff of the State Office in Prague as a guard for the discipline camp of Lety by Mirovice. The camp administrator was Josef Janovský who was there about two and a half years and then he was suspended. I was there three years in total. This camp was made for work-shy people; later Gypsies were sent there.

The conditions in the camp were poor and the inmates were very poorly dressed, not sufficiently fed and in winter they did not have sufficient heating. I saw three Gypsy women frozen to death in the winter.

I know from my own experience that the director Janovský was in charge of obtaining the entire food supply and also the clothes and everything else needed for the inmates. He went on his own to get and buy for the whole camp and told the accountant to do only the office work that was connected with the camp finances.

Janovský held German courses for the guards, he was very active and wanted us to salute him in the Hitler manner and ordered this as well among us.

Janovský made about 50 kids live in one wooden house that measured 2.5 by 3 square meters. The consequence of this "packing in" produced scabies among the children which infected the entire camp in addition to other skin illnesses. Later this over-crowding caused para-typhoid fever. As far as I know, Dr. Kopecký and his wife called attention to these conditions, but Janovský paid no attention and did not express any kind of interest in improving the conditions.

There were rumors in the camp that various food supplies sent to the camp were diverted away by Janovský. Only after the departure of Janovský when another administrator was appointed did the conditions improve markedly.

Signed: 20 April 1948, Hradec Králové, Šimkova 878.

Mr. Končický
(retired Orlík policeman)

I am embarrassed about what had happened at the camp by Lety. I would prefer not to talk about it.

Yes, I am eighty years old but it is not true, what you are saying, that I worked in the camp. I was a Czech policeman in those years and I did take Gypsies there, I admit to that, but I was never a guard at the camp.

No, I don't remember the names of any of the guards, but I do remember the names of several doctors who worked at the camp. Dr. Neuwirth was from Staré Sedlo, Dr. Kalbáč and Dr. Mráz, were both from Mirovice.

I remember that Marie Sklenářová from Orlík married a man who was working as a guard at Lety but after the camp was closed she and her husband had to move to Prague because the local people were so upset about what the guards had done to the inmates at Lety.

What did they do the them? Starved them to death. Beat them to death.

Did I ever see any of the prisoners? Sure. Some worked on a road gang, building highway 19. Others worked in the forest cutting down trees. Some were hired out to farmers. The fittest worked in the nearby stone quarries.

Mrs. Luzum? I don't want to talk about her. Ask the Schwarzenbergs. Don't ask me. Please, I don't want to talk about these things, about Lety.

Josef Matějka
(Lety guard, as told by his widow)

Yes, my husband was there in Lety. But not really as a guard. He was there like a soldier, because he was an officer in the army. My husband never told me about bad treatment of the prisoners. I never heard such things. I only heard that there was a typhus epidemic. Many, many prisoners died during that epidemic. The graveyard was so full in Mirovice that the priest wouldn't take any more bodies. They had to make a mass grave near the camp. I don't know where. But bad treatment, I never heard about that ever. On the contrary, the prisoners had a good time, there was plenty to eat because everyday I saw food being carried in: vegetables, fruit, bread, milk. They had plenty to eat.

Janovský, I knew he was the director of the camp. I remember Hejduk. I met him personally once when I was going shopping in Mirovice. I saw him with a violin under his arm. I think he was going to play in the pub.

I met my husband in Orlík, my home village. He was living in the camp at Lety, in the barracks for the officers. We saw each other almost everyday. I would ride my bicycle out there. It was a nice ride. A wonderful beautiful countryside with trees and hills. Later when we married he moved to Orlík with me.

The camp was very nice. Nice wooden buildings. Big buildings, built up nicely.

My husband told me that the prisoners were normal human beings. His parents were teachers and they were very liberal. But they didn't like Germans. My husband never liked the Germans. He was glad there were no Germans in Lety. He was a great Czech patriot.

He was given a picture from a Gypsy woman, one of the prisoners, a very pretty woman. On the back of the picture he wrote a poem about himself and her: *Regina, you are leaving, while your bread giver stays.*

My brother had a girlfriend in Lety village, so he and I rode over there every day, passing the camp. This is how I met my husband, there by the camp. I never saw any trouble at the camp. No beatings, no screams.

My husband never got ill at the camp because he had a very good relationship with Dr. Bohin. He visited him often, he was always getting a check up.

The only trouble my husband ever got into was in 1951. He was working at the border with passports and two American soldiers were in a pub in Furth Im Wald in Bavaria. They got lost in the forest and ended up in Česká Kubice, county Domažlice. Somebody called the police and my husband had big problems because of that. Because he was the vice chief and he was on duty that day he was responsible and he was in Pankrác prison in Prague for a short time because of this incident. He had a lot of problems in prison. After that he had to leave the police force. Then he worked as a miner in Plasy. But I really don't want to talk about that.

Yes, I remember the Schwarzenberg estate. I remember Karel when he was a little boy. I never saw any prisoners outside the camp. I never saw them working anywhere outside the camp. I never heard of people using the Gypsies to work for them. They certainly never worked on the Schwarzenberg estate. Karl's father was in Italy during the years of the Protectorate, working for the Pope.

My husband never saw any of the Lety guards again after the camp was closed. We lived in Orlík until 1945. Then we were transferred to the border in Česká Kubice.

I never heard of the guards marrying girls around Lety. I am sure I was the only one.[1] I still have a house in Orlík, but my husband and I never returned there.

There were no war battles around our area, and certainly none in Lety or around the camp at Lety. There was an attack by the Russians on retreating Germans troops near Příbram on the 11th of May 1945, but that was the closest battle to Lety that I know of.

I never heard that my husband testified against any Lety guards. He never had any problems because of Lety. I never heard of any brutality at Lety.

(1) In 1991 an old man in Orlík told me that after the war a Lety guard who married a local girl was chased from the village, not allowed to live there, because of his known brutality against the camp inmates.

Mrs. Luzumová
(Lety victim as told by a Schwarzenberg archivist)

The only story I remember about Lety is the one about Mrs. Luzum. The Gypsy camp was only a few kilometers from Orlík and this woman from Orlík, Mrs. Luzum, was arrested along with her two young daughters by the local police and taken to the camp.[1]

She was a Gypsy or half-Gypsy married to a local Czech farmer who lived near Orlík. One day the Czech police came and took her and her daughters away, saying they had to go to the Lety camp because they had Gypsy blood. Her husband was a white Czech and well off but that made no difference.

Mr. Luzum visited the camp nearly everyday but he never saw his wife and daughters again. Later, after the war, he became a well-known communist. He was so bitter he wanted to tear down all the churches in Bohemia because he was sure his wife had prayed but had not been saved.

(1) The surname Luzum appears nowhere in the Lety records in Třeboň Archive. However, I did find Mrs. Luzumová and her two daughters listed in the Auschwitz

records which noted that they came from Písek (the county seat for Orlík). Mrs. Luzumová and her two daughters died in Auschwitz.

Václav Veselý
(farmer by Lety)

I remember once when a Gypsy came out of the woods, asking me for a piece of bread. He told me that he got very little to eat at the camp. I gave him half a loaf of bread and told him to share it with the others. He ran away very fast.

In those days my job was to take potatoes to the camp. I went there with wagons pulled by cows. Once two Gypsy women came up to me, begging for potatoes. I told them to take whatever they needed, potatoes didn't cost much money in those days. They hid them in their dresses and ran to the camp. A short while later, the two women came back with another woman, so I thought I didn't give them enough. One of the woman came to ask me if the other two had stolen the potatoes. This third woman was a capo. At the camp they made capos out of some of the Gypsy women. I told her I gave them the potatoes and she could have some too. The capo told them they were very lucky they hadn't stolen the potatoes from me otherwise they would have been badly beaten. The capo told me she didn't need any potatoes, so I saw what kind of regime they had. The capo had a good life, I saw that. Those capos were supported by the guards. The capos must have had advantages, I don't know what kind of advantages.

I'm from a very poor family, I don't care if people are Jewish or Gypsy, only that they work and treat people nice.

When typhus broke out a doctor from Mirovice was suppose to come to the camp but he was afraid he would get the disease so he said he couldn't come to Lety with his car, that something was broken.[1] Later they asked the doctor from Staré Sedlo, Neuwirth, to come. So he went there, I don't know how often, or if he lived there. The villagers from Lety avoided the camp so they wouldn't catch typhus.

The dead bodies they buried in the forest. I didn't go near the camp when typhus broke out so I didn't see how the people were buried. After the Gypsies left, there was nothing there until they built a pig farm, some time after 1948.

In 1948 they negotiated in Lety whether there should be a pig farm or not. They wanted a collective farm, under the communist planned economy.

Near my house by the forest there were Gypsy men working. They were cleaning the irrigation ditches from the Schwarzenberg ponds. I never saw a guard with them, only a Gypsy capo. In Lety there were not many guards, I saw only four or five. I saw where they lived. Their office was separated from the camp. They also lived there. The Gypsy that came out of the forest asking for bread spoke Czech; there were no prisoners in the camp except Gypsies. We were the white people who brought things there, all the guards were white, but all the prisoners were Gypsies.

I can assure you that none of the Gypsies working here in the forest ever stole anything, never even a chicken. They came and asked us in a polite way for food. They were poor people.

When Heydrich was killed, Karel Frank said over the radio if they didn't find the assassins, every tenth person over 15 years old would be shot. We felt very bad. I could be the first or the tenth. But we were lucky, after three days they found the men hiding in the basement of a church; the Gestapo found them there; there was a big gun battle with both sides shooting at each other. The assassins knew they would die, so they saved some ammunition and later shot themselves. I was 25 years old then, married and had a son. It was not a rosy time to live under the Germans. We were always afraid.

I didn't see any beatings at Lety, but I heard about them. I lived here in Laziste. I came here in the year 1941; my wife was born here. All the guards were Czech. They were in the army before the war, then chosen by the government to be guards at Lety. I can't remember any names. I never introduced myself when I met them. I had my family here, I tried to stay away from them.

All of the land around here where the Gypsies worked belonged to the Schwarzenbergs. There were about thirty Jewish prisoners from another camp working in the Schwarzenberg forest too, in this forest right behind my home. I don't remember if they were guarded by Czechs or Germans. I talked to them once. They told me they would be very happy if they could survive the war here. But they weren't workers. They were educated people with diplomas. One of them was a doctor, one a professor, another the owner of a company. They worked about half a year in the Schwarzenberg forest, then one day these Jewish prisoners were taken away and we never saw them again. Schwarzenberg was here then. He spoke very good German. He went to Vienna when the communists took his land in about 1948.

I took the potatoes to Lety only three times, just in the winter. I didn't see much. I saw men working in the stone quarry, they used to bring the stones in small wagons from the quarry to the road. Two men were in front, pulling, while four in the back pushed. The land of the stone quarry also belonged to Schwarzenberg. All the land around here belonged to Schwarzenberg. Maybe even the land the camp was built on was owned by Schwarzenberg.

I don't know what the prisoners made with the stones, maybe they were working on the road, or expanding the camp. I saw with my own eyes how they worked hard pushing the wagons from the stone quarry to the camp.

When I gave this Gypsy half a loaf of bread he ran away very fast. I told him to share it. It was very dangerous for us to give food to the Gypsies. If the guards would have found a partisan around here the Gestapo would have killed the whole family. The Gestapo once found a partisan nearby in the hay and we never saw this man's family again. Everyone was afraid.

The Gypsy women wore long skirts, they looked like real Gypsies. The men wore normal work clothes, like me today. They had no prison clothes. The guards took away all their gold from them, everything, even shoes. I didn't see many prisoners working inside the camp. Most worked outside or they were in the barracks. The women prisoners also had to work but I never saw them. I didn't see them in the quarry.

I worked on the Schwarzenberg land in those days, most people around here did. The Schwarzenbergs owned everything. I worked in their forests. We never got paid for our work. They paid us by giving us the tops of the trees we cut down.

We had two pigs, two cows and four and a half hectares of land, so we worked for materials to build our house. Whoever at that time had three hectares of land had quite a good life. From this land you could get 80% of your needs.

The Schwarzenberg foreman treated us well. He gave us work. There were many foremen; I don't know how all of them acted. The forester we worked under was a good man. But whenever we needed firewood we had to work seven days for a load. Actually we worked for nothing.

It is better for society that there is a pig farm at Lety. They produce a lot of meat. It is better than individual farmers raising pigs. The government put the pig farm there because the Gypsy barracks were already there. That's why it was put there, that's why the Lety town hall decided to put a pig farm there, to use the buildings. I don't think people mind that the farm was put there, I don't mind it either. It's off the road.

I don't know how many people died there. The people were not buried where the pig farm is, the people were buried in the forest. The pig farm was only put where the camp was, not where the Gypsies were buried.

I've never seen the monument at Lety. I've only heard something was put there. What would I do there? People around here never talk about it.

There aren't many Gypsies around here today. There's a lot in the north. I've heard about the skinheads in Písek. I'll tell you what I think. It doesn't matter if people are Gypsy or Jewish or were born in the bush black, you can't do anything about it. The most important thing in life is that they work, they treat people nice.

I'm for the death penalty. If people kill, they should be killed. They shouldn't end up in jail for five or six years. They should think about the consequences. If I could make the rules they would be very strict. I think our government is worth zero when it comes to making penalties.

Those things at Lety happened fifty years ago. It makes no sense to talk about them today. You should leave it. I'm 79 years old today. You should forget those things.

I'm thinking about living another ten years but I could be dead tomorrow. I was happily married for 47 years. My wife died eight years ago. She had a weak heart. I take life as it is. I work on my home, in my garden. I sing songs about my youth. Retirement is a waiting room for death.

(1) Dr. Kalbáč. He is still alive today (1996) in Mirovice. He said Lety was a recreation camp for out-of-work Gypsies.

Václav Stuchlík
(head of all Protectorate labor camps from 1940-1942)

I was born 8 August 1904. I will be 92 years old this year. I was a soldier, I never wanted to work at the Ministry of the Interior. My boss made me work there. I was in charge of the work camps because as a soldier I did the same thing before, administering work camps in the Czech army. I remember my colleague at the ministry, Dr. Palák. He helped a Czech general escape to England.

I don't know a lot about Lety because after 1938 I came back from Slovakia where I was stationed. I never learned where all these camps were. Seidl was my boss.

I am from Hradec Králové. I went to school there, then into the army. I made my way up to the general headquarters. I was sent to Košice in Slovakia, helping the transfer of the Czech army back to the Czech lands.

It was the time when they built up these labor camps, that was when Mr. Seidl told me to work for him. I had to make a complete file for all the labor camps. I don't know how many camps there were. Mr. Palák translated my file into German to give it to the German government to let them know what we had. Mr. Palák was my colleague, we worked together.

I don't remember the name Janovský. I was only in charge of preparing the files on each camp. After they made the law about the Jews, I left the Ministry of the Interior voluntarily. I was lucky that the son of General Syrovy had a large gardening company; I knew him so I got a job there. I was lucky that I had the same grade as the General's son.

I don't know how many prisoners were sent to Lety. I didn't know there were Gypsies there. I don't know anything about Lety.[1] I wasn't involved there.

I don't know who ran the camps. I don't know if the Germans were involved or not. I just kept the files. Dr. Palák was the one in contact with the Germans. I was only there for two or three years.

I don't remember Minister Ježek, I don't remember the conference you mention.[2] It is possible that I attended this conference but I don't remember.

I never visited any of these camps. I remember Gypsies coming to my office, offering me anything not to be sent to these camps. I couldn't do this for them. It was impossible.

Possibly the police sent these Gypsies somewhere after they visited me. I don't know who sent the Gypsies to the camp. In this time I was already trying to get out of this office, out of this work. I was never in contact with Germans, they never worked in my office. Only Dr. Palák had contact with the Germans.

My boss Dr. Seidl was Czech. He was in Rychov as an employee of the Ministry of Interior, then he was transferred to Prague. After he was sent to Moravia, the Germans took over his work.

The guards at the work camps were employed by the town of Prague. Perhaps the guards at Lety were employed by town of Písek.

I never had any correspondence with the camps, I only made the files. I put in the files all the rules, how to work with the prisoners, instructions. After the mobilization, the government built up these work camps. I don't know the names of any of these camps. I would have to see the file to see if I did something special, but right now I don't remember. I don't remember what were the rules for the guards. I used to know.

Jiří Letov, I don't remember him. You should speak with Dr. Palak; he was a little bit older than me. He could tell you more. He could tell you what contact he had with the Germans.

I don't know what the guards did at the camp because I had no contact with them. All the guards and all the commanders had to be Czech when I was there. But I repeat these camps were just being built when I was there. After I left, I don't know what happened.

It's too long ago. I can't remember what kind of people were in these labor camps. It's possible that there was a kind of attitude then to send people to these work camps. I don't remember if it was the Czechs or the Germans who wanted to send people to these camps. I never heard if they sent Gypsies to Lety. By that time I was involved in my gardening. I think the Gypsies were deported and the Germans killed them.

I don't remember any problems about typhus in any of the camps. I was long away in this time. And I was glad that I worked with the son of the General.

The gardening company was on the island of Trója and I was there until the end of the war. I also worked as a gardener in the zoo. After the war I went right away back into the army. I was in the department of transport and was sent to North Bohemia to organize the railway management.

I never had to write a report about what I did during the war. Under the communists I had to spend two years in a labor camp in Mírov in Moravia from 1949-1951. There were 300 sergeants from the Czech army working in this camp. We weren't beaten but we had to work hard. In 1951 the Communists kicked me out of the army and sort of followed me. I ended up working from 1952 until my retirement in 1970 as a laborer.

(1) In his court testimony in 1947, the Lety guard František Kánský told the judge that the Lety guard Josef Bouda wrote a letter of protest about the conditions in the camp to Dr. Stuchlík. Stuchlík made a personal visit to the camp at Lety, called all the guards together and in front of them tore up Bouda's letter. According to Kánský's testimony, Stuchlík was in the camp quite often. Josef Bouda later died in Lety from typhus according to his official file. However, many Lety survivors say he was murdered. Bouda was remembered by many Lety survivors as the only good guard at Lety.
(2) In 1942 the Czech Minister of the Interior held a meeting to advise all labor camp commanders and their bosses in Prague how they should treat the Gypsies under their command. They were ordered to starve and beat the Gypsies within a breath of death. No Germans attended this meeting. According to the official files on this meeting, Stuchlík, Kuchař and Janovský were present.

Adolf Vondrášek[1]

I'm sixty years old. I was mayor of Mirovice from 1991-1994. As mayor I examined the documents that are in our town hall about Lety. I found out that 345 Gypsies are buried in our municipal cemetery. According to other documents, another 300 or 400 are buried around the camp near Lety. I brought up the issue in a town council meeting. We decided to make this little modest memorial plaque. It was my own initiative. No one ever asked me to do this. From this year on (1992), survivors and descendants of survivors come here on the day of the dead (November 1st) to light their candles.

Long before the plaque was put up, there were Gypsies visiting unmarked graves in our cemetery. About three times I talked to some of them but I don't remember what we talked about. They never came to visit me. I think the Gypsies from the Lety camp were all buried in mass graves in our cemetery, that's why there are no tombstones for them. There is only a little plaque that one survivor put on a wall for his family after the war.

Because of Polansky's efforts, the Czech people heard about the death camp at Lety for the first time. Wanting to be a democratic state, the government decided to make a memorial site at Lety.[2] Mrs. Gjuričová of the department of the Interior came to see me about it. She was sent by Minister Ruml and was surprised that we had put up a plaque already, two years before they had thought about it. She said there was a big movement in government circles to do something.

Mr. Prokopec, president of Písek county, was accused by the government that he never told them about the concentration camp at Lety. Mr. Prokopec found out that I had put up this plaque already and he immediately came to see me and told me, "Thank you for this, you have saved our country's reputation."

All the preparations were made in a big hurry. The government wanted to know who had been in Lety, what had happened there. On the 13th of May 1995 the government led by President Havel went to Lety to dedicate the small monument that is there now next to the pig farm.

I came to Mirovice in 1966. My father-in-law wanted to buy a house and the man living in this house decided to move. His name was Bedřich Pešek. He had once been a guard at Lety. His wife was from this town and this was their family home. Actually the house was his wife's dowry. She never wanted to sell this house, but as we found out later her husband had a reason to leave.

After the war the Pešeks were living in Mirovice without any problems. But suddenly some people began to throw stones through their windows, damaging their house. These people came at night with flashlights and shined them through his windows. The rumor in town was that these things were being done by Gypsies.

The Peseks sold the house to us and moved to Písek. When his wife died, Mr. Pešek moved to Prague where his son was working in the Ministry of the Interior.

I think Mr. Pešek sold the house because of some bad memories he had about Lety. He was always taking precautions. He even put barbed wire above his fence.

Of course, there are lots of things in this country that have yet to be resolved. Before 1989 nearly 70% of the population were communists or collaborating with the communists, then all of a sudden everyone had a clean record. Only now is there a law permitting people to look into the secret service files to see their own records.

I think it is to the credit of Mr. Polansky that he opened up this issue of Lety, but it would have been better if he hadn't created such a scandal. In some aspects he went too far with his accusations. Our people collaborated with the Germans but they did not invent the Holocaust. A lot of Czechs would not have done such things, but when the Germans came in and begun to do these things, many Czech were glad that they could finally get rid of some people in our society.

The pig farm should not be there at all. It's a national disgrace. It was built right over the original death camp. It should be an international remembrance site. When the government sent their people to research the matter they didn't even know where the graves were. It's a big shame.

Public awareness in the Czech Republic is not ready for this issue yet, but I would advise Mr. Polansky to keep up his pressure. It would be a good idea to make an information center at Lety but can you imagine how much money this would cost? Who would even go there? But at the very least the government should make a road to the site and put up a proper sign showing the way to the memorial. But even a proper memorial might not last long. If the Republican party ever gets to power what will they do with the Gypsies, liquidate them or drive them away?[3]

There are two men in Mirovice who could still know something. One is Mr. Toman, the town historian, but he is so old now that he is losing his memory. The other one is the old grave digger Mr. Kovář and maybe Mr Pospíšil, my neighbor. He told me a lot of rumors even about what had happened in this house. But I don't want to tell you any rumors.

Regarding war crimes, if it could be proved that the guards committed war crimes then they should be sentenced and punished, the same as war criminals were punished for crimes in Nazi camps. Even in Argentina war criminals now get sentenced for this. This country wants to be accepted in the world so we should do it as well.

This government is not able to do it yet, not capable. I think it will take another 20 years until this country will become a normal democracy. When you have at least two witnesses I think it is enough to take a war criminal to trial.

I have never heard any rumors about killing or drowning prisoners at Lety. I did hear that the Gypsies had to live there without any social infrastructure. There were no doctors, there was no real medical help.

The forest and the stone quarry where the prisoners worked belonged to Prince Karel Schwarzenberg. I wonder if he knows today how many people are buried on his land, how many people died on his land?

There are a lot more crimes that have never been investigated in this country. You can't imagine what the communists did to the farmers in this area. They took all their property, they expelled them from their homes, they sent them to prison, to a concentration camp in Jáchymov. My father was there three times. When the police tried to arrest him a fourth time he killed himself in front of them. These criminals are living among us. No one has been punished yet.

After 1948 they put the lower class people in power. They wanted to get rid of people. The same happened in Nazi Germany. Hitler was a primitive man and the same happened in Russia in 1918.

(1) Interview made by Ľubomír Zubák and Markus Pape on 28 April 1996.
(2) According to the Helsinki Agreements which the Czech Republic has ratified since 1989, any country that had a death camp on its territory at the end of World War II is suppose to conserve this camp as a remembrance site. In 1979 the Czechoslovakian government built a pig farm over the Lety death camp site. WW II American reconnaissance photos show the Lety camp was exactly where the pig farm is today.
(3) In their newspaper ad for the 1996 national elections, the Republican party called for a final solution to the parasite problem and in parenthesis put the word Gypsy.

Zdeněk Bárta
(mayor of Mirovice 1996)

I have some reports here about the Gypsy camp at Lety. In the beginning the camp dead were buried in our graveyard; when there was no more room they were buried in an emergency cemetery near the camp.

In 1992 the former mayor of Mirovice put up a plaque in our cemetery to honor those who had died in the Lety camp. Their graves will never be moved, even if no one pays the annual tax.

Today there is a pig farm on the site of the concentration camp. I think it should be moved. But Lety is an independent community so it's not my responsibility. Last year there was this memorial service and the government said, yes we will do something with the pig farm but nothing ever happened.

There are people coming here asking where is the concentration camp site and I tell them the way and I tell them there is a sign but they come back and tell me they can't find the sign or the site. The other day I went there and in fact there is no sign, it has vanished.

There are still people alive who know about Lety in our community: Mr. Toman, our local historian, Dr. Kalbáč who was a doctor at the camp, and Mr. Kovařík who dug the graves for the Gypsies buried in our cemetery. We don't have any death certificates, but we do have a book which lists every person buried in our cemetery.[1]

On 8 May this year, we had a short memorial service at the Gypsy plaque in our cemetery. I don't believe there will be a memorial service at Lety today.[2] The government has abandoned the site.

(1) I counted 359 burials in the chronicles of Mirovice for the Mirovice cemetery from the Lety camp from 20 August 1942 until the 23 April 1943. A Czech government report dated 7 July 1994 says that only 134 Lety Romany are buried in the Mirovice cemetery.
(2) 13 May 1996, the first anniversary of the Lety memorial.

Růžena

(an interview in Mirovice cemetery, June 1996)

She arrived on a rusted bicycle with a basket of yellow flowers on the handle bars. We were coming out of the gate of Mirovice cemetery when she almost ran over us. She apologized, saying she was 82 years old and it took her longer to stop nowadays.

Yes, I know where the prisoners of Lety are buried. Come with me. Over there to the right by the middle wall, they are all buried along the wall in a big trench. There are no names because there were so many of them, children mainly. The bodies were brought in trucks by the police. They also came with some prisoners to dig the trench and unload the bodies. Later the police took bread from Mirovice back to Lety in the same truck.

The prisoners all died from typhus, that's what we were told, still told to this day. But you know, there were many rumors about the Gypsies dying in Lety. I went to the Lety area every day to work on a farm, but I never saw what happened.

I remember there was one bad man at Lety. I don't know his name, but after the war the Czech police came looking for him. He left our town to live somewhere around Písek, then he moved somewhere where no one could find him. I don't think he went abroad.[1]

Hejduk? Fiala? Černý? Pešek? *Yes, that was the man, Pešek.*

267

I knew him personally, I met him many times. He had to escape because Gypsies were looking for him. He must have done something bad to have so many people looking for him after the war. Even people in our village were throwing stones though his windows until he left. Everyone knew he was a bad man, he did bad things to the Gypsies at the Lety camp.

He had a wife from Mirovice, that's why I saw him so often. I am sure he is already dead. He was older than me, or maybe the same age.

There were some Jews living here in Mirovice, families by the na- me of Kohn and Pik but they were expelled to Germany after the war.

We had a good mayor four years ago, Vondrášek, who put up the plaque in this cemetery for the Lety victims. That was a nice gesture, before the government ever thought of putting up those stones at Lety, don't you think?

No, I can't tell you my last name. I don't want any problems. Things here are still not so good. Yes, I'm still scared about what could happen. These are things you still don't talk about.

(1) He died in Prague. His son lives there today, working for the Ministry of the Interior.

Lety 1996

(two interviews)

An old man with a withered arm was working in his garden. He looked like a very poor man. He said:

Yes, there was a camp with Gypsies, but I don't know anything about a bunker.[1] There was typhus and they died. Some worked there, others were sent to other camps. I don't know anything else. Do you see that house with the yellow stripe? There's another old man living there. He may know more.

He was very weak. It took him five minutes to walk me to the gate.

The other old man was sitting in front of the house with the yellow stripe. When he saw me he took his cane and came to the gate. I told him what I wanted. He said:

Yes, there was a camp there. The prisoners worked on the highway, but they were not prisoners. I don't know about any bunker, but they built a cellar in the forest for potatoes. I don't think it exists anymore. They leveled the ground there after the camp closed. They filled in the cellar with earth and planted some new trees over it.

The prisoners were mainly people who played cards instead of working. There were also some Gypsies but mainly they took people there to work.

The only ones who would know [where the cellar was] were the guards but they are all dead. Only the Blažeks or the Klímas would know something. They are the families of the wives of the guards. Some guards married local girls but they are not here anymore. After the war the communists came and took all their property and said they were guilty. So they moved somewhere else. You know when you are guilty but are not found guilty you move away; you never come back to your village.

Now I remember it was typhus, lots of them died of typhus, then they dug a trench and they put all the bodies in there. But I was not here in this time. I came back after the war. But you know these prisoners were people who played cards and gambling games. There were also Gypsies but most of the prisoners were just people who were punished for gambling. I don't think that the guards were bad. They had to do their duty. I don't know any names, I've never heard the names Hejduk or Janovský.

Today the government should punish these people who did something in the communist times but they don't. During the war the guards had to do these things because of the Germans.

There are only a few locals left in this village. You see the people across the road, I don't even know them. There is only one more old person in this town, a relative of ours, but she is in bed, too old to move.

(1) I visited Lety seeking information about the gas chamber Eduard Čermák said had been built behind the camp. I did find some rusted pipes near the spot where Čermák told me the gas chamber had been built in the forest.

Epilogue

April 15, 1998: From the *Prague Post:*

The Office for the Investigation of Communist Crimes has been unable to prove that genocide took place in Lety, a World War II concentration camp where hundreds of Czech Romanies died. Investigator Pavel Brett of the investigation office said about 50 Romany survivors were questioned but their testimony did not clearly indicate that genocide had been committed. Survivors of the camp have pressed for the prosecution of two Czech camp guards who they say cooperated in genocide. President Václav Havel unveiled a memorial on the site of Lety, which is now occupied by a pig farm. Romany lobbies are pressing for the removal of the farm so that the entire place can become a memorial.